D0021751

Stumbling On Wins

Stumbling On Wins

Two Economists Expose the Pitfalls on the Road to Victory in Professional Sports

David J. Berri
Martin B. Schmidt

HARMONY LIBRARY
Fort Collins, Colorado

Vice President, Publisher: Tim Moore
Associate Publisher and Director of Marketing: Amy Neidlinger
Acquisitions Editor: Kirk Jensen
Editorial Assistant: Pamela Boland
Development Editor: Russ Hall
Operations Manager: Gina Kanouse
Senior Marketing Manager: Julie Phifer
Publicity Manager: Laura Czaja
Assistant Marketing Manager: Megan Colvin
Cover Designer: Joy Panos Stauber
Managing Editor: Kristy Hart
Project Editor: Anne Goebel
Copy Editor: Geneil Breeze
Proofreader: Sheri Cain
Indexer: Erika Millen
Compositor: Nonie Ratcliff
Manufacturing Buyer: Dan Uhrig

FT Press offers excellent discounts on this book when ordered in quantity for bulk purchases or special sales. For more information, please contact U.S. Corporate and Government Sales, 1-800-382-3419, corpsales@pearsontechgroup.com. For sales outside the U.S., please contact International Sales at international@pearson.com.

Company and product names mentioned herein are the trademarks or registered trademarks of their respective owners.

Printed in the United States of America

Second Printing June 2010

ISBN-10: 0-13-235778-X
ISBN-13: 978-0-13-235778-4

Pearson Education LTD.
Pearson Education Australia PTY, Limited.
Pearson Education Singapore, Pte. Ltd.
Pearson Education North Asia, Ltd.
Pearson Education Canada, Ltd.
Pearson Educación de Mexico, S.A. de C.V.
Pearson Education—Japan
Pearson Education Malaysia, Pte. Ltd.

Library of Congress Cataloging-in-Publication Data

Berri, David J.
  Stumbling on wins : two economists expose the pitfalls on the road to victory in professional sports / David J. Berri, Martin B. Schmidt.
    p. cm.
  ISBN 978-0-13-235778-4 (hardback : alk. paper) 1. Professional sports—Economic aspects—United States. 2. Professional sports—Social aspects—United States. I. Schmidt, Martin B. II. Title.
  GV716.B466 2010
  338.4'77960973—dc22
                                    2009040397

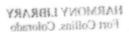

To Lynn and Susan:
We couldn't have done this
without you.

Contents

Acknowledgments

The stories we present are drawn both from our research, and the research of others. Obviously, we are indebted to the authors of all the studies we cite. Our own research, though, is not simply the product of our efforts. Specifically we are indebted to the following list of coauthors: Stacey Brook, J.C. Bradbury, Aju Fenn, Rod Fort, Brad Humphreys, Anthony Krautmann, Young Hoon Lee, Michael Leeds, Eva Marikova Leeds, Michael Mondello, Joe Price, Rob Simmons, Brian Soebbing, and Peter von Allmen. We would also like to thank all of the economists who have participated in sessions on sports economics at the Western Economic Association and with the North American Association of Sports Economists. These sessions have been a tremendous help in our work.

We also wish to thank Stefan Szymanski, who urged us to focus on these stories for our next book; and Dean Oliver, who once again provided invaluable insights and assistance for our study of basketball statistics.

Several people read early drafts of chapters and made many valuable suggestions. This list includes J. C. Bradbury, Owen Breck, Stacey Brook, Juliane Clapp, Rich Campbell, Jason Eshleman, Jim Peach, Kevin Quinn, Raymond Sauer, and Stephen Walters. Special thanks go out to Leslee Watson-Flores and Fred Flores, who took the time to read and offer valuable comments on every single chapter.

The Wages of Wins Journal—a blog we started at the suggestion of J. C. Bradbury—has proven to be an invaluable resource. Our audience consistently provides insightful comments into the stories we try and tell.

The people of FT Press, specifically Martha Cooley, Kirk Jensen, Russ Hall, Anne Goebel, and Tim Moore have all been extremely patient and helpful. This book would not have been possible without Martha, so she certainly deserves a great deal of credit. And Kirk's editorial assistance was essential in transforming our ideas into this final product.

Finally, the list of people we have to thank includes our families, whose support is very much appreciated. Dave Berri would like to thank his wife, Lynn, as well as his daughters, Allyson and Jessica. Lynn read each and every chapter of this book, and her suggestions went far to overcome the limitations in our writing abilities. Martin Schmidt would also like to thank his wife, Susan, as well as his children, Michael, Casey, and Daniel.

About the Authors

David J. Berri is an associate professor of economics at Southern Utah University. He is coauthor of *The Wages of Wins* (Stanford Press). Additionally, he has authored or coauthored more than 30 academic papers, most in the area of sports and economics. His nonacademic writing has appeared in *The New York Times*, *VIBE Magazine*, and online at The Wages of Wins Journal (dberri.wordpress.com). In 2009, he was elected president of the North American Association of Sports Economists and is currently serving on the editorial board of both the *Journal of Sports Economics* and the *International Journal of Sport Finance*. He lives with his wife (Lynn) and two daughters (Allyson and Jessica) in Cedar City, Utah.

Martin B. Schmidt is a professor of economics at the College of William and Mary. He is coauthor of *The Wages of Wins* and also the author of nearly 40 articles primarily in the areas of monetary economics and sports economics. In addition, his writing has appeared in *The New York Times* and *The Sports Business Journal*. He lives with his wife and three kids in Williamsburg, Virginia.

Preface

Once upon a time, the word "moneyball" was only heard in reference to a winning shot in billiards. A few years ago, though, the phrase moved out of the pool hall and onto the baseball diamond. The man responsible for this move was Michael Lewis. In 2003, Lewis published *Moneyball*, a book that tells the remarkable story of the Oakland A's and General Manager Billy Beane. From 1996 to 2006, Beane managed to consistently field a winning baseball team without spending very much money on players. According to Lewis, this feat was accomplished because Beane knew something about measuring player performance that other decision-makers in baseball didn't know.

One year before *Moneyball* appeared, we published an article examining the coaches voting for the All-Rookie team in the National Basketball Association (NBA). This article suggested that coaches in the NBA were not evaluating rookies correctly. Then in 2006 we published, along with Stacey Brook, *The Wages of Wins*. Our first book explored a variety of issues in sports and economics, including labor strikes, competitive balance, and the ability of a player to "turn it on" in the playoffs. Within this list, we presented evidence that decision-makers in the NBA—like their counterparts in baseball—had problems measuring the value of free agents.

The idea that people in baseball and basketball have trouble evaluating players is certainly interesting to sports fans. Such stories, though, have implications beyond sports. In recent years, research has shown that, in general, people have trouble making "good" decisions. For example, Daniel Gilbert's *Stumbling on Happiness*, a book that inspired our own title, showed how people's efforts to find happiness are often sabotaged by their own actions. Dan Ariely, in *Predictably Irrational*, presented a number of experiments that show the difficulty people have in evaluating new information and making good decisions. And Richard Thaler and Cass Sunstein—in *Nudge*—not only describe the troubles people have making choices, but also how the presentation of choices can lead to better outcomes.

Much of this research is based on experimental evidence, and we find such evidence to be persuasive. Still, in the world of professional sports one might expect a different story. Sports come with an abundance of data to inform decisions. Plus, the consequences of failure are both quite severe and very public. In such an environment, we should expect that the experts employed in the industry get it "right."

The two stories told in *Moneyball* and *The Wages of Wins*, though, suggest otherwise. And these tales are actually just the tip of the iceberg. As the following pages reveal, similar stories can be found throughout the world of sports. We believe these stories should not only change the way sports fans perceive the choices made by their favorite teams, but also impact the way economists and other social scientists think about human decision-making.

1

Maybe the Fans Are Right

"I must say, with all due respect, I find it very hard to see the logic behind some of the moves you have made with this fine organization. In the past 20 years, you have caused myself, and the city of New York, a good deal of distress, as we have watched you take our beloved Yankees and reduce them to a laughing stock."

George Costanza upon meeting George Steinbrenner (owner of the New York Yankees): Seinfeld, "The Opposite" (season 5, 1994)

"What the hell did you trade Jay Buhner for?! He had 30 home runs and over 100 RBIs last year. He's got a rocket for an arm. You don't know what the hell you're doin'!"

Frank Costanza (George's father) upon meeting George Steinbrenner: Seinfeld, "The Caddy" (season 7, 1996)[1]

Few sports fans ever meet the people who operate their beloved sports teams. Such a meeting, though, would probably inspire many fans to get in touch with their inner "Costanza." Given the opportunity, fans would love to ask:

- Why do you keep signing such lousy free agents?
- Why can't we ever draft players who actually help us win?
- Why can't we ever find a better goalie?
- Why does the coach keep making that decision on fourth down?
- Why does the coach keep playing that point guard?

Obviously, this is just a sample of the questions asked. And, just as obviously, we have cleaned up the language. What may not be obvious is the economic implication of these questions.

Fans often suggest that decision-makers in sports are less than perfect. Managers and coaches are not only accused of making bad choices, fans often accuse these people of making the same bad choices over and over again. Many economists, though, find such stories unbelievable. After all, traditional economics clearly teaches that decision-makers are supposed to be "rational."

What does it mean to be a "rational" decision-maker? Thorstein Veblen sarcastically argued in 1898 that economists tend to see people as "hedonistic lightning calculators."[2] In more recent years, Richard Thaler and Cass Sunstein have just as sarcastically suggested that the rational decision-makers described by economists "can think like Albert Einstein, store as much memory as IBM's Big Blue, and exercise the willpower of Mahatama Gandhi."[3]

Both these remarks comment on the simple idea that rational decision-makers "choose efficiently the means that advance their goals."[4] Let's imagine the behavior of a manager and coach that "chooses efficiently." Such a person would tend to make the correct decision given the circumstances they observe. Perhaps more importantly, as the game changes, these same coaches and managers would change their point of view and make different decisions. Therefore— and contrary to what sports fans often contend—it's not possible for coaches and managers to make the same mistake over and over again.

So who is right: fans or economists? The emerging field of behavioral economics—via a collection of laboratory experiments—seems to side with the fans. Experiments have shown that people are not quite as rational as traditional economics contends.[5] Some economists have argued, though, that how people behave in a laboratory experiment is different from how they behave in the "real world."[6] In the real world, people face real consequences for making mistakes, and real consequences force people to be rational.

Sporting Rationality

To settle this debate, it might help to move out of the laboratory and look at decisions in the "real world." Sports are often described as being removed from reality. Yet for the people in this particular reality, what happens in sports matters. Consequently, we can learn about the rationality—or irrationality—of human decision-making by examining the "real world" of sports. This examination, consistent with the experimental evidence, will show again and again and again (actually we will present at least 20 "agains") that decisions in sports are not completely rational.

Before we get to this examination, let's emphasize that the word "irrational" is not synonymous with the word "stupid." When we eventually argue that decision-makers in sports are "irrational," we will not be saying that people in sports are not as smart as people are in other industries or other occupations. In fact, people in sports are often better prepared for their jobs than people employed elsewhere.[7] Furthermore, it seems likely that whatever "irrationalities" are observed in sports are likely to be found elsewhere.

We make this claim because at first glance decision-makers in sports perhaps more than anyone else should be "rational." There are two characteristics of the sports industry that bolster this expectation. First, despite being a relatively small industry in the American economy,[8] sports receive an inordinate amount of attention from the media. After all, no other industry has an entire section of each local paper devoted to its happenings. Such coverage raises the cost of failure to the participants in sporting contests. Losing in sports, as noted earlier, is not a private affair. Sports fans both near and far witness your failure and are often not shy in expressing their disappointment. Although people do pay some attention to failures in non-sports industries, it's rare to see interested observers in other industries pay money to yell obscenities at those who fail to achieve success.

Sports are not only different in terms of attention received. In sports, success and failure would seem to be—relative to other industries—somewhat easy to understand. To illustrate, ask yourself this question: At your place of employment, who is the most productive worker? Yes, we know. It must be you. But is this something you could prove? We suspect, for many people, this would be difficult. For workers in many non-sports industries, measuring worker productivity is difficult.

Take our profession, college professors. We both think of ourselves as above average professors. But such a self-assessment may be dubious. In fact, a survey at the University of Nebraska revealed that 94% of college professors thought they were better teachers than the average at that same institution.[9] We don't think this obvious delusion is unique to Nebraska. Neither of us can recall meeting a fellow professor who thought he or she was below average.

It also turns out that professors are not the only people who overestimate their abilities. Thaler and Sunstein find evidence of this phenomenon in surveys of MBA students, drivers, and new business owners,[10] and this is just a partial list. They go on to note that "unrealistic optimism is a pervasive feature of human life; it characterizes most people in most social categories."[11]

In sports, though, there's a brake on this natural tendency. If we asked Jeff Francoeur of the Atlanta Braves how his hitting in 2008 compared to the league average, Francoeur would be hard pressed to argue he was above average. With respect to most of the standard measures of hitting performance, Francoeur was below average. Likewise, Francoeur's teammate Chipper Jones can be pretty confident that he really was an above-average hitter in 2008. Again, that's what the stats indicate.[12]

Because sports come with numbers, evaluating worker performance in sports would seem to be easier. Consequently, the path to success would seem—relative to what's seen in other industries—easier to navigate. Unfortunately, there are a few stumbling blocks on the path to victory.

The stumbling blocks can be separated into two broad categories. First, numbers have to be understood. Coaches and general managers can see the numbers associated with each player's performance. But how these numbers connect to wins is not always appreciated. Even if the numbers were understood, though, another stumbling block gets in the way. Understanding the past doesn't have much value if the past can't predict the future. Some numbers in sports are simply inconsistent across time. When that's the case, following the unpredictable numbers makes the path to victory hard to find.

What the numbers mean for the present and future is the foundation of our story. But before we get to that story, we need to address a fundamental objection to any sports analysis offered by academics. Specifically, is it likely that academics would be able to say anything that the "experts" employed in the sports industry don't already know?

Crunchers, "Experts," and the Wrath of Randomness

Even if you don't believe people are perfectly rational, you might still expect decision-makers in sports—where there is an abundance of information, clear objectives, and severe consequences for failure—to get it "right." After all, these people are the "experts." There is no reason to think that some college professors armed with a slide rule can do any better.

Let's respond to that by noting that neither of us owns a slide rule (or knows how to use one). We do, though, have spreadsheets and some fairly sophisticated econometric software. There are a number of examples where people armed with such tools can see things that "the experts" miss. Some of our favorite examples come from places as diverse as the wine industry,[13] analysis of Supreme Court decisions,[14] and the treatment of heart patients in the emergency room.[15] In essence, it appears that human beings—who are not actually lightning calculators—tend to lose in a contest against actual lightning calculators.[16] Such an outcome is observed whether or not the human being is an "expert."

Related to the obvious point that people are not lightning calculators is a classic finding in psychology. People in sports often claim they can simply watch a player during a game and "know" if he is good or bad. The seminal work of George Miller, though, has shown that the human mind can only track about seven items at one time.[17] In sports, though, a multitude of events are happening throughout the contest. All these events not only have to be seen and noted, the impact of these factors on wins must be ascertained. To claim that you can simply watch a player and see his or her overall contribution to wins suggests that you believe your mind can do something that research suggests is difficult. Despite the limitations of personal observation, though, human beings still tend to believe the analysis based on this approach is correct. Such overconfidence can often cause people to ignore contradictory information.

Statistical analysis, though, can overcome these issues. Spreadsheets and statistical software can evaluate more games than a person can ever personally observe. These evaluations can also allow us to look past the "most dramatic factors" and identify which factors truly matter most in terms of wins. Furthermore, the analysis can also easily change as new data arrives. Perhaps most importantly, statistical models come with confidence intervals.[18] In other words, statistical models can assess the quality of the prediction being made. Try getting that kind of service from a human expert!

Number crunching does more than offer better explanations than what we get from "experts." It can also tell us when there really isn't an explanation. In other words, number crunching can help us see when a process is inherently random.

Let's illustrate this last point with an oddity from the Super Bowl. As of 2009, the National Football Conference (NFC) team has won the coin toss at the Super Bowl for 12 consecutive years. Such a streak clearly indicates that the NFC has some secret that allows it to better predict coin tosses; and the American Football Conference (AFC) better do some work if it hopes to close the "coin toss predicting gap." Then again, maybe there's another possibility. Flipping a coin is a random process.[19] Even if you flipped a coin 12 times in a row with the same result, the process is still random. The outcomes don't tell us anything about the skill level of the NFC teams. This point should be obvious, since predicting a coin toss is not an actual skill.

This simple story highlights an additional advantage of analyzing sports data, and another potential pitfall for decision-makers. Some numbers that we associate with an athlete represent the skills of the performer. Other numbers, though, are not about a player's skill, but instead are determined by the actions of the player's teammates (or coaching or some random process). The analysis of numbers can actually clue us in on the skills versus non-skills argument. In the absence of such analysis, though, a decision-maker can actually suffer from the "wrath of randomness." Specifically, a decision-maker can be fooled by numbers that are as reliable predictors of the future as the numbers generated by our coin-flipping game. When that happens, money can be wasted on players who are not really helping. Or on the flip side, a player with some supposedly poor numbers can be removed from the roster when in fact the player is actually helping the team win.

A Century of Mistakes in Baseball

Although the "wrath of randomness" does rear its head in the study of sports, often the numbers do tell a story. Let's start with a great story that reveals a century of mistakes in Major League Baseball (MLB).

In 1997, the Oakland A's ranked toward the bottom in Major League Baseball, in respect to both team payroll and winning percentage. The next season, Billy Beane became general manager, and part of this story stayed pretty much the same. Specifically, the lack of spending on players didn't change. What did change were the outcomes achieved by the A's. From 1999 to 2002, only the New York Yankees, a team that spent three times more on playing talent than Beane, managed to win more games in the American League. The term "more" is a bit misleading. The Yankees actually won only two more games than the A's across these four seasons.

How was this possible? It's been argued[20] that the key was Beane's ability to recognize specific inefficiencies in baseball's labor market. Such inefficiencies allowed Beane to pick up talent that was both cheap and productive.[21]

At least, that's the story that's been told. For the empirical evidence supporting this tale, we turn to the work of Jahn Hakes and Raymond Sauer. These economists decided to investigate whether the baseball player market was, as they say, "grossly inefficient." Before we get to their answer, however, let's briefly describe an efficient labor market. A basic tenet in economics is that workers are paid in line with their expected productivity, that is, workers who are expected to be the most productive get paid the most. This suggests that baseball players who are expected to perform the best are paid the highest salaries (at least, once they become free agents). In a world where some teams are "rich" and others "poor," the best players typically end up on teams that have the ability to pay the most. In other words, we would expect the Yankees—or the "rich" team—to get the best talent, and a "poor" team like the Oakland A's should end up with the less capable players.

The key to the above reasoning is the phrase "ballplayers who are expected to be the most productive." This tells us that having money isn't enough. Teams have to be able to identify the "most productive" players. If one team can do a better job at identifying the "most productive," then that team might be able to field a very good team that's not very expensive.

To see if the Oakland A's actually followed this blueprint, Hakes and Sauer needed to connect three dots:

- They needed to uncover how various performance characteristics impact wins in Major League Baseball.
- They needed to figure out what individual teams were willing to pay for each performance characteristic.
- They needed to determine whether the salaries that various performance characteristics command is consistent with how those measures impact wins.

To cut to the chase, Hakes and Sauer found that "...hitters' salaries during this period (2000-2003) did not accurately reflect the contribution of various batting skills to winning games." Furthermore, "this inefficiency was sufficiently large enough that knowledge of its existence, and the ability to exploit it, enabled the Oakland Athletics to gain a substantial advantage over their competition."[22]

How did they reach this conclusion? First, data was collected on team winning percentage, team on-base percentage,[23] and team slugging percentage[24] for all 30 MLB teams from 1999 to 2003. They then ran a simple regression.

Okay, we get ahead of ourselves. What's a "simple regression?" Regressions[25] are essentially the test tubes of economics. When a chemist seeks to understand the world, he or she steps into a laboratory and starts playing around with test tubes. These test tubes allow a chemist to conduct controlled experiments. Hakes and Sauer, though, could not conduct a controlled experiment with Major League Baseball (at least, Major League Baseball probably wouldn't let them do this). What they could do, though, is employ regression analysis. This is simply a standard technique economists employ to uncover the relationship between two variables (like player salary and on-base percentage), while statistically holding other factors constant.

When properly executed, regression analysis allows one to see if the relationship between two variables exists; or more precisely, if the relationship between two variables is statistically significant.

Beyond statistical significance, we can also measure the economic significance of a relationship,[26] or the size of the impact one variable has on another. Consider how on-base percentage and slugging percentage relate to team wins. Hakes and Sauer found both to be statistically significant. On-base percentage, though, had twice the impact on team wins. Such a result suggests that players should be paid more for on-base percentage. The study of salaries, though, suggested that prior to 2004, it was slugging percentage that got a hitter paid. In fact, in many of the years these authors examined, on-base percentage was not even found to have a statistically significant impact on player salaries.

After 2004, though, the story changed.[27] An examination of data from 2004 to 2006 reveals that on-base percentage had a bigger impact on player salaries than slugging percentage. In other words, an inefficiency exploited by Billy Beane was eventually eliminated.[28]

It's important to note, though, how long this took. The National League came into existence in 1876. All of the data necessary to calculate on-base percentage was actually tracked that very first season in the 19th century. However, it was not until the 21st century—or after more than 100 years—that these numbers were understood by decision-makers in baseball. It appears that decision-makers in baseball made the same mistake in evaluating talent year after year, and this continued for a century. Such a tale suggests that maybe all those fans are on to something. Maybe coaches and general managers are capable of repeating the same mistakes.

Of course, one story from the real world of sports doesn't make a point. What we need is a multitude of stories. And that's what we provide. The stories we tell give insight into how free agents are evaluated, how teams make decisions on draft day, and even how choices are made on game day. We even present evidence that the evaluation of coaches in the National Basketball Association (NBA) is less than ideal.

All of these tales from the world of sports tell one very important story. Decision-making is not often as rational as traditional economics argues. And that story has an impact on our understanding of both sports and economics.

2 ————————————————————————

Defending Isiah

The New York Yankees spent more than $1.5 billion on acquiring playing talent between 1999 and 2008. Across these years, no team in baseball won more regular season games. Although critics would note that a World Series title proved elusive from 2001 to 2008, a list of top teams in baseball across the past ten years would certainly begin with the Yankees.

The Yankees' experience suggests that innovations like those employed by Billy Beane are not the only way to achieve victory. If you simply have more resources than your competition, this can also lead to success. Of course, you need to know how to use those resources. It also helps to have some luck on your side.

The importance of knowledge—and perhaps luck—can be illustrated when we look at other sports. From 2000 to 2008, the Washington Redskins spent the most in the National Football League (NFL) yet failed to win half their games. The New York Rangers of the National Hockey League (NHL) paid its players more than anyone else from 2000-01 to 2007-08. Despite this spending, 19 other teams—in a league with 30 franchises—achieved better results on the ice. So the link between spending and success is not that clear.

If we look at all teams in North American sports, the link is even murkier. Table 2.1 examines[1] the relationship[2] between a team's relative payroll (a team's payroll in a given season divided by the average payroll in a league that season) and its regular season winning percentage. In all of these sports, more than 75% of the variation in winning percentage is *not* explained by a team's spending.[3] In basketball and football, a team's spending explains less than 10% of the variation in wins. Contrary to what we see when we look at the Yankees, simple statistical analysis demonstrates that it takes more than money to find success in sports.

TABLE 2.1   The Link Between Payroll and Wins in the Major North American Sports

League	Percentage of Wins Explained by Relative Payroll
National Hockey League	24%
Major League Baseball	18%
National Basketball Association	6%
National Football League	2%

Isiah Thomas Illustrates How Money Can't Buy You Love

To further illustrate this point, let's look at the New York Knicks. From 1997-98 to 2003-04, the Knicks finished either first or second in league payroll every single year. Although the team did reach the NBA Finals in 1999, their average finish was...well, quite average. Across these seven seasons the Knicks only won six more games than they lost. The consistent "averageness" of the team led the Knicks to hire Isiah Lord Thomas III in December 2003.

Today it's understood that Isiah's tenure in New York was not exactly successful. But that's not the way it started. William Rhoden of the *New York Times* stated soon after the Knicks announced the hiring of Isiah: "If you love the Knicks and don't like this move, you must be delirious. This was a great move for the home team."[4]

When we look over Isiah's resume before he came to the Knicks, we suspect that Rhoden was not the only one to think Isiah was going to make the Knicks better. As an All-American point guard, Isiah led Indiana University to the NCAA championship in 1981. After winning this title he left the Hoosiers for the NBA. Taken by the Detroit Pistons with the second overall choice in the 1981 draft, Isiah quickly became a fixture at the midseason All-Star game. When his 13-year career was over he had appeared in the All-Star game 12 times and was widely believed to be the primary reason the Pistons (i.e., the Bad Boys) won the NBA title in both 1989 and 1990. Isiah retired in 1994, and two years later, he was named one of the 50 greatest players in the NBA's first 50 years. This honor was followed by election to the Hall of Fame in 2000.[5]

After his playing days were over, Isiah spent time as a front office executive with the Toronto Raptors, a broadcaster with NBC, and head coach with the Indiana Pacers. At each stop he was hired because it was believed that Isiah was a winner who was an expert on the subject of basketball.[6] So when the New York Knicks were looking for someone to convert their league-leading payroll into league-leading performance on the court, Isiah's name rose to the top of the list.

Few people in the NBA could claim in December 2003 that they knew more about basketball than Isiah Thomas. Of course, after Isiah left the Knicks in 2008, the assessment of Isiah in many circles had changed. The path toward changing this assessment actually began with the very first move Isiah made as general manager. Within days of taking the job, Isiah sent several players and draft picks to the Phoenix Suns for a collection of players that included point guard Stephon "Starbury" Marbury.

It's not hard to conclude that when Isiah looked at Starbury, he essentially saw himself. Like Thomas, Marbury was a very high draft choice, taken with the fourth pick in the 1996 draft. Like Thomas, he was named to the All-Rookie first team. And like Thomas, Marbury also had many All-Star appearances on his resume. Beyond being a high draft choice and an All-Star, Marbury and Thomas have some clear statistical similarities.

Before discussing the similarities between the statistics of Marbury and Thomas, let's briefly talk about the NBA box score numbers. The numbers the NBA tracks for its players can be separated into three categories: scoring factors, possession factors, and help factors. With respect to scoring we have points scored, which are derived from the number of shots a player takes and the player's ability to convert these shots into points. Shots are divided into two categories, field goal and free throw attempts. Because players can take both two-point and three-point shots, for shooting efficiency from the field we focus on adjusted field goal percentage.[7] Beyond scoring are two additional categories. Possession factors include rebounds, steals, and turnovers; or actions that measure how well a team keeps—or acquires—possession of the ball.[8] Then, there are help[9] factors. Within this category are assists (passes that help a teammate score), blocked shots (which can be thought of as defensive help), and personal fouls (which can be thought of as actions that help your opponent).

Table 2.2 reports the career averages of each player at the age of 26 (the age when Marbury arrived in New York). The first numbers listed tell us that, relative to the average point guard, both Thomas and Marbury were very good at scoring. There is an issue, though, with how these scoring totals were accumulated. Scoring totals depend on both shooting efficiency and the number of shots taken. Both Isiah and Marbury were slightly below average in shooting efficiency, but they were able to accumulate lofty point totals by simply taking more shots.

This issue of shot attempts is important. Except for Isiah's rookie season in 1981-82, he led the Detroit Pistons in field goal attempts in each season during the 1980s. Prior to arriving in New York, Marbury played for the Minnesota Timberwolves, New Jersey Nets, and Phoenix Suns. With the latter two teams, Marbury was consistently the leader in field goal attempts. Remember, each of these players was a point guard, and relative to the level of shooting efficiency we typically see from this position, both Isiah and Marbury were below average. Despite being inefficient scorers, though, each player tended to call his own number on offense first.

TABLE 2.2   The Career Numbers of Stephon Marbury and Isiah Thomas at Age 26 (Numbers Are Per 48 Minutes Played)

Statistic	Average Point Guard[10]	Stephon Marbury	Isiah Thomas
Scoring Factors			
Points Scored	19.1	25.6	26.9
Field Goal Attempts	16.2	21.3	22.2
Free Throw Attempts	4.7	7.4	7.9
Adjusted Field Goal Percentage	48%	47%	47%
Free Throw Percentage	79%	78%	76%
Possession Factors			
Rebounds	4.6	3.8	5.0
Steals	2.2	1.6	2.8
Turnovers	3.6	4.1	5.0
Help Factors			
Blocked Shots	0.3	0.2	0.4
Assists	9.0	10.2	13.1
Personal Fouls	3.8	3.1	4.5
WP48	**0.100**	**0.093**	**0.156**
Career Wins Produced	**na**	**39.7**	**66.1**

In a moment, we will get to our explanation for this behavior. Before we do, though, let's finish our assessment of Marbury and Thomas. Beyond scoring totals, Marbury was only above average with respect to assists and personal fouls. Isiah brought a bit more to the table, exceeding the marks of an average point guard with respect to rebounds, steals, blocked shots, and assists.

Given all these numbers, what is needed is some way to sum-
marize each player's impact. And that something is presented in the
last lines of Table 2.2. In our earlier book, *The Wages of Wins*—and
in Appendix A, "Measuring Wins Produced in the NBA"—are
details on how the box score statistics tabulated for individual
players can be used to measure each player's contribution to team
wins.[11] This metric—called Wins Produced—essentially argues that
a player's contribution to wins is driven by shooting efficiency,
rebounds, turnovers, and steals.[12] Yes, assists, blocked shots, and
personal fouls do matter. But teams win because they score when
they have the ball, and they prevent their opponent from doing
likewise. That means players help a team win when they hit their
shots and dominate the factors that take and keep the ball from
their opponent.

To evaluate how much a player is helping or hurting, one needs to
consider the performance of an average player. As reported in Table
2.2, an average player in the NBA produces 0.100 Wins per 48 Minutes (WP48). Marbury's career mark prior to coming to the Knicks
was close to, but slightly below, average. To be fair to Marbury, his
WP48 with the Phoenix Suns in 2003-04 was 0.136, a mark quite
close to what Isiah achieved across his first seven seasons. In other
words, Marbury's performance at 26 years of age was similar to Isiah's
career average at the same age.

As we will emphasize, Wins Produced can be described as a
measure that accurately captures a player's contribution to wins. But
it doesn't accurately capture the perceptions of a player's value. These
perceptions are driven by scoring. Consequently, in the 1980s, people
believed Isiah Thomas was the most important player on the Bad
Boys.[13] Given this belief—which we suspect Isiah shared—one
should not be surprised to see Isiah find a player just like himself to
rebuild the New York Knicks.

Isiah, though, didn't stop with the acquisition of Marbury. After
bringing Starbury into the fold, Isiah behaved as if he believed that if

one scorer is good, then a whole team of scorers must be better. By the start of the 2005-06 season, every single player who was on the roster when Thomas took over in December 2003 was gone. The list of players he added[14] included Jamal Crawford, Eddy Curry, Quentin Richardson, Channing Frye, and Zach Randolph. What do these players have in common? All of these players were above average scorers before they arrived in New York.

Unfortunately, all of these players had something else in common. Although each was an above-average scorer, each player also had flaws that undermined his overall effectiveness. For example, Marbury, Crawford,[15] Richardson,[16] Frye, and Randolph[17] were below average in shooting efficiency. Curry[18] was above average in shooting efficiency, but below average with respect to almost every other aspect of the game. Specifically, although Curry is 6'11" and weighs 285 pounds, he has consistently been below average on the boards. He's also prone to commit turnovers. The problems Curry had getting and keeping the ball actually negated the positives his scoring created.

The 2005-06 season was the first year that Marbury, Crawford, Richardson, Frye, and Curry played together. In that season, the Knicks spent $126.6 million on players, the highest mark in NBA history.[19] All this money, though, only produced 23 wins. And since the regular season is 82 games long, this expensive collection of flawed scorers also lost 59 games. The next season, with Isiah adding head coach to his list of duties, the Knicks spent the second highest amount in NBA history and won just 33 games.

In the summer of 2007, Isiah made his last major acquisition, acquiring Randolph from the Portland Trail Blazers. With Randolph on board, the Knicks looked to have enough fire power to contend in the Eastern Conference. But when the season ended, the Knicks—in a repeat of the 2005-06 season—only won 23 games.

That's how Isiah's tenure in New York ended. In the four complete seasons with Isiah leading the team, the Knicks only won 112 games.

This works out to only 28 victories—and 54 losses—per season. Only two teams—the Atlanta Hawks and Charlotte Bobcats—were less successful during the Isiah years in New York. Atlanta and Charlotte, though, ranked last in the NBA in payroll, combining to spend only $339 million on player salaries. In contrast, Isiah's Knicks spent $442 million on players, a mark that led the NBA across these four seasons. To put the level of inefficiency in perspective, in these same years, the San Antonio Spurs, Miami Heat, and Boston Celtics spent between $245 and $258 million on playing talent. These were the three teams that won the NBA titles—the titles Isiah was hired to win—from 2005 to 2008.

Isiah's record in New York led many to conclude that he was simply very bad at his job.[20] Despite years of success in the NBA, he simply didn't know how to build a winner. Although this might seem obvious in hindsight, we think there is evidence that Isiah was just as smart as his fellow general managers. Unfortunately, the immense budget the Knicks gave him to build a winner led Isiah to build a loser.

Getting Paid in the NBA

How can we blame the budget? To understand our argument, one has to understand what gets a player paid in the NBA.[21]

We have already noted that wins are primarily impacted by shooting efficiency, rebounds, and turnovers. One might suspect that these would be the factors that primarily determine a player's salary. But such suspicions are dashed by the empirical evidence. Just as we saw in baseball—where on-base percentage historically had a larger impact on wins than it had on player salaries—the factors that have the largest impact on wins are not the factors that get an NBA player more money.

To see what determines the flow of money, a statistical model[22] was estimated linking the average salary paid to NBA free agents to how these players had performed on the court, as well as a variety of nonperformance factors.[23] The results, summarized in Table 2.3, indicate that an NBA player is paid more money if he stayed healthy, played on a winning team, signed with the same team, and was a starter. He gets less money as he ages and if he played the shooting guard position.

TABLE 2.3   What Explains Free Agents' Salaries in the NBA?

Statistically Significant and Positive Factors	Statistically Insignificant Factors
Points Scored	Shooting Efficiency from the Free Throw Line
Shooting Efficiency from the Field	Steals
Rebounds	Turnovers[24]
Blocked Shots	Size of Market Where Player Signs
Assists	Playing the Center Position
Games Played Last Two Seasons	Playing the Power Forward Position
Signing with the Same Team	Playing the Point Guard Position
Regular Season Wins for Player's Team Last Season	Race of Player
Ratio of Games Started to Games Played	
Statistically Significant and Negative Factors	
Personal Fouls	
Age	
Playing the Shooting Guard Position	

With respect to performance on the court, steals and turnovers do not impact a player's pay. Yes, these possession factors impact wins. But players like Eddy Curry don't appear to lose money when they fail to hang on to the ball.

What performance factors do get a player paid? The dominant factor is the number of points a player scores. If an average free agent[25] increased his scoring by roughly 5 points per 48 minutes played (i.e., one standard deviation[26]), then his salary would increase by $1.4 million. The same approach applied to other statistics—such as rebounds, blocked shots, assists, and shooting efficiency—fails to unearth a single measure where a one standard deviation increase in performance leads to a $1 million increase in pay.[27]

Okay, scoring matters. But doesn't trying to score more points impose a penalty? Specifically, it's believed that a player who tries to take more shots will see his shooting efficiency decline, and the model indicates that declines in shooting efficiency lead to lower pay. Consequently, players who decide to take as many shots as their coach allows might not see much more money.

At least, that's a story one might tell. There are three problems, though, with this tale. First of all—as detailed later on—the actual link between shooting efficiency and shot attempts is not very large. In other words, a large increase in shot attempts doesn't have much impact on a player's adjusted field goal percentage.[28] Furthermore, although shooting efficiency is listed among the statistically significant factors, the result is somewhat tenuous and depends on how the model is specified.[29] Finally, even if one ignored the issues with statistical significance, the actual impact shooting efficiency has on player salary is quite small. Remember, about 5 more points per 48 minutes will increase pay by about $1.4 million. To offset this increase in salary, shooting efficiency would have to decline from 49.0%—the mark of an average NBA free agent—all the way to 26.1%; or well below the lowest level of shooting efficiency (36%) found in our sample.

In sum, the payoff to scoring easily trumps any payoff to shooting efficiency, or any other statistic. This tells us that players have a clear incentive to take as many shots as they can. More shots will lead to more points, and more points will lead to more money. Now it is clear why both Isiah and Marbury consistently led their respective teams in shooting attempts. Although there's a payoff to assists, scoring is simply worth more.

And this is exactly the story told by Marbury. Tommy Craggs, writing for *New York* Magazine[30] in November 2007, asked Marbury about his style of play.

Marbury defended this style as follows: "If I didn't play the way how I played, I wouldn't have gotten no max contract," he said. "They can talk about whatever they wanna talk about me, because I got maxed. I'm a max player. Don't get mad at me, because I'm telling you what's real. One plus one is two, all day long, and it's never gonna change. And that's factorial."

A "max player" is a player paid the maximum salary allowed by the NBA's collective bargaining agreement. Marbury was such a player, and he clearly understood that his focus on scoring got him that money.

Coaching Contradictions

Unfortunately for coaches, the lesson taught by the salary numbers—and emphasized by Marbury—presents a problem. Teams will struggle to win if every player only focuses on his own scoring. Consequently, coaches are often imploring their players to focus on something besides their own shots.

For example, consider the legendary Red Auerbach, who coached the Boston Celtics from 1950 to 1966. His tenure saw the team win nine championships, including eight consecutive titles from 1959 to 1966. In an era when Wilt Chamberlain was consistently leading the league in points scored, it was the Celtics that kept winning the title.

How did Auerbach's team consistently frustrate Wilt the Stilt?[31] For many, it might be Auerbach's obsession with winning. After all, he is the one who once said, "Show me a good loser and I will show you a loser."

Wanting to win, as many losers have discovered, is never enough. Auerbach did more than just tell his team to focus on winning. For Auerbach, the key was to look beyond individual honors and focus on the team. Specifically, Auerbach and the Celtics are considered to be the first organization to popularize the concept of a "role player." According to Auerbach, a role player is someone "who willingly undertakes a thankless job that has to be done in order to make the whole package fly." Auerbach went on to add that the Celtics represent a philosophy that in its simplest form maintains that victory belongs to the team: "Individual honors are nice, but no Celtic has ever gone out of his way to achieve them," he said. "We have never had the league's top scorer. In fact, we won seven league championships without placing even one among the league's top ten scorers. Our pride was never rooted in statistics."

The wisdom of Auerbach—that is, wins are about more than scoring—has not been lost on today's coaches.[32] Doc Rivers,[33] who coached the Celtics to their latest championship, also complained that younger players focus too much on scoring.

> "People seem to think it's easier to coach younger players than older players, but it's really the opposite. Most veterans in our league have had their day and chased the idea of being a star, and now they've fallen back to whatever they really are. They know who they are. Young guys always want to prove they're better than whatever role you give them. They won't buy into the system. They always say that they will, but the minute they have the chance to score, they'll try to prove that they can be a scorer."

Jerry Sloan, the only coach the Utah Jazz has known since 1988, faced an epidemic of young players focusing on scoring during the 2008 preseason.[34] First, there was Morris Almond. After a preseason game where Almond scored 10 points in 19 minutes, Sloan made the following observation:

> "Well, he scored points, but I'm disappointed with the way he runs the floor. He looks like he's not concerned about running

the floor and helping defensively. We can't afford to have that, especially out of our mid-sized people. I mean, everybody likes to score. But if that's all you're going to do, then it's hard to play to win. Numbers are one thing, but you can win with less numbers and more effort on the other side. He's got to rebound the ball, pass the basketball, learn to do some other things, rather than just being a one-dimensional player."

Almond was not the only player to get on the wrong side of Sloan. In a preseason game against Portland, C. J. Miles started off the half by taking jump shots on consecutive possessions. Sloan was "neither surprised or amused" by the play of Miles. "It's like I don't get any shots the first half, so I've got to show you I can get them off the second half. That's not a good way to do it."

Kosta Koufos had a similar problem in the same game, missing all five shots he took in the second quarter. After the game, Sloan was observed scolding Koufos for "shooting every time he touched the ball."

Such comments are consistent with the teachings of Larry Brown. For more than three decades Brown has coached numerous teams in the NBA and college ranks. At each spot, Brown has taught his teams to play the "right way." What is the "right way?" The 2004 Pistons won the NBA championship with a leading scorer—Richard Hamilton—who didn't even rank among the top 25 in the league in points scored per game. The construction of Brown's lone NBA championship team suggests that scoring is not his primary focus.

Rick Bonnell of the *Charlotte Observer*[35] noted that Shannon Brown was introduced to Brown's perspective during the 2008 training camp of the Charlotte Bobcats:

Charlotte Bobcats guard Shannon Brown had a simple, yet stark, question for one of his coaches a couple of weeks ago:

Why don't you like me?

Brown now says he was joking, but assistant coach Dave Hanners had a serious reply. He liked Brown just fine. It was Brown's game Hanners didn't like.

"I said Coach (Larry Brown) is asking you to do certain things, and you're not doing them," Hanners recalled. "Most guys are misguided about how to do well. They think, 'If I score 15 or 18 points, Coach has to play me!'

"We have Jason Richardson and Adam Morrison and a whole lot of guys who can make shots. We need Shannon to do something else to help."

The quote from Brown's assistant Dave Hanners doesn't just reiterate the message that goes back to Red Auerbach. It also illustrates the conflicting signals young players receive. Hanners noted that Adam Morrison was one of the players the Bobcats had to take shots. Morrison was selected with the third choice in the 2006 NBA draft, and he went on to lead all rookies in shot attempts. Unfortunately, Morrison's only apparent skill was taking shots. His adjusted field goal percentage of 42.2% was well below average for an NBA small forward. Except for turnovers and personal fouls,[36] he was also below average in every other statistic. Morrison's -6.7 Wins Produced (yes, that's a negative number) ranked 458th—out of 458 NBA players—in 2006-07. Despite this performance, Morrison was voted by the NBA's head coaches to the All-Rookie second team, and if just one more coach had voted him to the first team, Morrison would have been a first-team selection.[37]

In the summer of 2007, Adam Morrison suffered an injury that caused him to miss the entire 2007-08 season. So Hanners—and coach Larry Brown—only had Morrison's rookie season from which to draw conclusions. Given how poorly Morrison shot as a rookie, one would suspect that Morrison shouldn't be given a green light to fire away. But that's exactly the message Shannon Brown was hearing. Morrison was being encouraged to shoot while Shannon was being discouraged. Consequently, his conversation with Hanners might have left Shannon Brown a bit confused.

Morrison is not the only rookie rewarded for taking shots. If one examines voting for the All-Rookie team,[38] it's clear that despite the arguments of Auerbach, Rivers, Sloan, and Larry Brown, young NBA players receive a definite signal from coaches to focus primarily on scoring.

Voting for the All-Rookie team was connected to the 19 factors listed in Table 2.4. The results suggest that that the voting by the coaches is influenced by the number of games a player plays, the wins of the player's team, how often the player starts, and a player's draft position. This last result is somewhat surprising. At the time the coaches vote the player has already logged a complete season in the NBA. One would expect that whatever the coaches thought about the player on draft day would be trumped by what the player actually did in the NBA. The data says otherwise.

TABLE 2.4   What Explains Voting for the All-Rookie Team in the NBA?

Statistically Significant and Positive Factors	Statistically Insignificant Factors
Points Scored	Shooting Efficiency from the Field
Rebounds	Shooting Efficiency from the Free Throw Line
Steals	Blocked Shots
Assists	Turnovers
Games Played	Size of Market Where Player Plays
Regular Season Wins for Team	Age
Ratio of Games Started to Games Played	Playing the Center Position
	Playing the Power Forward Position
	Playing the Shooting Guard Position
	Playing the Point Guard Position

Statistically Significant and Negative Factors
Personal Fouls
Place Taken in Draft

Turning to performance on the court, the model indicates that points scored, rebounds, steals, and assists statistically impacted vote totals. From this list, points scored were found to be the dominant factor. Increasing scoring totals will increase the player's vote totals seven times faster than improvements in rebounds, steals, or assists.[39] Just as was seen in the discussion of free agent salaries, scoring dominates the coaches' evaluation of players.

All of this suggests that decision-makers in the NBA suffer from scoring illusion. Players who score more points are regarded as better players, even if a player misses many shots to score his additional points, or if they don't do any other things well. Hence, if all you looked at was points scored, you could be convinced—as people were with respect to the rookie performance of Morrison—that an unproductive player is actually helping his team win.

Isiah's Defense

The evidence indicates that NBA players have an incentive to shoot as much as possible. More shots lead to more points, and more points lead to more money and recognition. Given the primacy of scoring, players who can accumulate points become expensive. The limited budgets of most general managers, though, limit how many scorers teams can collect. Isiah Thomas, though, was far less constrained.[40]

Isiah's collection of scorers, however, didn't produce many wins. Since the number of wins didn't match the size of the payroll, people concluded that Isiah's players were vastly overpaid. This, though, is not the story seen when players are examined via the lens of the aforementioned salary model.

Table 2.5 looks at the primary players Isiah traded for as general manager of the Knicks. One can see what each of these players was paid his first year in New York. In addition one can estimate, given what the players did before coming to New York, what these players should have been paid if Isiah had to acquire these players on the NBA's free agent market.

TABLE 2.5 Predicting the Salary of the Primary Players Isiah Thomas Acquired

Player	First Season in New York	Actual Salary	Predicted Salary	Difference
Stephon Marbury	2003-04	$13,500,000	$15,392,655	−$1,892,655
Jamal Crawford	2004-05	$5,760,000	$7,714,251	−$1,954,251
Eddy Curry	2005-06	$7,390,000	$9,508,557	−$2,118,557
Quentin Richardson	2005-06	$6,940,000	$11,439,212	−$4,499,212
Zach Randolph	2007-08	$13,333,333	$13,437,639	−$104,306
Summation		**$46,923,333**	**$57,492,313**	**−$10,568,980**

In each case, these players appear to be bargains. For example, Marbury was paid $13.5 million in 2003-04. The salary model indicates, though, that Marbury's contract was $1.9 million less than his hypothetical free agent value. Even larger differences are seen for Jamal Crawford, Eddy Curry, and Quentin Richardson. In all, the five players listed in Table 2.5 cost the Knicks $10.6 million less than what the salary model indicates they would have commanded in a free market. So it looks like Isiah was making—according to the logic of the NBA's free agent market—very sound decisions.

The problem, therefore, was not with Isiah's decisions. No, the problem lies in how the free agent market values a player's contribution. Player evaluation in the NBA places too much emphasis on scoring. Unfortunately for Isiah—and fans of this team—Red Auerbach was right. Wins in the NBA are about more than scoring.

Although the salary model indicates that the Isiah's primary acquisitions were generally "good" choices, a different picture emerges when we look at Wins Produced, a measure that looks at more than points scored per game.

Table 2.6 reports the Wins Produced of each player listed in Table 2.5 in the two seasons prior to arriving in New York. In looking at this table the key is "WP48" (or Wins Produced per 48 minutes). Remember, an average player will post a WP48 of 0.100. Only Stephon Marbury was above average in each of the two seasons listed. One should note, though, that Marbury's WP48 in 2001-02 was 0.069, and his career mark before his first game in New York was only 0.093. A similar story can be told of the other four players. Only Quentin Richardson had a career mark that was above average before coming to New York, and his WP48 of 0.107 was only slightly above par.

TABLE 2.6   The Performance of Primary Players Isiah Acquired Before Coming to New York

Player	Team	Season	WP48	Wins Produced
Stephon Marbury	Phoenix	2003-04	0.136	4.0
	Phoenix	2002-03	0.110	7.5
Jamal Crawford	Chicago	2003-04	0.063	3.7
	Chicago	2002-03	0.075	3.1
Quentin Richardson	Phoenix	2004-05	0.103	6.1
	LA Clippers	2003-04	0.084	4.1
Eddy Curry	Chicago	2004-05	0.007	0.3
	Chicago	2003-04	0.042	-1.9
	Chicago	2003-04	0.042	-1.9
Zach Randolph	Portland	2006-07	0.147	7.4
	Portland	2005-06	−0.003	−0.1
		Average	**0.064**	

Turning to the average WP48 of these players—reported in the last line of Table 2.6—we see a mark of 0.064. This is consistent with a team that wins 26.4 games. As noted earlier, Isiah's Knicks only

averaged 28 wins per season, so the prior performance of these players—when examined via Wins Produced—indicated that the team
Isiah was assembling would struggle.

Of course, that's just what happened. These five players played a
combined 15 seasons under the leadership of Thomas. As Table 2.7
indicates, in only four of these seasons did a player's WP48 exceed the
mark of an average player. The cumulative average WP48 for this
group was actually quite similar to what these players tended to offer
before coming to the Big Apple.

TABLE 2.7   The Performance of Isiah's Primary Acquisitions in New York

Player	Season	WP48	Wins Produced
Stephon Marbury	2007-08	0.036	0.6
	2006-07	0.070	4.0
	2005-06	0.092	4.2
	2004-05	0.208	14.2
Jamal Crawford	2007-08	0.032	2.1
	2006-07	0.019	0.9
	2005-06	0.109	5.8
	2004-05	0.042	2.4
Quentin Richardson	2007-08	0.017	0.6
	2006-07	0.194	6.6
	2005-06	0.042	1.3
Eddy Curry	2007-08	−0.060	−1.9
	2006-07	0.002	0.1
	2005-06	0.049	1.9
Zach Randolph	2007-08	0.143	6.7
	Average	**0.072**	

The Wins Produced numbers tell us why the Knicks failed to
achieve much under Isiah. The players he acquired were simply not

very good. This was clear both before and after each player joined the Knicks. These players generally had a problem with shooting efficiency, and the one player without this problem—Eddy Curry—had significant trouble hitting the boards and avoiding turnovers.

Although accumulating scorers didn't ultimately lead to much success, it's not clear that other general managers would have made different choices given the budget Isiah had at his disposal. In other words, it's clear—from both the study of free agents and the study of the coaches' voting for the All-Rookie team—that scorers are generally prized by NBA decision-makers. Only a lack of funds appears to prevent other general managers from following Isiah's path.

3 ————————————————————————

The Search for Useful Stats

Why do teams track statistics in the first place? The primary purpose is to separate a player from his team. We know at the end of a contest who won. What we don't know is which players were responsible for a team's success (or failure).

The history of baseball statistics begins in the 19th century.[1] Eventually, the idea of tracking numbers carried over to other sports, and today sports fans are presented with a dizzying array of statistics. All these numbers are supposed to tell us which players are "helping" or "hurting." For that to happen, though, one has to identify which numbers are "useful."

Identifying the Most "Useful" Numbers

What makes for a "useful" number? J. C. Bradbury[2] argues that there are two criteria for evaluating a specific statistical measure. First, one must look at how the measure connects to current outcomes. Then, one must look at the consistency of the measure over time.

The first criterion can be illustrated by an examination of batting average and OPS (on-base percentage plus slugging percentage). Batting average is one of the oldest and most popular performance measures for a hitter in baseball. However, only 65% of the variation in a team's runs scored can be explained by a team's batting average.[3]

In contrast, OPS can explain 89% of the variation in runs scored.[4] These results tell us that if you want to know who had the biggest impact on team success, a hitter's OPS is a better indicator than batting average.[5]

Connecting a statistic to outcomes certainly helps identify the "better" measures; but this is really only half the story. Statistics are used to make decisions about the future. Therefore, decision-makers need to know if what a player did last season says something about what he will do this season. In other words, one needs to consider the consistency of the measure. As Bradbury argued, a measure that's consistent over time is probably measuring a skill. In contrast, inconsistent metrics are probably capturing luck or the impact of teammates.[6]

Consistency is measured by looking at how much of the variation in this year's performance can be explained by what a player did last year. For example, Table 3.1 reports that 22% of the variation in a hitter's batting average is explained by the hitter's batting average the previous season. Turning to OPS, we see that 43% of this year's performance is explained by what a player did last season. Once again, batting average is shown to be the inferior measure.

Performance measures for pitchers are more difficult to evaluate. Baseball fans traditionally look at Earned Run Average (ERA)—or the number of earned runs a pitcher allows per nine innings pitched—when evaluating pitchers. A team's ERA is certainly highly correlated with runs allowed per game,[7] but ERA, as Table 3.1 notes, is also quite inconsistent across time. This suggests that ERA is not measuring a pitcher's contribution to team success. More specifically, it appears that ERA depends somewhat on the quality of the defensive players around the pitcher. If these defensive players are good, then the pitcher will tend to have a lower ERA, but if defensive play is poor, a pitcher will see his ERA soar.

TABLE 3.1   The Consistency of Hitters and Pitchers in Baseball[8]

Statistic for Hitter[9]	How Much of the Variation in Current Season Performance Is Explained by Performance Last Season?
Batting Average	22%
On-base percentage (OBP)	41%
On-base percentage plus slugging average (OPS)	43%
Slugging average (SLG)	45%
Statistic for Pitcher	
Earned Run Average (ERA)	14%
Home runs per nine innings	19%
Walks per nine innings	42%
Strike-outs per nine innings	62%

Source: Bradbury (2008)

Given the inconsistency we see in ERA, baseball researchers have argued that decision-makers should focus more attention on home runs, walks, and strike-outs. These factors—also known as Defensive Independent Pitching Statistics (DIPS)[10]—are more consistent across time. This suggests that the DIPS factors are a better representation of a pitcher's specific contribution to team success.

Finding "useful" numbers is not just a problem seen with respect to pitchers in baseball. As Table 3.2 highlights, we can see similar problems in football, hockey, and basketball. For football, the problem is quite severe, especially with respect to turnovers. Interceptions and fumbles are often considered crucial to outcomes in football. Turnovers, though, are almost impossible to predict. For quarterbacks, less than 1% of the variation in a quarterback's fumbles and interceptions can be explained by what the quarterback did the previous season. For running backs, explanatory power is not much better. When we move past turnovers one sees more consistency, although predicting the future performance of football players appears difficult.[11]

Appendix B, "Measuring Wins Produced in the NFL," illustrates that the box score statistics tracked in football can be linked to outcomes. But these same statistics show very little consistency across time. As a consequence, we should not be surprised that the link between payroll and wins in the NFL is weak. Payroll decisions are statements about the future, and in football, the future is hard to see.

TABLE 3.2 Consistency Across Sports

Statistics...	How Much of the Variation in Current Season Performance Is Explained by Performance Last Season?
...Tracked for Quarterbacks[12]	
Fumbles lost, per play	0.03%
Interceptions, per pass attempt	0.5%
Fumbles, per play	3%
Touchdowns, per pass attempt	8%
Yards, per pass attempt	18%
Completion percentage	24%
Sacks, per pass attempt	25%
Rushing yards, per attempt	26%
...Tracked for Running Backs	
Receiving yard, per reception	1%
Fumbles lost, per play	2%
Fumbles, per play	7%
Rushing yards, per attempt	13%

TABLE 3.2   Consistency Across Sports

Statistics...	How Much of the Variation in Current Season Performance Is Explained by Performance Last Season?
...*Tracked for Hockey Skaters*[13]	
Plus–minus	9%
Shooting percentage	39%
Assists, per minute	55%
Goals, per minute	63%
Points, per minute	69%
Penalties, per minute	71%
Shots on goal, per minute	80%
...*Tracked for Basketball Players*[14]	
Plus–minus	23%
Field goal percentage	47%
Free throw percentage	59%
Turnovers, per minute	61%
Steals, per minute	68%
Free throw attempts, per minute	71%
Personal fouls, per minute	70%
Field goal attempts, per minute	75%
Points, per minute	75%
Defensive rebounds, per minute	86%
Offensive rebounds, per minute	86%
Blocked shots, per minute	87%
Assists, per minute	87%
Total rebounds, per minute	90%

The inconsistency we see with respect to football statistics can be traced to two issues: inexperience and teammate interactions. With respect to the former, we need to remember that the NFL has a

16-game regular season. Both the NHL and NBA play an 82-game regular season. An NFL player would have to play for five years to accumulate this much experience. In addition, a player in basketball and hockey can participate in a game every day of his life. A football player, though, can't simply get together a bunch of friends and truly simulate an NFL game.

Beyond a lack of experience is the issue of interdependency. Baseball pitchers are inconsistent because so much of what happens on defense depends on the players around the pitcher. Quarterbacks and running backs have the same problem. Quarterbacks need receivers to catch their passes. Running backs need linemen to block. Consequently, the numbers used to track the performance of these players likely capture the quality of these players' teammates. As the performance of these teammates changes, the numbers tracked for quarterbacks and running backs will also be different.

Teammate interactions are not unique to football. Table 3.2 reveals the plus-minus statistic in both hockey and basketball is also inconsistent across time.[15] In each sport, the plus-minus statistic essentially measures how well a team performs with and without the player in the game.[16] The definition of plus-minus tells us why we see so little consistency. Again, the purpose of tracking statistics is to separate a player from his teammates. A player's plus-minus, though, depends crucially on his teammates. If you happen to play with very good players, your plus-minus will tend to be high. If the quality of your teammates is low, your plus-minus will fall. As a consequence, the plus-minus statistic appears to contradict the very purpose of tracking numbers in sports. Rather than separate the player from his teammates, the plus-minus statistic defines a player by the quality of his teammates.[17]

Examining the box score statistics in hockey and basketball suggests the plus–minus statistic is unnecessary. Relative to what is seen in baseball and football, the box score statistics in hockey and basketball generally exhibit a great deal of consistency. Such a result appears to contradict the idea that a player's performance on the ice or the court depends on his teammates. Consider rebounds per minute. One might think that how many rebounds a player grabs is heavily dependent on the quality of his team's defense. After all, an opponent has to miss a shot before there is a rebound. When we look at consistency, though, we see that 90% of the variation in a player's per-minute rebounds is explained by a player's per-minute rebounds the previous season. There appear to be no statistics in baseball or football that are as consistent as rebounds in basketball.[18]

Appendix A, "Measuring Wins Produced in the NBA," illustrates that the box score statistics tabulated for basketball players can be connected to wins in basketball. Now we see that those same statistics are quite consistent across time. These two pieces of information tell us that basketball statistics are quite useful.[19]

Like football, payroll and wins in basketball have a relatively weak connection. Performance, though, is consistent. One can explain these two results by repeating the story told about how performance is evaluated in the NBA. Scorers tend to be overvalued. Non-scorers are undervalued. As a consequence, although performance is predictable, teams make systematic errors in acquiring players. Therefore, the link between team payroll and wins is weaker than one might expect.

The Most Important Position in Team Sports?[20]

Martin Brodeur—perhaps the greatest goalie in the history of the NHL—has argued that "the goaltender position is arguably the most important in team sports."[21] Although we are not sure about Brodeur's contention, we will argue that no other position in North American sports illustrates more powerfully the need for decision-makers to understand consistency in player performance.

Brodeur is the NHL's all-time leader in career wins. He is also second on the all-time list for career shut-outs. Furthermore, he was a four-time winner of the Vezina Trophy (an award given by general managers to the best goalie in a given season) and had been the goalie on three teams that won the Stanley Cup. Therefore, one could make an argument that Brodeur is the greatest goalie in the history of the NHL. If being a goaltender is the most important position in all of team sports, then Brodeur ranks pretty high on the list of all-time great athletes in North American professional sports.

Although one might question the importance of the goalie position, it's difficult to question the proposition that goalies are the easiest players to evaluate in North American sports. A goalie has essentially one task on the ice. He must stop the puck from entering the net. Consequently, evaluating this position simply requires that one note the value of completing this task and how often a goalie fails in his duty.

The value of allowing the puck to enter the net is easy to determine. Outcomes in hockey are defined by standing points.[22] With some simple statistical analysis, one can determine the impact that scoring a goal—and allowing a goal—has on standing points.[23] With these impacts measured, one need only evaluate whether or not a goalie is "good" or "bad" at preventing goals. The terms "good" and "bad" require a reference point, and for goalies, the appropriate reference point is the performance of the average goalie.

To illustrate, let's compare Martin Brodeur to an average goalie. For his career (after the 2008-09 season), Brodeur faced 25,126 shots on goal. Of these, 2,172 resulted in a goal. So Brodeur's save percentage was 91.4%. Although this might sound impressive, the average goalie during Brodeur's career, as Table 3.3 notes, had a save percentage of 90.4%. Therefore, an average goalie—facing the same number of shots as Brodeur—would have allowed about 217 more goals across Brodeur's career. This may sound like quite a few, but one must remember Brodeur has played 16 seasons in the NHL. So per season, an average goalie would have only allowed about 13.6 additional pucks to enter the net.

TABLE 3.3 Comparing Martin Brodeur to an Average Goalie

Year	Wins	Martin Brodeur Save Percentage	Wins Above Average	Saves Above Average	Average Goalie Facing Brodeur's Shots on Goal Estimated Wins	Save Percentage
2008-09	19	91.6%	1.0	6.6	18.0	90.8%
2007-08	44	92.0%	3.4	21.8	40.6	90.9%
2006-07	48	92.2%	5.5	35.8	42.5	90.5%
2005-06	43	91.1%	3.2	20.8	39.8	90.1%
2003-04	38	91.7%	1.6	10.3	36.4	91.1%
2002-03	41	91.4%	1.3	8.5	39.7	90.9%
2001-02	38	90.6%	–0.5	–3.3	38.5	90.8%
2000-01	42	90.6%	0.7	4.5	41.3	90.3%
1999-00	43	91.0%	1.7	10.8	41.3	90.4%
1998-99	39	90.6%	–0.4	-2.7	39.4	90.8%
1997-98	43	91.7%	2.6	17.1	40.4	90.6%
1996-97	37	92.7%	5.5	35.6	31.5	90.5%
1995-96	34	91.1%	3.9	25.5	30.1	89.8%
1994-95	19	90.2%	0.2	1.3	18.8	90.1%
1993-94	27	91.5%	3.8	24.9	23.2	89.5%
1991-92	2	88.2%	–0.1	–0.5	2.1	88.8%
Career	**557**	**91.4%**	**33.5**	**216.9**	**523.5**	**90.4%**

Given the link between goals allowed and standing points, 217 additional goals would have cost the New Jersey Devils about 66.9 standing points across Brodeur's entire career. Since a win is worth two standing points, Brodeur's career performance after the 2008-09 season was only worth 33.5 Wins Above Average. Remember, Brodeur is the all-time leader in career wins. If Brodeur was replaced by an average goalie, though, this average goalie would currently be ranked second all-time with about 524 career wins.

To put this in perspective, consider the career performances of Magic Johnson, Michael Jordan, and Larry Bird. Magic, MJ, and Bird are three of the greatest players in NBA history. Utilizing the methods detailed in Appendix A, one can measure each player's Wins Produced across his respective careers. One can also look at how many wins an average player would have produced in the minutes these three legends played. The results, reported in Table 3.4, reveal a very different picture than what is seen when the all-time greatest goalie was examined. Magic, MJ, and Bird each produced about 200 more wins than an average NBA player. In other words, replacing each of these NBA stars with an average player would have dramatically altered the outcomes of their respective teams. The data suggests one cannot tell the same story about Brodeur.

TABLE 3.4   The Career Wins Produced of Three Basketball Legends

Player	Career Wins Produced	Career Wins Produced of an Average Player	Wins Produced Above Average
Magic Johnson	297.3	69.3	**228.0**
Michael Jordan	283.6	85.4	**198.1**
Larry Bird	261.9	71.8	**190.2**

What we say about Brodeur applies to all goalies. Consider the top 20 goalie performances—ranked in terms of Wins Above Average—from 1983-84 to the 2008-09 season.[24] As shown in Table 3.5, Curtis Joseph tops the list. His performance in goal was worth 8.9 wins more than the average goalie in 1992-93. Joseph was one of only three goalies to post eight wins beyond an average goalie. At the end of the list is Tim Thomas from the 2008-09 season, who finished with 6.3 beyond average. Yes, that's all it takes for a goalie's performance to rank in the top 20 across the more than 20 years considered.

TABLE 3.5   The Top 20 Goalie Performances 1983-84 to 2008-09

Rank	Player	Season	Save Percentage	Saves Above Average	Wins Above Average
1	Curtis Joseph	1992-93	91.1%	57.4	8.9
2	John Vanbiesbrouck	1993-94	92.4%	55.6	8.6
3	Dominik Hasek	1997-98	93.2%	54.5	8.4
4	Dominik Hasek	1996-97	93.0%	54.4	8.4
5	Dominik Hasek	1998-99	93.7%	54.1	8.3
6	Dominik Hasek	1993-94	93.0%	53.8	8.3
7	Roberto Luongo	2003-04	93.1%	48.4	7.5
8	Pelle Lindbergh	1984-85	89.9%	47.9	7.4
9	Patrick Roy	1989-90	91.2%	47.2	7.3
10	Patrick Roy	1991-92	91.4%	47.0	7.2
11	Kelly Hrudey	1985-86	90.6%	45.9	7.1
12	Jose Theodore	2001-02	93.1%	45.9	7.1
13	Ed Belfour	1990-91	91.0%	44.6	6.9
14	Patrick Roy	1993-94	91.8%	44.2	6.8
15	Bob Froese	1985-86	90.9%	43.7	6.7
16	Curtis Joseph	1991-92	91.0%	43.4	6.7
17	Dominik Hasek	1995-96	92.0%	43.3	6.7
18	Ron Hextall	1986-87	90.2%	41.9	6.5
19	Miikka Kiprusoff	2005-06	92.3%	41.6	6.4
20	Tim Thomas	2008-09	93.3%	41.0	6.3

Once again, we need some additional perspective. Table 3.6 reports the top 20 players in terms of Wins Produced Above Average from the 2008-09 NBA season. Chris Paul leads the list. His perform-ance was worth 22.0 wins more than the average NBA player. After Paul we see seven additional NBA players who were at least ten wins beyond the average. So the very best NBA players can produce far more than an average basketball player. The same story cannot be told about the very best goalies in hockey.[25]

TABLE 3.6   The Top 20 Players in the NBA in 2008-09

Rank	Player	Wins Produced	Wins Produced of an Average Player	Wins Produced Above Average
1	Chris Paul	28.2	6.3	22.0
2	LeBron James	27.8	6.4	21.4
3	Dwight Howard	22.2	5.9	16.4
4	Dwyane Wade	22.2	6.4	15.9
5	Troy Murphy	19.1	5.2	13.9
6	Jason Kidd	19.8	6.0	13.8
7	Rajon Rondo	17.2	5.5	11.7
8	Gerald Wallace	15.7	5.6	10.2
9	Pau Gasol	15.6	6.2	9.4
10	Brandon Roy	15.3	6.0	9.2
11	Mike Miller	13.9	4.9	9.0
12	Kobe Bryant	15.0	6.2	8.9
13	Tim Duncan	13.9	5.3	8.7
14	Marcus Camby	12.4	4.0	8.4
15	David Lee	14.1	5.9	8.3
16	Kevin Garnett	11.6	3.7	7.9
17	Joel Przybilla	11.7	4.1	7.7

TABLE 3.6   The Top 20 Players in the NBA in 2008-09

Rank	Player	Wins Produced	Wins Produced of an Average Player	Wins Produced Above Average
18	Antonio McDyess	11.0	3.9	7.1
19	Andris Biedrins	10.7	3.9	6.9
20	Jose Calderon	11.5	4.9	6.6

One might look at these numbers and still say that the top goalies are doing more than the average, and these small differences really do matter. With this line of reasoning in mind, let's return to the issue of consistency. Table 3.7 reports how much variation in a goalie's performance this season is explained by what he did the previous season.[26] The middle term is Goals Against Average,[27] or the number of goals surrendered by a goalie per 60 minutes played. The consistency of this measure is similar to what was reported for a pitcher's ERA in baseball.

TABLE 3.7   The Consistency of NHL Goalies

Statistic	How Much of the Variation in Current Season Performance Is Explained by Performance Last Season?
Save Percentage	6%
Goals Against Average	15%
Shots on Goal, Minute	34%

The relative inconsistency seen with respect to ERA is tied to the fact that a pitcher's performance depends somewhat on the quality of a team's defense. A similar story can be told about Goals Against Average. Essentially, this measure is comprised of two other statistics. First we have shots on goal, which is the most consistent statistic

listed in Table 3.7. A goalie, though, has little control over this number. What a goalie can control is save percentage, and save percentage
is very inconsistent. To illustrate this observed inconsistency, consider
the top goalies in terms of save percentage[28] for each season from
1983-84 to 2007-08. Of the goalies ranked in the top ten across these
23 seasons, only 70—or about 30%—were able to repeat a top ten
ranking in the next season. So 70% of top ten goalies in a given regular season will generally be out of the top ten the next regular season.

Hockey lore teaches, though, that the regular season is not what
matters when it comes to goalies. The key to winning a Stanley Cup
title is to ride a hot goalie to victory. Unfortunately, it appears that outstanding performances in hockey's postseason are also hard to predict.
Only 7% of the variation in postseason save percentage can be
explained by what a goalie did in the regular season.[29]

Perhaps, though, the playoffs and the regular season are just different. Maybe there are goalies that are just really good in the postseason. Although some may believe this to be true, there doesn't
appear to be any evidence in the data. A study of goalies who played
substantial time in two consecutive postseasons revealed that none of
the variation in save percentage in a current postseason was explained
by what a goalie did in the previous postseason.[30] Certainly there are
goalies who have played well in the playoffs, but it doesn't appear that
the ability to play well in the postseason is a skill. Whether or not
someone becomes a "hot" goalie appears to be mostly about luck.

Okay, goalies are inconsistent, and one can't predict who is going
to be a "hot" goalie come playoff time. Now we come to the big question: Do the people who write the checks understand this story?

To answer this question, let's consider the market for free agent
goalies.[31] Again, productivity at the goalie position can be easily measured with save percentage. Fans and the media, though, might look at
wins, winning percentage, or Goals Against Average in evaluating a
goalie. Decision-makers in the NHL, though, ignore these other

measures. Of all these performance measures examined, only past save percentage statistically impacts a goalie's current salary. The key phrase in the last sentence, though, is "past save percentage." There is no statistical link between current save percentage and current salary.[32] This tells us that decision-makers in hockey look at the correct statistic in evaluating goals (i.e., save percentage), but these same decision-makers are not able to predict future save percentage. Unfortunately, that's what the salary determination process is all about. Athletes are paid for what they are going to do in the future, and it appears for goalies, this future is essentially unknown. Decision-makers, though, behave as if they are able to predict the future.[33]

Assigning Wins and Losses

The evaluation of goalies is part of a larger story in sports. At the onset of this story it was noted that player statistics are collected to separate the player from his teammates. In essence, statistics are kept so decision-makers can connect wins and losses to individuals.

For most individual players in sports, the process of connecting wins to the player's actions involves first collecting the individual statistics. Some effort is then made to define these numbers in terms of wins. This can be done explicitly via statistical analysis. Or it's done implicitly by the decision-maker as he or she watches the player in action. Whether one follows the explicit or implicit route, the process is essentially the same. First collect the data; then connect data to wins.

For three specific individual positions in sports, though, the process is different. For pitchers in baseball, quarterbacks in football, and goalies in hockey; wins are directly assigned to the individual. Essentially, if you play at one of these positions and your team wins, then you are given a win. If your team loses, you are given a loss.

The analysis of consistency, though, suggests that this practice is misguided. Remember, the less consistent a player, the less his performance is about his own abilities. So who are the least consistent players in North American sports? It's the very players who are traditionally assigned wins and losses. Pitchers, quarterbacks, and goalies are believed to be the players most responsible for winning. But what these players do is heavily dependent on their teammates. Pitchers don't tend to catch the ball when it's hit in play. Quarterbacks can't block for themselves and generally don't catch their own passes. And goalies can do little to control the number of shots on goal they are asked to deflect.

Why are wins and losses assigned to these specific players? In watching these games, we see that no one else touches the object the players are fighting over more frequently. Every play in baseball and football begins with the pitcher and the quarterback. In hockey, except for empty-net goals, every goal and shot on goal involves the goalie. Given how frequently these players are the focus of the action, it's natural to assume these players are the primary determinants of outcomes. The study of consistency, though, tells us that what people assume about pitchers, quarterbacks, and goalies is incorrect. These players are not solely responsible for team success. These players are not even solely responsible for many of the numbers people attach to their performance.

We should emphasize that we are not saying that pitchers, quarterbacks, and goalies fail to make a contribution to outcomes. These positions do have a positive—or negative—impact on team success (or failure). So the search for these players is worthwhile, and these searches—as we will now demonstrate—are certainly something that can be studied.

4

Football in Black and White

Athletes are supposed to be rewarded for what they can do, not for what they are or who they know. Teams shouldn't care whether a player is black or white, rich or poor. All they should care about is whether the player helps the team win.

Although this simple view of sports might be true today, sports have historically failed to live up to this vision. Prior to 1947, a black player regardless of his ability was denied the opportunity to play Major League Baseball.[1] When the National Basketball Association came into existence in 1949, it was also an all-white league.[2] In the latter half of the 20th century, each of these professional sports leagues integrated, and sports moved closer to fulfilling the equal-opportunity ideal.

Tales of racial integration tend to focus on social justice. Such tales, however, are also stories of innovation. Consider the story of integration in Major League Baseball.[3] In the first decades after integration, the average black player outperformed the average white player.[4] It was not until the 1980s that the average performance of each group converged. A study of integration in the Atlantic Coast Conference (ACC) told a similar story.[5] The ACC didn't integrate its basketball teams until the 1960s. In the years that followed, teams that employed more black players tended to win more games.

With a bit of thought, these results shouldn't be seen as surprising. When teams begin to integrate, they first choose the very best players from the minority group. Such players will tend to outperform the average from the majority group, and consequently, teams that integrate first will have an advantage.

Given the impact integration has on team success, we shouldn't be surprised that integration in professional sports, which generally began in the late 1940s in North America, appeared complete by the 1970s and 1980s. At least, that's what we see if we don't look too closely at the National Football League.

A Brief History of the Black Quarterback

The story of integration in professional football followed a somewhat different path from what was observed in baseball and basketball. The story started in 1904 when the Shelby Athletic Club signed Charles W. Follis, the first known black professional football player.[6] Across the next three decades, professional football teams employed 16 additional black players.[7] After the 1933 season, though, the NFL adopted a de facto color barrier.[8]

In 1946, this barrier was removed when the Los Angeles Rams of the NFL signed both Kenny Washington and Woody Strode.[9] At the same time, the Cleveland Browns of the All-American Football Conference signed both Bill Willis and Marion Motley.[10] Across the next decade, more and more black players were added, although progress was slow. From 1948 to 1958, an average of nine black players joined the professional ranks each season. In 1959, the NFL drafted 142 players and only 12—or 8.5%—were black. In other words, more than a decade after reintegration the NFL was still predominantly a white man's league.

In 1960, the American Football League (AFL) came into existence, and not coincidently, 51 black players began a career in professional football.[11] Initially, the AFL was thought of as inferior to the NFL. By the end of the decade, though, the story had changed. On January 11, 1970, the Kansas City Chiefs of the AFL—with a roster where 50% of the players were black[12]—defeated the Minnesota Vikings of the NFL in the Super Bowl. Such success encouraged other teams to seek out the best talent regardless of race and furthered the pace of integration. By the late 1990s, 68% of the league was black.[13]

Although much of the league is black today, there is one glaring exception. Historically the black quarterback has been relatively rare in the NFL. The first was Willie Thrower, who threw the only eight passes of his entire career for the Chicago Bears on October 18, 1953.[14] It wasn't until 1968 that Marlin Briscoe became the first starting black quarterback, leading the Denver Broncos of the AFL.[15]

In the 1970s, the black starting quarterback came to the NFL. The first was James Harris, who was drafted by the Buffalo Bills of the AFL in 1969. In 1970 the NFL and AFL merged. Consequently, when Harris attempted 103 passes for the Bills in 1971 he became the first black quarterback to receive "significant" playing time (where significant is defined as attempting at least 100 passes in a single season)[16] in the history of the NFL. Harris was cut from the Bills after the 1971 season and didn't play professional football in 1972. In 1973 he joined the Los Angeles Rams, performing well enough to be named to the Pro Bowl in 1974. Three years later, though, Harris was traded to the San Diego Chargers, where he ended his career in 1979.

Although Harris had some success on the field, teams still proved reluctant to employ black quarterbacks. In the entire decade of the 1970s, there were only three other black quarterbacks—Joe Gilliam, Dave Mays, and Doug Williams—who attempted 100 passes for an NFL team in one season.[17] Unlike Harris, Gilliam, and Mays, Williams went on to receive significant playing time in the next decade. But after Williams, only four more black quarterbacks—Vince Evans, Warren Moon, Randall Cunningham, and Rodney Peete—received significant playing time at the quarterback position in the 1980s.

By the end of the 1993 season—nearly 50 years after the NFL reintegrated—only eight black quarterbacks had ever attempted 100 passes in a single season in the NFL. When we look at Table 4.1, which lists all 31 black quarterbacks to ever attempt 100 passes in a single season (as of 2008), we see that in the mid-1990s, blacks finally began to make substantial progress at this position.

TABLE 4.1   Black Quarterbacks Who Have Attempted at Least 100 Passes in a Single NFL Season in League History

Black Quarterbacks	Years with 100 Passes Attempted	Years
James Harris	5	1971, 1974-77
Joe Gilliam	1	1974
Dave Mays	1	1977
Doug Williams	7	1978-82, 1987-88
Vince Evans	4	1980-81, 1983, 1995
Warren Moon	15	1984-98
Randall Cunningham	12	1986-90, 1992-95, 98-00
Rodney Peete	10	1989-93, 95-98, 2002
Jeff Blake	8	1994-97, 1999-00, 2002-03
Tony Banks	7	1996-01, 2003
Steve McNair	12	1996-07
Kordell Stewart	7	1997-03
Charlie Batch	4	1998-01
Shaun King	2	1999-00
Ray Lucas	2	1999, 2002
Donovan McNabb	10	1999-08
Akili Smith	2	1999-00
Aaron Brooks	7	2000-06
Daunte Culpepper	9	2000-08
Quincy Carter	3	2001-03

TABLE 4.1   Black Quarterbacks Who Have Attempted at Least 100 Passes in a Single NFL Season in League History

Black Quarterbacks	Years with 100 Passes Attempted	Years
Michael Vick	6	2001-06
Byron Leftwich	4	2003-06
Anthony Wright	2	2003, 2005
David Garrard	4	2005-08
Jason Campbell	3	2006-08
Seneca Wallace	2	2006, 2008
Vince Young	2	2006-07
Quinn Gray	1	2007
Tarvaris Jackson	2	2007-08
Cleo Lemon	1	2007
JaMarcus Russell	1	2008

In 1994, Jeff Blake became the starting quarterback for the Cincinnati Bengals. The next season, Blake, Moon, Evans, Cunningham, and Peete all attempted at least 100 passes. As Table 4.2 indicates, 1995 was the first time that more than five black quarterbacks received significant playing time in the same season. Participation by blacks continued to increase in the latter 1990s, with the number of black quarterbacks rising from five to eleven by the end of the decade. The mark of eleven was again matched in 2000 and 2003. Eleven, though, remains the maximum number, and in 2008 only seven black quarterbacks received significant playing time.

Relative to what was seen in the 1970s and 1980s, blacks certainly have more opportunity to play quarterback in the NFL today. Even with an increase in the number of black quarterbacks, though, this position is still dominated by whites. From 2000 to 2008 there were 343 instances where a quarterback attempted 100 passes in a single

season. Black quarterbacks only accounted for 84 of these instances,
or 24.5%. When one notes that about two-thirds of the NFL is black,
it's easy to conclude that progress still remains to be made in the
effort to integrate the quarterback position.

**TABLE 4.2   Percentage of NFL Quarterbacks Who Are Black:
1971-2008 Minimum 100 Passes Attempted in a Season**

Year	Black Quarterbacks	All Quarterbacks	Percent Black
1971	1	35	3%
1972	0	31	0%
1973	0	36	0%
1974	2	38	5%
1975	1	33	3%
1976	1	36	3%
1977	2	36	6%
1978	1	33	3%
1979	1	33	3%
1980	2	36	6%
1981	2	40	5%
1982	1	30	3%
1983	1	38	3%
1984	1	41	2%
1985	1	43	2%
1986	2	41	5%
1987	3	41	7%
1988	3	44	7%
1989	3	37	8%
1990	3	37	8%
1991	2	38	5%
1992	3	42	7%
1993	3	44	7%

TABLE 4.2 Percentage of NFL Quarterbacks Who Are Black: 1971-2008 Minimum 100 Passes Attempted in a Season

Year	Black Quarterbacks	All Quarterbacks	Percent Black
1994	3	43	7%
1995	5	39	13%
1996	5	43	12%
1997	6	41	15%
1998	7	42	17%
1999	10	42	24%
2000	11	35	31%
2001	9	31	29%
2002	10	37	27%
2003	11	36	31%
2004	6	37	16%
2005	8	39	21%
2006	10	36	28%
2007	9	51	18%
2008	7	41	17%
Totals	**156**	**1,456**	**11%**

Updated from Berri and Simmons (2009a)

Performance in Black and White

Such a conclusion is bolstered when one considers performance on the field. Before we get to the topic of performance and race, though, we first have to address how a quarterback's performance can be measured. The measure most frequently cited is the NFL's Quarterback Rating. As detailed in Appendix B, "Measuring Wins Produced in the NFL," the NFL's method is complicated, and furthermore, incomplete and inaccurate. Our approach is to calculate each quarterback's Wins Produced and a simplified measure we call QB Score. Each of these measures connects a quarterback's performance with respect to both passing and rushing to team wins.

Appendix B provides further details behind Wins Produced and QB Score. For the purpose of the present discussion, two issues need to be noted. First, we argue that a quarterback's performance should be evaluated per play. Specifically, we focus on Wins Produced per 100 plays (WP100). In addition, we are going to examine quarterbacks from 1970 to 2008. Across this time period the performance of a typical quarterback has changed. Consequently, when we compare performances across several decades we need to consider Relative WP100, or WP100 that has been adjusted for the average performance in each year.

With a measure of player performance, let's discuss the performance of James Harris. As the first black quarterback to lead an NFL team, Harris is essentially the Jackie Robinson of NFL quarterbacks. Unlike Robinson, though, Harris was never elected Rookie of the Year, Most Valuable Player, or into the Hall of Fame. In other words, Harris is not considered one of the all-time greats in his sport. But how fair is this evaluation?

As noted, Harris was named to the Pro Bowl in 1974. He didn't begin that season, though, as the starting quarterback of the L.A. Rams. John Hadl, who went to the Pro Bowl in 1973 with the Rams, began the season as the starter. However, after five games Hadl was traded to the Green Bay Packers, and Harris became the team's starter. Harris's Relative WP100 in 1974 was 0.730. To put this number in perspective, the average quarterback from 1970 to 2008 posted a 0.377 Relative WP100. So Harris was well above average; and of the quarterbacks who attempted 100 passes in 1974, Harris ranked fifth in per play performance.

The next season, Harris played in 13 games with a 0.550 Relative WP100. In 1976 his playing time was limited, but Harris's per play performance was outstanding; his Relative WP100 of 0.928 ranked second in the league. Despite this performance, though, the Rams decided to hire an aging Joe Namath in 1977. With the New York Jets in 1974, Namath was above average (Relative WP100 of 0.490). In 1975, though, his Relative WP100 fell to 0.184, and the next season he posted a -0.106 mark. Despite these performances, though, the Rams decided to trade Harris to the Chargers and install Broadway Joe as their starting quarterback.[18] Harris was the primary starter for the Chargers in 1977, but by 1979 his NFL career was over.

Consider now the case of the second black quarterback to start an NFL game. Back in 1974, Joe Gilliam was the first black quarterback to start the season as a team's number-one quarterback. Gilliam was given the job over Terry Bradshaw, the first player taken in the 1970 draft. Although Bradshaw is considered one of the all-time great quarterbacks today, in 1974, it was unclear whether he was ever going to be an effective player. During his first four seasons—whether you look at the NFL's Quarterback Rating or Relative WP100—he had never posted above average numbers.

Bradshaw was especially bad in 1973. Among the 39 quarterbacks who attempted 100 passes, Bradshaw ranked in the bottom five in Relative WP100. Consequently, it wasn't surprising that the Steelers looked elsewhere in 1974. Although Gilliam was above average with respect to Relative WP100, after six games Gilliam was back on the bench. Bradshaw then went on to post below average numbers the rest of the season. After the Steelers won the Super Bowl—primarily because of their defense—Bradshaw became entrenched as the team's starter and went on to the Hall of Fame career people remember. Meanwhile, Gilliam was out of football after the 1975 season.[19]

The Harris and Gilliam story is not unique. Doug Williams began playing for the Tampa Bay Buccaneers as a rookie in 1978. After two below-average seasons, Williams posted above average numbers from 1980 to 1982. Prior to the 1983 season, though, Williams left the Buccaneers over a salary dispute and played the next two seasons in the

USFL. The USFL folded in 1986, and Williams returned to the NFL with the Washington Redskins. In 1987, due to an injury to Jay Schroeder (Washington's starting quarterback), Williams was named the team's starter[20] toward the end of the season. Williams then led the Redskins to the Super Bowl title in 1988, becoming the first black quarterback to start for a team in the NFL's biggest game. After this success, Williams continued as Washington's starter the next season. However, injuries eventually forced him from the starting lineup, and by 1989, his career was over.

The stories of Harris, Gilliam, and Williams suggest that the first black quarterbacks struggled to get a chance. Furthermore, despite often performing at an above-average level, these chances were often fleeting. Such is the same story for Warren Moon, the only black quarterback in the Hall of Fame.

Since 1969, there have been ten quarterbacks who entered the NFL and eventually were named to the Hall of Fame. Looking at the career performances of these players, reported in Table 4.3, reveals some interesting patterns. With respect to Relative WP100, all of these quarterbacks—with the exception of Roger Staubach and Joe Montana—posted below-average numbers in at least one season. In fact, John Elway was below average in five different years. Such a result, as noted in the previous chapter, is not surprising. Quarterbacks tend to be inconsistent. Despite this inconsistency, though, these Hall-of-Fame quarterbacks tended to keep their job with their respective teams.[21] At least, the white quarterbacks tended to keep their job. For Warren Moon it was a different story.

Moon first became nationally known when he led the Washington Huskies to a Rose Bowl victory over the Michigan Wolverines in 1978. But in the 1978 draft, no NFL team called his name. So, Moon headed to the Canadian Football League, where he led the Edmonton Eskimos to five consecutive Grey Cup championships.

This record finally proved good enough to get the attention of an NFL team. Unfortunately for Moon, that team was the Houston

Oilers. In 1983, the Oilers finished 2-14, and it was with this team that Moon began his NFL career at the age of 27 in 1984.

TABLE 4.3   Ten Recent Hall-of-Fame Quarterbacks

Quarterback	Years	Team(s)	Above Average Seasons	Below Average Seasons	Career Relative Wins Produced	Career Relative WP100
Roger Staubach	1969-79	Dallas	8	0	24.8	0.674
Terry Bradshaw	1970-83	Pittsburgh	8	4	21.0	0.452
Dan Fouts	1973-87	San Diego	12	2	37.1	0.603
Joe Montana	1979-94	San Francisco-Kansas City	13	0	38.2	0.621
Dan Marino	1983-99	Miami	15	1	53.2	0.596
John Elway	1983-99	Denver	11	5	39.7	0.465
Warren Moon	1984-98	Houston-Minnesota-Seattle-Kansas City	10	5	35.8	0.457
Steve Young	1985-99	Tampa Bay-San Francisco	8	1	35.0	0.670
Jim Kelly	1986-96	Buffalo	9	2	26.1	0.482
Troy Aikman	989-00	Dallas	9	3	25.0	0.471
		Average for these 10 QBs	**10.3**	**2.3**	**33.6**	**0.549**

Average Relative WP100 for all quarterbacks from 1969 to 2008 is 0.377.

As Table 4.4 indicates, Moon's performance across his first three campaigns was inconsistent. Then, in year four—at the age of 30—Moon embarked on a string of six seasons where his Relative WP100 numbers were well above average. After this streak, though, the story of Moon's performance—and the identity of his employers—is dominated by inconsistency.

TABLE 4.4   The Career of Warren Moon

Team	Season	Games Played	Relative WP100
Houston	1984	16	0.448°
Houston	1985	14	0.268
Houston	1986	15	0.305
Houston	1987	12	0.447°
Houston	1988	11	0.667°
Houston	1989	16	0.531°
Houston	1990	15	0.680°
Houston	1991	16	0.518°
Houston	1992	11	0.596°
Houston	1993	15	0.331
Minnesota	1994	15	0.456°
Minnesota	1995	16	0.462°
Minnesota	1996	8	0.308
Seattle	1997	15	0.488°
Seattle	1998	10	0.246
Kansas City	1999	1	0.807°
Kansas City	2000	2	0.039

°Above average numbers

In 1993, the Oilers finished 12-4. Moon's performance, though, was below par. Although this was the first below-average season since 1986, Moon was traded to the Minnesota Vikings. The Vikings in 1994—with Moon once again offering an above average performance—finished 10-6. (Meanwhile, the Oilers slipped to 2-14, the same mark the team had before Moon arrived.)

In 1995, Moon was again an above-average performer, but in 1996 his performance slipped and he changed teams. At the age of 41, playing for the Seattle Seahawks, Moon was once again above average. The next season, though, Moon's performance declined and yet again, he changed teams.

Let's review the pattern. The white Hall-of-Fame quarterbacks tended to play for the same team throughout their careers. Although most of the quarterbacks had at least one poor season, these poor seasons didn't generally cause the quarterback to change employers. In contrast, Moon had to wait five years just to find an NFL employer, and his first job was with the very worst NFL team. Eventually, with Moon leading the way, the Oilers became a consistent playoff team. After six above-average campaigns, though, one poor season caused the Oilers to trade Moon to the Vikings. One poor season then caused the Vikings to let Moon go to Seattle, who repeated the same pattern two years later.

Of course, Moon did get to play; and he did post the numbers necessary to get into the Hall of Fame. Harris, Gilliam, and Williams never quite got the same chance. What would have happened, though, if this trio got to play as much as a typical Hall-of-Fame quarterback?

The average Hall-of-Famer in Table 4.3 participated in 6,187 plays. If the first black quarterbacks got to appear in that many plays they would have each produced, as noted in Table 4.5, more than 27 wins in their careers. Such productivity would have at least rivaled the career mark of Terry Bradshaw. In other words, the first black quarterbacks—given the same opportunity as the typical Hall-of-Fame quarterbacks—might have also made it into the Hall of Fame. Consequently, each of these pioneers in football might today be remembered in the same way many remember the first black players in baseball history.

Our game of what-if only examined three quarterbacks. Although that game revealed the first black quarterbacks were above-average performers, a sample of three is hardly conclusive. What do we see if we examine the average performance of all black and white quarterbacks?

TABLE 4.5   Playing What-If with the First Black Quarterbacks

First Black Quarterbacks	Career RWP100	Career Relative Wins Produced with Career Plays of an Average Hall-of-Famer
James Harris	0.451	27.9
Joe Gilliam	0.442	27.3
Doug Williams	0.492	30.4

From 1971 to 1993, the average black quarterback posted better numbers than the average white quarterback. This is seen in Table 4.6 whether one looks at the NFL's Quarterback Rating or WP100. With respect to the latter metric, there is a 30% difference between the average per-play performances from each group. In more recent years, although the differences narrow, the average black quarterback still offered more production.

TABLE 4.6   Comparing the Average Black and White Quarterback

Statistics	Black QB 1971-93	White QB 1971-93	Black QB 1994-08	White QB 1994-08
Number of Quarterbacks	39	824	117	548
Completion Percentage	54.5%	54.6%	57.6%	58.4%
Touchdown Passes per Passing Attempt	4.1%	4.1%	3.8%	3.9%
Interceptions per Attempt	4.1%	4.5%	3.0%	3.3%
Passing Yards per Passing Attempt	7.08	6.84	6.70	6.72
Quarterback Rating	73.89	71.05	78.18	77.88
Passing Yards per Game	190.9	168.6	186.7	191.3
Rushing Yards per Game	16.3	7.4	18.3	6.8
Yards Lost from Sacks per Game	15.8	15.2	13.5	12.7
Yards Gained per Game	191.3	160.8	191.5	185.5
Plays per Game	32.2	28.4	33.7	32.4
Fumbles Lost per Game	NA	NA	0.3	0.2

TABLE 4.6 Comparing the Average Black and White Quarterback

Statistics	Black QB 1971-93	White QB 1971-93	Black QB 1994-08	White QB 1994-08
Interceptions per Game	1.0	1.1	0.8	0.9
Wins Produced per Game	0.118	0.080	0.126	0.116
Wins per 100 Plays (WP100)	0.346	0.260	0.363	0.347

Updated from Berri and Simmons (2009a)

Not only do black quarterbacks offer more production than whites, how each group plays the game is also somewhat different. Specifically, black quarterbacks are far more likely to run with the football. The average black quarterback from 1971 to 2008 ran with the ball on 11% of his plays. In contrast, white quarterbacks only ran 7% of the time. To put these averages in perspective, let's consider Warren Moon in 1997 at the age of 41. At this advanced age, Moon still ran on 3% of his plays. Of all black quarterbacks, only Doug Williams—in the second to last season of his career—was less likely to run. If we look at the season observations from white quarterbacks in our data set, though, 11% of these seasons came from white quarterbacks who were less likely to run than the 41-year old Moon. Included in this sample was Peyton Manning's 1998 season. This was Manning's first season in the NFL, and at the age of 22, he was less likely to run with the football than the aging Moon.

Quarterback Pay in Black and White

The difference in how black and white quarterbacks perform is important to the discussion of the salaries earned by each group.[22] Such a discussion begins with average salaries, where we see a 3.3% advantage for white quarterbacks. If we focus on the highest paid white and black quarterbacks, though, we see a 10% difference.[23]

Although simple averages are revealing, to understand the compensation of an NFL quarterback one must consider the factors, listed in Table 4.7, that determine pay.[24] Let's focus on player performance. Aggregate measures such as the NFL's QB Rating or QB Score (a simplified version of Wins Produced detailed in Appendix B) are statistically related to salary. Although QB Score explains more of a player's salary than QB Rating, one can explain even more if one considers the individual performance statistics separately. Such an approach doesn't just improve explanatory power, it also reveals something about decision-making in the NFL.

TABLE 4.7   What Explains the Pay of an NFL Quarterback?

Statistically Significant and Positive Factors	Statistically Insignificant Factors
Player Performance (various measures)	Player Performance (various measures)
First or Second Round Draft Choice[25]	Pro Bowl Appearances
Experience[26]	Market Size[27]
Quality of Skill Players around Quarterback[28]	

Statistically Significant and Negative Factors	
Changing Teams	

The performance measures considered included passing yards, touchdowns per attempts, completions per attempts, interceptions per attempts, and rushing yards. Of these, only passing yards was consistently significant. In fact, a salary model that only considers passing yards does a better job of explaining salaries than a salary model that considers any aggregate performance measure (i.e., QB Rating, QB Score, etc.).

The importance of passing yards is not surprising. Passing yards for quarterbacks is much like scoring points for a basketball player. What may be surprising is the insignificance of interceptions. In evaluating quarterbacks, fans tend to focus on interceptions. However, as noted in the previous chapter, one cannot predict turnovers. There-fore, decision-makers are correct to ignore interceptions when deter-mining a quarterback's salary.[29]

Where there may be an issue with decision-making is with respect to rushing yards. Again, black quarterbacks are much more likely to run with the football than their white counterparts, but all this run-ning is not statistically connected to salary. It would appear that black quarterbacks are doing something that helps their respective teams win games, but this extra effort is uncompensated.

The insignificance of rushing yards suggests that black quarter-backs are paid differently. More evidence behind this proposition can be seen by looking at how much teams pay for passing yards. At lower levels of productivity and salary, there is not much difference between how black and white quarterbacks are treated. A difference is observed when one looks at the very best quarterbacks in the game. Specifically, white quarterbacks who excel are paid more than simi-larly productive black quarterbacks.[30]

It appears there's a difference in how the best quarterbacks are perceived. This can be illustrated by examining the careers of Brett Favre, Donovan McNabb, and Steve McNair. Of these three, who is mostly likely to be in the Hall of Fame someday? Before answering, consider the numbers reported in Table 4.8.

TABLE 4.8   Comparing Favre, McNair, and McNabb

Quarterback	Years	Career Relative WP100
Brett Favre	1993-2008	0.454
Steve McNair	1995-2007	0.502
Donovan McNabb	1999-2008	0.478

Both McNair and McNabb have a slight edge in Relative WP100. Consequently, one could make the argument that both McNair and McNabb were at least as effective as Favre. Certainly the perform-ance of McNair and McNabb compares favorably to Favre, as well as to Hall-of-Fame quarterbacks like Jim Kelly, Troy Aikman, and John Elway. One suspects, though, that while Favre will be voted into the Hall of Fame on the first ballot, McNair and McNabb will have a much harder time.[31] It's not that people don't think these two black quarterbacks are good. It does appear—as the study of salaries indicates—that the very best black quarterbacks are not perceived to be as good as the very best white quarterbacks.

The racial differences in perceptions of the very best signal callers are certainly the most important story the study of salaries reveals. It's not the only story, though, one can tell about decision-making. Previously it was noted that the performance of quarterbacks is quite inconsistent. This inconsistency is also revealed in the study of salaries. Specifically, the study of salaries revealed a statistical link between current salary and past performance. When one looked at the link between current salary and current performance, no relationship was revealed. Such a result is similar to what was uncovered for goalies in hockey. When performance is difficult to predict, as is the case for goalies and quarterbacks, the checks a player cashes today are not related to what he's currently doing on the field.[32]

Decision-makers, though, behave as if performance is predictable, and this is a theme that we are going to revisit next, when we examine the NFL draft.

5

Finding the Face of the Franchise

Imagine you are completing a journalism degree at Columbia University. As graduation day approaches, it becomes clear that you are one of the top students in your class. Your lofty ranking starts you dreaming of working at places like the *New York Times* or the *Los Angeles Times*. Just before you graduate, though, you are notified that your rights have been acquired by the *Lincoln Journal-Star*. The notification goes on to add that if you want to work as a journalist, this will only happen in Lincoln, Nebraska.[1]

When you hear this news, you become angry and contact your lawyer. Surely, someone cannot require that you—a top graduate of Columbia—begin your career in Lincoln. Your lawyer, though, tells you that journalists have signed a collective bargaining agreement, giving newspapers the right to assign new talent in this fashion. Furthermore, this collective bargaining agreement has been upheld numerous times in court. In essence, there is nothing for you to do if you want to work as a journalist. For your career to happen, it must start happening on the plains of Nebraska.

Outside the world of sports, the scenario we just described is unthinkable. We are accustomed to a labor market where workers are free to apply to any employer, and employers are free to hire any worker. To have the "rights" to our labor simply assigned to a firm, without our consent, runs contrary to the ideals of a free and open labor market.

Birth of the Draft

Due to the effort of Bert Bell,[2] this very scenario is now an accepted way of life in North American sports. In 1935, the Brooklyn Dodgers (yes, there was an NFL team with this name) and Bell's Philadelphia Eagles both desired the services of a star fullback with the Minnesota Golden Gophers named Stanislaus ("Stockyard Stan") Kostka.[3] At this time there was no college football draft. Consequently, a bidding war for Kostka ensued between the Dodgers and Eagles. When the war ended, Kostka signed a $5,000 contract with the Dodgers.

Such a contract doesn't sound very impressive today. A salary of $5,000 in 1934 is only worth about $80,000 in 2009 dollars,[4] a figure well below the minimum salary of $295,000 paid to NFL rookies in 2008.[5] Although it pales in comparison to what rookies are paid today, it did rival the pay of Kostka's hero, Bronco Nagurski. Nagurski began playing in the NFL in 1930 and was selected to All-Pro First-Team in 1932, 1933, and 1934. For a player with no NFL experience to get the same money paid to one of the league's stars seemed like a problem for many NFL observers.

It certainly was a problem for Bell. The owner of the Eagles argued that NFL teams should no longer compete for the services of college talent. For Bell, a better system would be a reverse-order draft, where the worst teams from the previous season get to select the best college talent. Upon being drafted, the players would only be allowed to negotiate a contract with the team that held his rights. Consequently, a player who wanted to play in the NFL had to come to terms with the team that chose him on draft day.

Instituting the NFL draft clearly benefitted Bell. Bell's Eagles were the worst team in 1935; and when the draft was instituted in 1936, Bell got to choose first. Despite Bell's obvious self-interest, defenders of this institution have often argued that a reverse-order draft is necessary to maintain a league's competitive balance, or the degree of parity in a league.[6] By funneling the best amateur talent to the worst teams, the worst teams are given an opportunity to improve. Theoretically the differences between the best and worst should lessen over time. At least, that's the theory offered by defenders of the draft. Unfortunately, more than 50 years of economic theory suggests a reverse-order draft wouldn't actually alter the level of competitive balance.[7] Furthermore, there's very little empirical evidence supporting the notion that a draft impacts the level of parity in a league,[8] or even that a league's level of competitive balance has much impact on league attendance.[9]

If the draft is not about competitive balance, what is its purpose? Bell proposed the institution of a draft after he lost a bidding war for Kostka. It's difficult to read this story and not conclude that Bell was primarily motivated by a desire to spend less on players. Because the draft eliminates the bidding war for new talent, the cost of these players falls. Whether this was Bell's ultimate objective or not (and we suspect it was), the draft has had that effect. Research has shown[10] that an NFL player with less than three years of experience is paid a wage that's 50% below what they would earn in a free market. Such findings suggest that Bell's institution—at least from the perspective of lowering the cost of new talent—has been remarkably successful.

The Problem with Picking First

One might think that the draft—as a tool to extract money from new talent—would be most successful with respect to the very first picks. After all, the best players should be chosen first, and therefore, teams that hold the rights to the first picks should be reaping the greatest benefit from the draft.

A recent study by Cade Massey and Richard Thaler,[11] though, suggests otherwise. This study examined the surplus value of each drafted player, or the difference between each player's salary and the economic value of the player's production if he was allowed to be a free agent. If the draft worked according to conventional wisdom, the greatest surplus value would be found at the top of the draft. However, the data suggests that the picks in the top half of the second round have the greatest surplus value.[12] This means that teams in the first round, especially at the top of the first round, should be making every effort to trade down.

In contrast, teams have traditionally taken the opposite approach. A premium is often paid by teams to move up in the first round. To illustrate, in 2004 the New York Giants and San Diego Chargers completed a trade, with the Giants getting the first pick in the first round and the rights to quarterback Eli Manning. For this pick, the Chargers acquired the fourth pick in the first round, a pick that gave San Diego the rights to quarterback Philip Rivers. In addition to the rights to Rivers, the Chargers were also given a third round pick in 2004, and a first round and a fifth round pick in the 2005 draft. So to move up just three spots in the draft—to a pick with a lower expected surplus value—the Giants surrendered three additional picks.[13]

The Massey and Thaler examination of surplus value considered all positions on the field. Thus, the study could only consider factors like games played, game started, and Pro Bowl selections to evaluate the quality of a player.[14] A different approach is to consider the statistics tracked for individual players. Such an approach, though, requires that one pick a position, and the obvious position to focus on is the quarterback.[15]

Quarterbacks are often thought of as the "face of the franchise," and quarterbacks are the only players in football assigned responsibility for wins and losses. Given the stature of this position and the money invested, one would expect decision-makers would get the decision to draft a specific quarterback "right."

To address the "rightness" of this decision, let's first look at Table 5.1. This table reports the productivity of the first quarterback taken in the draft from 1990 to 2004. In looking at these numbers, we have to remember that the average quarterback posts a Relative WP100 of 0.377. As we can see, the top signal callers across these 15 drafts were, on average, below average. In fact, only five of these 15 top choices were above-average players after five NFL seasons.

TABLE 5.1 Performance of the First Quarterback Selected From 1990 to 2004 (Performance After Five Seasons in the NFL)

First Quarterback	Year Drafted	Round Drafted	Pick Number	Relative Wins Produced	Relative WP100
Eli Manning	2004	1	1	7.5	0.298
Carson Palmer	2003	1	1	11.3	0.477°
David Carr	2002	1	1	6.3	0.244
Michael Vick	2001	1	1	8.2	0.435°
Chad Pennington	2000	1	18	6.7	0.540°
Tim Couch	1999	1	1	4.9	0.243
Peyton Manning	1998	1	1	16.5	0.534°
Jim Druckenmiller	1997	1	26	-0.3	-0.441
Tony Banks	1996	2	42	6.5	0.290
Steve McNair	1995	1	3	9.4	0.511°
Heath Shuler	1994	1	3	0.7	0.094
Drew Bledsoe	1993	1	1	11.3	0.355
David Klingler	1992	1	6	1.3	0.153
Dan McGwire	1991	1	16	-0.3	-0.189
Jeff George	1990	1	1	6.4	0.276
Averages			**8.1**	**6.4**	**0.255**

°Above average numbers, where Average Relative WP100 is 0.377.

This list includes a number of choices that in retrospect look less than desirable. For example, consider Dan McGwire, the first choice in 1991. McGwire is the brother of baseball player Mark McGwire, who set the record of home runs in a single season in 1998. Dan was not quite as successful as a football player. Although he stood 6'8" in height, making him the tallest quarterback listed in Table 5.1, McGwire's height didn't translate into much production. He only started five games in his career, and his production of wins fell into the negative range. Another choice that didn't quite work out was Heath Shuler. Shuler finished second in the Heisman vote in 1994 and was taken with the third overall choice in the subsequent draft by Washington. Washington also selected Gus Frerotte with the 197th overall choice in 1994. Frerotte went to the Pro Bowl in 1996, and in 2008 was still playing in the NFL (as the starting quarterback of the Minnesota Vikings). Shuler's career ended in 1997, and in 2005 he was elected to the United States Congress. If the Redskins were looking for leadership—and if people in Congress are examples of leaders— the choice of Shuler might make sense. With respect to production on the field, though, it's pretty clear Washington's choice of Shuler didn't quite work out as they hoped in 1994.

The stories of McGwire and Shuler indicate that those selecting quarterbacks make some spectacular mistakes, but the analysis might be unfair. It's possible that, as badly as some of these quarterbacks played, these were really the best choices available in each year. With this issue in mind, each draft class was ranked in terms of career Relative Wins Produced after five years in the league.[16] The results, reported in Table 5.2, indicate that of the 15 drafts examined, the first quarterback taken was the leader in Relative Wins Produced only six times.

Frequently, the leader in Relative Wins Produced was taken much later in the draft. Perhaps the most amusing case is the aforementioned Shuler-Frerotte draft of 1994. Washington clearly missed on Shuler in the first round. But they were not the only teams to miss. The two most productive quarterbacks available to be drafted were Jeff Garcia and Kurt Warner. Neither quarterback, though, was drafted. The most productive quarterback selected on draft day was Gus Frerotte, and he didn't hear his name called until the very last round of the draft. Therefore, the order that quarterbacks were chosen in 1994 was almost the inverse of their eventual productivity.

TABLE 5.2   The Top Quarterbacks in Each Draft in Terms of Wins Produced: 1990-2004 (Performance After First Five Seasons in the NFL)

Quarterback	Year Drafted	Order Taken in Draft	Relative Wins Produced
Ben Roethlisberger	2004	3	10.0
Carson Palmer	2003	1	11.3
David Carr	2002	1	6.3
Drew Brees	2001	2	8.4
Marc Bulger	2000	5	12.7
Daunte Culpepper	1999	4	12.4
Peyton Manning	1998	1	16.5
Jake Delhomme	1997	Not Drafted	7.9
Tony Banks	1996	1	6.5
Steve McNair	1995	1	9.4
Jeff Garcia	1994	Not Drafted	15.4
Drew Bledsoe	1993	1	11.3
Jeff Blake	1992	8	9.0
Brett Favre	1991	3	11.2
Neil O'Donnell	1990	5	9.4

Although productivity doesn't always follow draft order, compensation most certainly does. In addition, very small changes in draft position can have a very large impact on pay. Table 5.3 reports the first-year compensation of each quarterback selected in the 2002 draft.

TABLE 5.3   Reviewing the First-Year Compensation of the 2002 Quarterback Draft Class[17]

Quarterback	Team	Round	Pick	First-Year Base Salary	Signing Bonus	First-Year Base Salary + Signing Bonus
David Carr	Houston	1	1	$1,040,000	$10,920,000	$11,960,000
Joey Harrington	Detroit	1	3	$1,300,000	$6,000,000	$7,300,000
Patrick Ramsey	Washington	1	32	$344,000	$3,100,000	$3,444,000
Josh McCown	Arizona	3	81	$225,000	$483,000	$708,000
David Garrard	Jacksonville	4	108	$225,000	$424,000	$649,000
Rohan Davey	New England	4	117	$225,000	$330,000	$555,000
Randy Fasani	Carolina	5	137	$225,000	175,000	$400,000
Kurt Kittner	Atlanta	5	158	$225,000	111,000	$336,000
Brandon Doman	San Francisco	5	163	$225,000	106,000	$331,000
Craig Nall	Green Bay	5	164	$225,000	$104,000	$329,000
J.T. O'Sullivan	New Orleans	6	186	$225,000	$68,000	$293,000
Steve Bellisari	St. Louis	6	205	$225,000	$45,000	$270,000
Seth Burford	San Diego	7	216	$225,000	$38,000	$263,000
Jeff Kelly	Seattle	7	232	$225,000	$31,000	$256,000
Wes Pate	Baltimore	7	236	$225,000	$29,000	$254,000

The very first pick in this draft was David Carr. His contract with the Houston Texans included a $10,920,000 signing bonus with a first-year base salary of $1,040,000; so Carr received $11,960,000 his first year. Joey Harrington was chosen two spots later by the Detroit Lions and signed a contract that called for him to be paid, via base salary and signing bonus, $7,300,000. So, two spots at the top of the draft resulted in a difference of $4,660,000 in first-year compensation. This difference eclipsed the gap between the first-year compensation of Harrington and Patrick Ramsey, the quarterback chosen by Washington with the last pick of the first round. Ramsey, selected 29 picks after Harrington, was paid $3,444,000 his first year, or $3,856,000 less than Harrington.

When you move past the first round of the draft the differences in pay are even smaller. Josh McCown was selected in the third round by the Arizona Cardinals. According to ESPN.com, McCown's entire three-year contract was only worth $1,388,000. Contracts in the NFL are not guaranteed. Therefore, at the time he signed, McCown was only sure to receive his signing bonus of $483,000 and—if he made the team—his first-year salary of $225,000.

This is essentially the same situation that David Garrard faced. Garrard was selected in the fourth round by Jacksonville, 27 picks after McCown was chosen by Arizona. As was the case for McCown— and every quarterback selected after McCown—Garrard's first-year base salary was also $225,000. With a signing bonus of $424,000, Garrard's first-year compensation of $649,000 was only $59,000 less than the amount of money paid to McCown.

It's obvious that a quarterback reaps substantial benefits when he is picked early in the draft. The teams paying out these benefits, though, don't seem to see much of a return on their investment. To illustrate, across the first five seasons of their respective careers, Garrard was much more productive than Carr (0.417 Relative WP100 versus 0.244 Relative WP100). Eventually, this productivity difference impacted playing time. By the start of the 2007 season, Garrard was named the starting quarterback in Jacksonville. Meanwhile, Houston allowed Carr to sign with the Carolina Panthers in 2007, where Carr began the season as a backup.

Although it is clear that teams make mistakes drafting quarterbacks, it should be noted that more than 30 years of data suggests there is a statistical link between a quarterback's draft position and his production of wins in the NFL.[18] Draft position, though, only explains about 4% of the variation in a quarterback's performance. In other words, 96% of the variation in a quarterback's productivity was unrelated to where he was chosen in the draft. Although that doesn't sound too good, 4% is better than nothing. There is at least a suggestion that decision-makers in the NFL know something on draft day.

Then again, after a bit more investigation this hint of a suggestion seems to vanish. How many wins a quarterback produces depends on two factors: the number of plays a quarterback participates in and a quarterback's per-play productivity. Draft position and how often a quarterback appears on the field (i.e., number of plays) have a very clear statistical link.[19] Once the link between draft position and productivity per play (i.e., Relative WP100) is investigated, though, the statistical link vanishes. Draft position gets a quarterback on the field, but draft position doesn't appear to tell us anything about how well the quarterback plays when he's on the field.[20]

As Table 5.4 illustrates, the quarterbacks taken with one of the first ten choices did get more plays, and their Relative Wins per Game were also higher. However, the per play numbers (i.e., Relative WP100 or the NFL's QB Rating) reveal that the players taken with picks 11 to 50 were more productive than those taken at the top of the draft. In fact, quarterbacks taken from picks 51 to 90 were—on a per-play basis—as productive as the quarterbacks taken with one of the first ten picks. Remember, the quarterbacks taken first are much more expensive. It doesn't appear, though, that these highly touted quarterbacks are any better than those taken in the second and third rounds.[21]

Such results cast serious doubt on the decision made at the start of the 2009 NFL draft. The Detroit Lions—after failing to win a single game in 2008—selected Matthew Stafford with the first pick in the 2009 draft with the hope that he would become the team's franchise quarterback. Stafford signed a six-year contract worth $72 million, with $41.7 million guaranteed.[22] To put these numbers in perspective, a few months after Stafford signed his contract, the New

York Giants re-signed the aforementioned Eli Manning to a new contract that guaranteed Manning $35 million.[23] As of 2009, Manning had already led his team to a Super Bowl victory and Stafford had obviously never played in the NFL. Nevertheless, fans of the Lions hoped the investment in Stafford would prove to be wise.[24] The data suggests, though, that the only guarantee with Stafford's contract is the vast sums of money he will collect. On the day this contract was signed, the quality of Stafford's future performance on the field was still unknown.

This is not the story, though, told by the "draft experts" during ESPN's widely watched broadcast of the NFL draft.[25] The Lions also express certainty that their millions are not going to be wasted. As the review of past drafts has indicated, though, it's hard for a team to know what it is getting on draft day. Matthew Stafford could be the next Peyton Manning. Then again, he could be the next David Carr, Tim Couch, or—as fans of the Lions remember—Joey Harrington. All of these quarterbacks were hailed as future stars on draft day. When the players actually took the field for their respective NFL teams, though, the guarantee of success simply failed to materialize.

TABLE 5.4   Performance of NFL Quarterbacks Chosen at Different Points in the NFL Draft Years: 1970-2007[26]

Picks	Season Observations	Total Plays	Relative Wins per Game	Relative WP100
Picks 1-10	396	131,965	0.111	0.368
Picks 11-50	400	108,765	0.104	0.381
Picks 51-90	372	72,958	0.085	0.373
Picks 91-150	413	68,689	0.070	0.335
Picks 151-250	362	54,293	0.067	0.354

Source: Berri and Simmons (2009b)

How to Get Picked First?

Certainly, there is some sadness when these future stars fail to shine. Then again, each of these top picks did get paid millions of dollars. For a college quarterback, that might be the most important part of the story. What matters most is not how a college quarterback plays in the NFL, but how he can secure a place at the top of the draft and the millions of guaranteed dollars that go with this honor.

The key to this story is what people in the NFL are thinking about on draft day. At the time of the draft it is known where a quarterback attended college and how his college team performed. One can also look at various performance statistics, which can be examined separately or via aggregate measures like Wins Produced and the NFL's Quarterback Rating.

The NFL also has information from each quarterback's job interview. The job interview for the NFL takes place each year in Indianapolis at the NFL's Scouting Combine.[27] Potential draft picks come to the Combine each year and undergo a series of physical tests. These tests reveal a quarterback's height, weight, body mass index (BMI),[28] and how fast he runs. Beyond the physical tests, quarterbacks are also asked to take the Wonderlic test. Because much of what a quarterback accomplishes on the field of play depends on his decision-making ability, future quarterbacks are asked to take an intelligence test that typically ignores the subject of football. Nevertheless, it's hoped the Wonderlic test gives some insights into the mental skills of the player.[29]

All of these factors could theoretically impact where a quarterback is selected. To see which factors mattered in a statistical sense, a model was designed[30] to explain where a quarterback was selected on draft day. This model tells us that when it comes to performance, Wins Produced—relative to the NFL's Quarterback Rating—does a better job of explaining draft position.[31] Such a result echoes what was found when free agent quarterbacks were examined.

Although college performance impacts draft position, it's not the factor that dominates this decision. The NFL Combine factors actually explain more of the variation in a quarterback's draft position.[32] Looking at the individual Combine measures reveals that each additional inch in height will improve a quarterback's draft position by more than one round. Although height can't be changed, a similar leap can be made by a quarterback who can trim about 0.2 seconds off his 40-yard dash time.[33] Turning to BMI, the average quarterback examined had a BMI of 27.8, a mark that traditionally indicates a person is overweight. Despite this indication, increases in this value will actually enhance draft position, but only up to a point. Once the value surpasses 29.1, further increases in BMI will lower a quarterback's draft position. Finally, a quarterback can improve his draft position by about one round[34]—or 30 slots—if he can score about seven points higher on the Wonderlic[35] test.

TABLE 5.5   What Determines a Quarterback's Draft Position

Statistically Significant Factors	Statistically Insignificant Factors
Player Performance (various measures)	Performance of a Quarterback's College Team
Player's Height	Race of the Quarterback
Player's Body Mass Index	
40-Yard Dash Time	
Wonderlic Score	
Playing for an FCS School[36]	

The next step in the analysis is to connect the factors that get a player drafted to what that he does in the NFL. Unfortunately, that step doesn't meet with any success. Specifically, Wonderlic scores, 40-yard dash times, height, BMI, a quarterback's production in college (measured via Wins Produced, WP100, or the NFL's Quarterback Rating), and where a quarterback played in college generally are unrelated to future NFL performance.[37] It appears that all the factors that explain where a quarterback is taken in the draft fail to predict how well he will play in the NFL.

Let's slightly amend that statement. One can look at individual stats and find something. Completion percentage in college is related to completion percentage in the NFL, although the explanatory power is relatively low.[38] Although college completion percentage tells us something about NFL performance, it doesn't tell us much about draft position. In other words, completion percentage doesn't appear to be something on which people focus on draft day.[39]

Perhaps such results are not that surprising. Remember, the productivity of veteran NFL quarterbacks is hard to predict. So we should not be surprised that projecting from the college ranks to the pros is even more difficult.

What is surprising, though, is that decision-makers in the NFL behave as if they can predict future performance. These people are betting millions of dollars that they can see a difference in college quarterbacks. The data strongly suggests, though, that these decision-makers are wrong. It seems that decision-makers are fooled by the inherent randomness of quarterback performance. People look at a host of information and conclude that they can differentiate the quarterback talent observed on draft day; but we have seen that much of this information is nothing more than "fool's gold." As a consequence, a few lucky young men collect a great deal of gold. Teams, though, don't consistently get much of a return from these investments.

Back to Kostka

Let's return to the story of Stan Kostka. When we left this story, the Brooklyn Dodgers had won a bidding war for Kostka's services. The owner of the Eagles, Bert Bell, responded to the loss of this bidding war by proposing a reverse-order draft. What happened, though, to Kostka?

Kostka's entire NFL career lasted only one season. In 1935, Kostka played nine games, starting only five. In these games, he rushed 63 times for 249 yards. Seventeen players ran for more yards in 1935, and twelve other backs ran for more yards per game. It appears the Dodgers failed to find the second coming of Bronco Nagurski.

The career of the player who inspired the draft illustrates the primary problem NFL decision-makers have in selecting players. No matter what's learned about a player on and off the college gridiron, until he faces NFL talent it can't be known what kind of professional player a team has acquired. This was true in 1935, and it appears to be just as true today.

6

The Pareto Principle and Drafting Mistakes

There is no "I" in team.

This one sentence captures the essence of teamwork. Teams are more likely to succeed when each team member places the group ahead of himself or herself. This ethos often leads people to conclude that individuals don't matter on a team. In essence, a team is a community of equals.

When we think of the NBA, though, it's clear that everybody isn't equal. Players like Magic Johnson, Hakeem Olajuwon, Tim Duncan, and LeBron James are not "just as good" as everyone else on their respective teams. There simply is a significant disparity between the productivity of these players and the productivity of their teammates.

The Pareto Principle and Losing to Win

This disparity can be illustrated by an application of the Pareto Principle. Around the start of the 20th century the noted economist Vilfredo Pareto observed that 80% of the wealth in Italy was owned by 20% of the population. This observation led to a general rule of thumb: 80% of observed outcomes come from 20% of the people. For example, people believe that 80% of a firm's sales come from 20% of its clients; or 80% of a firm's production comes from 20% of its employees. The Pareto Principle seems far too simplistic;

consequently, economists like us tend to discount this particular insight from Pareto.[1]

At least, we did before examining wins production in the NBA. From 1977-78 to 2007-08, 80% of all Wins Produced in the NBA came from 22.6% of all player season observations. To apply this to the analysis of a typical NBA team, let's start with the fact that the average NBA team employs about 16 players.[2] Following the Pareto Principle, this means 80% of a team's wins are generally produced by about three players.

Consider the 32 teams that won an NBA title from 1978 to 2009. Table 6.1 presents the top three players—in terms of regular season Wins Produced—on each of these champions. Some of these results are not too surprising. The Boston Celtics teams that won titles in 1984 and 1986 were led by Hall of Famers Larry Bird, Robert Parish, and Kevin McHale; the Lakers in 1985 were led by Hall of Famers Magic Johnson, Kareem Abdul-Jabbar, and James Worthy; and Michael Jordan, Scottie Pippen, and Horace Grant were the most productive players on the Chicago Bulls teams that won championships in 1991, 1992, and 1993. In each case, the analysis appears to conform to conventional wisdom. However, there are some surprises. Hall of Famers Isiah Thomas and Joe Dumars were not among the top three producers of wins for the Pistons when they won the NBA title in 1989. It's also commonly believed that the Boston Celtics in 2008 were led by Kevin Garnett, Paul Pierce, and Ray Allen. Wins Produced, though, indicates that Rajon Rondo was more productive than Allen.

On these title teams, 73.1% of team wins are produced by the top three players on the roster. This is not exactly the 80-20 Pareto rule, but it's close enough to highlight the observation that everyone in the NBA isn't equal. A few players produce far more than the typical employee of the Association.

TABLE 6.1   The Top Three Producers of Wins on the NBA Champions: 1978–2008

Year	Champion	Team Wins Produced	Actual Wins	Top Three Producers of Wins[3]	Wins Produced of Top Three	Percentage from Top Three
1978	Washington	43.5	44	Unseld, Hayes, Dandridge	30.4	69.9%
1979	Seattle	48.3	52	Sikma, Williams, Johnson	28.9	59.7%
1980	LA Lakers	57.7	60	Abdul-Jabbar, Johnson, Wilkes	50.2	87.0%
1981	Boston	56.8	62	Bird, Parish, Maxwell	46.6	82.0%
1982	LA Lakers	54.2	57	Johnson, Abdul-Jabbar, Nixon	45.7	84.4%
1983	Philadelphia	61.7	65	Malone, Cheeks, Erving	48.3	78.2%
1984	Boston	58.9	62	Bird, Parish, McHale	47.2	80.1%
1985	LA Lakers	60.7	62	Johnson, Abdul-Jabbar, Worthy	44.6	73.5%
1986	Boston	66.4	67	Bird, Parish, McHale	49.5	74.5%
1987	LA Lakers	65.9	65	Johnson, Green, Worthy	44.6	67.7%
1988	LA Lakers	56.5	62	Johnson, Scott, Green	40.3	71.4%
1989	Detroit	56.4	63	Rodman, Laimbeer, Mahorn	37.3	66.2%
1990	Detroit	57.1	59	Rodman, Laimbeer, Dumars	40.8	71.5%

TABLE 6.1   The Top Three Producers of Wins on the NBA Champions: 1978–2008

Year	Champion	Team Wins Produced	Actual Wins	Top Three Producers of Wins[3]	Wins Produced of Top Three	Percentage from Top Three
1991	Chicago	65.0	61	Jordan, Pippen, Grant	59.8	92.1%
1992	Chicago	68.7	67	Jordan, Pippen, Grant	62.7	91.3%
1993	Chicago	57.7	57	Jordan, Pippen, Grant	50.4	87.3%
1994	Houston	52.4	58	Olajuwon, Thorpe, Horry	41.0	78.2%
1995	Houston	46.4	47	Olajuwon, Drexler, Horry	30.3	65.3%
1996	Chicago	73.3	72	Jordan, Rodman, Pippen	57.5	78.5%
1997	Chicago	69.4	69	Jordan, Pippen, Rodman	51.3	74.0%
1998	Chicago	59.8	62	Rodman, Jordan, Harper	43.5	72.7%
1999	San Antonio	37.8	37	Robinson, Duncan, Elie	25.0	66.0%
2000	LA Lakers	63.5	67	O'Neal, Bryant, Harper	46.3	72.8%
2001	LA Lakers	50.3	56	O'Neal, Bryant, Fox	36.3	72.1%
2002	LA Lakers	65.5	58	O'Neal, Bryant, Horry	39.7	60.6%
2003	San Antonio	55.2	60	Duncan, Robinson, Rose	38.6	70.0%
2004	Detroit	56.2	54	B. Wallace, Billups, Prince	38.7	68.7%

TABLE 6.1 The Top Three Producers of Wins on the NBA Champions: 1978–2008

Year	Champion	Team Wins Produced	Actual Wins	Top Three Producers of Wins[3]	Wins Produced of Top Three	Percentage from Top Three
2005	San Antonio	61.5	59	Duncan, Ginobili, Parker	38.6	62.8%
2006	Miami	51.1	52	Wade, O'Neal, Haslem	33.1	64.8%
2007	San Antonio	63.1	58	Duncan, Ginobili, Parker	43.9	69.5%
2008	Boston	68.0	66	Garnett, Pierce, Rondo	41.3	60.7%
2009	LA Lakers	61.2	65	Gasol, Bryant, Odom	41.3	67.5%
	Averages	**58.4**	**59.5**		**42.9**	**73.2%**

To acquire the dominant players every championship team requires, teams often turn to the NBA draft. The NBA employs the familiar reverse-order draft, although the specifics are different from what we observed in the NFL. In football, the worst team from the previous season picks first in the draft. In the NBA, the system has generally been a bit more involved.

From 1966 to 1984, the worst teams from each conference flipped a coin to see who would draft first.[4] Then in 1985, a lottery system was put in place. The initial approach was to randomly assign the first seven slots in the draft to the teams that didn't make the playoffs. This was modified for the 1987 draft when only the first three slots were randomly assigned. In 1990 the draft was modified again when a weighted lottery was put in place. These weights, which were modified again in 1994, gave the worst teams in the NBA a better chance to secure one of the first three spots.

Each of these moves was motivated by two competing concerns. First, it's generally believed—at least in North American sports—that competitive balance is improved by allocating the best amateur talent to the worst teams in a league. Although the empirical evidence contradicts this, the belief persists. It's also suspected that NBA teams prior to 1985 intentionally lost games to secure a better draft position.[5] These two perspectives motivate how the NBA draft is structured. Like other North American sports leagues, the NBA believes it should help the worst teams improve, but it doesn't want teams to lose games on purpose to acquire the best amateur talent.

It's important to understand why teams would lose on purpose. Table 6.2 reports the productivity of the first and second players taken in each draft from 1977 to 2004. After five seasons[6] in the NBA, the first player chosen produced on average 19.1 more wins than the second choice.

TABLE 6.2   Evaluating the First and Second Pick in the NBA Draft: 1977 to 2004, Wins Produced After First Five Seasons in the NBA

Year	First Pick	Wins Produced	Second Pick	Wins Produced
1977	Kent Benson	9.7	Otis Birdsong	33.8
1978	Mychal Thompson	33.8	Phil Ford	20.5
1979	Magic Johnson	118.6	Dave Greenwood	41.1
1980	Joe Barry Carroll	8.4	Darrell Griffith	10.6
1981	Mark Aguirre	21.8	Isiah Thomas	51.8
1982	James Worthy	37.8	Terry Cummings	53.4
1983	Ralph Sampson	32.2	Steve Stipanovich	29.4
1984	Hakeem Olajuwon	91.7	Sam Bowie	22.0
1985	Patrick Ewing	56.3	Wayman Tisdale	16.9
1986	Brad Daugherty	42.4	Len Bias°	—
1987	David Robinson	120.2	Armon Gilliam	19.8
1988	Danny Manning	23.9	Rik Smits	4.3

TABLE 6.2 Evaluating the First and Second Pick in the NBA Draft: 1977 to 2004, Wins Produced After First Five Seasons in the NBA

Year	First Pick	Wins Produced	Second Pick	Wins Produced
1989	Pervis Ellison	23.6	Danny Ferry	0.4
1990	Derrick Coleman	51.0	Gary Payton	38.6
1991	Larry Johnson	45.6	Kenny Anderson	24.5
1992	Shaquille O'Neal	89.9	Alonzo Mourning	51.7
1993	Chris Webber	43.7	Shawn Bradley	13.9
1994	Glenn Robinson	18.5	Jason Kidd	61.4
1995	Joe Smith	8.1	Antonio McDyess	20.9
1996	Allen Iverson	21.6	Marcus Camby	32.7
1997	Tim Duncan	90.0	Keith Van Horn	17.0
1998	Michael Olowokandi	-3.0	Mike Bibby	25.7
1999	Elton Brand	61.0	Steve Francis	53.6
2000	Kenyon Martin	19.9	Stromile Swift	12.1
2001	Kwame Brown	10.3	Tyson Chandler	37.4
2002	Yao Ming	51.4	Jay Williams	1.0
2003	LeBron James	85.1	Darko Milicic	0.0
2004	Dwight Howard	93.2	Emeka Okafor	44.8
	Averages	**46.7**	**Averages**	**27.6**

*Len Bias died before he ever played in the NBA.

The overall averages understate the immense differences seen in specific years. Consider the 1979 draft. In 1978-79, the two worst teams in the NBA were the Chicago Bulls and the New Orleans Jazz. The subsequent coin flip awarded the first pick to the Jazz, but unfortunately, New Orleans had already sent its first-round pick to the Lakers in a trade that gave Gail Goodrich to the Jazz. Goodrich was a Hall of Fame player, but probably not for what he did in New Orleans. The Jazz acquired Goodrich in 1976, and he only played three seasons before retiring at the end of the 1978-79 season. In his first season in New Orleans, Goodrich only played 609 minutes. During his last two seasons, he played 4,683 minutes but only produced 4.6 wins. It was for those wins, New Orleans surrendered the rights to the first pick in the 1979 draft. With that pick, the Lakers selected Magic Johnson. Magic went on to produce 118.6 wins across his first five seasons. The Chicago Bulls with the second choice in the 1979 draft selected David Greenwood. After five seasons in Chicago, Greenwood produced only 41.1 wins.

A similar story can be told about the draft that inspired the institution of the NBA's lottery system. Heading into the 1984 draft, the consensus top choice was Hakeem Olajuwon of the University of Houston. There was a suspicion that the Houston Rockets deliberately lost games to secure the worst record in the Western Conference. At that time, the worst teams in each conference flipped a coin for the top pick and as fate would have it, the Rockets won the coin flip. In other words, if Houston lost games on purpose, fate rewarded their bad behavior. Houston took Olajuwon and during the next five seasons received 91.7 Wins Produced. The Blazers took Sam Bowie with the second choice. Although Bowie was quite good his rookie season, injuries limited Bowie's production, and after five seasons he had produced nearly 70 wins fewer than Olajuwon.[7]

Such stories can be also told about the 1987 draft (David Robinson vs. Armon Gilliam), the 1997 draft (Tim Duncan vs. Keith van Horn), and the 2003 draft (LeBron James vs. Darko Milicic). In each of these seasons, the first pick was expected to be a very productive player, and in each instance those expectations were realized. Meanwhile, the team picking second in those seasons was left to wonder "what might have been."

The difference seen with respect to wins actually understates the advantages of picking first. Often, the first pick is considered a "star" before he ever plays a game, and as a "star" he can increase revenue beyond his impact on wins.[8]

Before reviewing the evidence of the first pick's "star power," let's briefly discuss the factors that get people into an NBA arena. Table 6.2 reports that Allen Iverson was one of the least productive number-one picks.[9] This lack of productivity is primarily tied to Iverson's inefficient scoring. Whether one considers Iverson a point guard or shooting guard, his career-adjusted field goal percentage of 45.2% is below average. Although Iverson frequently ranked among the top five players in the league in points per game, his scoring—because it was done inefficiently—didn't help his team as much as his fans would like to believe.

Of course, basketball teams are trying to sell tickets. If Iverson puts people in the seats, then maybe it doesn't matter that he doesn't win many games. Unfortunately, the empirical evidence doesn't support this argument. Table 6.3 reports the determinants of a team's gate revenue.[10] This list indicates that both wins and star power are statistically significant. Of these two factors, though, team wins are much more important. To see this point, imagine two piles of money. The first has $680,000 while the second has $5.7 million. The first pile represents how much Iverson's star power[11] was worth to the Philadelphia 76ers from 1999-00 to 2005-06. The second—and much bigger—pile of cash represents the amount of revenue Iverson's production of wins created for the 76ers. Iverson produced 30.8 wins across these years, or only about 4.4 per season. Such production for a "star" player is low. Nevertheless, when one thinks about Philadelphia's ticket sales, the impact of Iverson's meager production of wins trumped his star power.[12]

Given our previous findings about the star power of veteran players, we originally expected that the impact of a high draft choice would be similar. As is often the case, the empirical evidence defies prior expectations. Independent of a first pick's on-court performance, employing the first pick in the draft increases gate revenue[14] an estimated $1.8 million his first season and $1 million in his second campaign. As Table 6.4 shows, the first pick also averages 16.3 Wins

Produced across his first two seasons. Although this level of production is above average, the gate revenue generated from these wins is actually less than the gate revenue generated from the first pick's star appeal.

TABLE 6.3   What Explains Gate Revenue in the NBA: 1992-93 to 2007-08[13]

Statistically Significant and Positive Factors	Statistically Insignificant Factors
Regular Season Wins in the Current Season	Employing Number Three Pick in Draft
Regular Season Wins Last Season	Employing Number Two Pick in Draft from Last Season
Star Power on Team	Employing Number Three Pick in Draft from Last Season
Stadium Capacity	
Championship Won in the Past	
Being an Expansion Team	
Having a New Stadium	
Employing Number One Pick in Draft	
Employing Number Two Pick in Draft	
Employing Number One Pick in Draft from Last Season	

TABLE 6.4   The Value of the First Three Picks in the NBA Draft: 1985–2006, Value in Terms of Gate Revenue for First Two Seasons of a Player's Career (An Average NBA Player Has a 0.100 WP48)

	Value of First Pick in Draft	Value of Second Pick in Draft	Value of Third Pick in Draft
Average Wins Produced	16.3	6.7	7.8
Average WP48	0.143	0.062	0.064
Value of Wins	$1,616,527	$678,648	$803,778
Value of Draft Position	$2,816,072	$1,615,512	$0
Total Value	**$4,432,599**	**$2,294,160**	**$803,778**

The second and third picks tend to be less productive than an average player across his first two seasons. The second pick, though, does seem to possess some star power. As a consequence, the second pick produces nearly $1.5 million more in revenue than the third pick. The revenue generated by the second and third choices, though, pales in comparison to the top overall choice.

In evaluating draft picks, one needs to think about more than the impact these players have on revenue. The NBA has employed a rookie salary scale since 1995. For example, the first pick in the 2005 draft (Andrew Bogut) only received about $790,000 more in salary than the second pick (Marvin Williams) across the first two seasons of his career.[15] Furthermore, Bogut—an above average NBA talent—was paid less than the average NBA player in 2005-06.[16] Consequently, top picks tend to come at a discount.

Now we see why NBA teams have an incentive to lose games in an effort to secure the first pick in the draft. The first pick in the draft, unlike the second or third pick, tends to produce wins at an above-average rate. His star power also has a substantial impact on gate revenue. Finally, he is paid a wage that is below average for an NBA player. This pick can literally be worth millions of dollars, and consequently, the NBA has had to take steps to make sure teams do not lose games on purpose to improve their chances to acquire these players.

The NBA Draft and NBA Performance

Thus far, the decision-makers in the NBA appear quite rational. The first choice in the draft provides substantial benefits. A team can reap these benefits if it manages to secure the number one pick and then turn that pick into a productive player. An examination of the history of the number one pick reveals that NBA teams—despite the steps taken by the league—have made an effort (i.e., lose to win) to capture this pick, and it appears teams that get this pick tend to draft very good players.

Looking at all draft picks, though, reveals some issues with decision-making on draft day. For example, consider the top players in terms of Wins Produced and WP48 in each draft from 1985 to 2005. Table 6.5 reports that seven of the 21 players chosen first from 1985 to 2005 led their respective class in Wins Produced after four seasons. The second pick, though, never led his class while the third pick took the title on just three occasions. This means a player taken with one of the top three choices leads his class in Wins Produced less than 50% of the time.

TABLE 6.5 The Top Player in Each Draft in Terms of Wins Produced (Performance After Four Seasons in the NBA)

Player	Year Drafted	Draft Position	Wins Produced
Chris Paul	2005	4	83.2
Dwight Howard	2004	1	71.0
LeBron James	2003	1	64.5
Yao Ming	2002	1	44.1
Andrei Kirilenko	2001	24	50.1
Jamaal Magloire	2000	19	26.4
Shawn Marion	1999	9	68.5
Paul Pierce	1998	10	46.2
Tim Duncan	1997	1	65.0
Shareef Abdur-Rahim	1996	3	32.7
Kevin Garnett	1995	5	45.7
Grant Hill	1994	3	73.9
Anfernee Hardaway	1993	3	51.6
Shaquille O'Neal	1992	1	76.6
Dikembe Mutombo	1991	4	67.9
Derrick Coleman	1990	1	44.9
Tim Hardaway	1989	14	40.0

TABLE 6.5   The Top Player in Each Draft in Terms of Wins Produced (Performance after Four Seasons in the NBA)

Player	Year Drafted	Draft Position	Wins Produced
Dan Majerle	1988	14	33.8
David Robinson[20]	1987	1	97.9
Dennis Rodman	1986	27	57.0
Charles Oakley	1985	9	50.9
Averages		**7.4**	**56.8**

Such a result suggests—but only "suggests"—a problem with how college players are evaluated. More evidence can be found when one considers the link between where a player is taken in the draft and his subsequent performance in the NBA.[17] A statistical examination of performance after four NBA seasons reveals that only 5.5% of the variation in a player's career Wins Produced is explained by where he was taken in the draft.[18] This weak link actually exaggerates the relationship between draft position and NBA productivity. A player's Wins Produced depends on the number of minutes a player plays[19] and his productivity per minute. Turning to the latter, which is captured with Wins Produced per 48 minutes (WP48), one sees that only 1.6% of the variation in a player's career WP48 can be explained by his draft position.[21]

The weak link between draft position and NBA performance leads one to wonder what factors decision-makers focus upon on draft day. A list of possible factors[22] is reported in Table 6.6.

Although on-court performance is important, the non-performance factors tell an interesting story. All else being equal, players will be drafted higher if the player is younger, recently appeared in the Final Four, and is relatively taller.[23] The Final Four result is especially noteworthy. A player who appears in the Final Four can improve his draft position by about 12 spots. This effect, though, is only seen if the player enters the draft the year he appears in the Final Four. If a player appears in the Final Four and then returns to school, the value of the Final Four appearance vanishes. This result suggests that decision-makers in the NBA are overly influenced by recent observations. Looking past the fact that a Final Four appearance might only show that a player has good teammates, it's odd for decision-makers to take into account a Final Four appearance in the year the player is drafted, yet completely ignore an appearance in earlier years. After all, if a Final Four appearance meant something, surely the meaning would last more than a few months.

TABLE 6.6   What Explains Draft Position the NBA?

Statistically Significant Factors That Lead to a Better Draft Position	Statistically Insignificant Factors
Points Scored°	Rebounds°
Shooting Efficiency from Two-Point Range	Turnovers°
Shooting Efficiency from Three-Point Range	Free Throw Percentage
Assists°	Player's Race
Steals°	Playing Center
Blocked Shots°	Playing Power Forward
Height, Relative to Position Played	Playing Point Guard
Playing in the Final Four the Year Drafted	
Playing for an NCAA Champion the Year Drafted	

Statistically Significant Factors That Lead to a Lower Draft Position

Player's Age When Drafted

Personal Fouls°

Playing Shooting Guard[24]

° Per 40 minutes played, adjusted for position played[25]

The importance of a recent Final Four appearance also provides an interesting incentive to players. Players clearly have an incentive to declare the year their team reaches the Final Four, and the result with respect to age reinforces this incentive. A player loses about five slots in the draft for each year he stays in school. This means that a freshman who keeps returning to college could lose 15 slots by the time he completes his college education. Of course, additional schooling can lead to higher levels of productivity in college. If a player doesn't improve, though, having additional education can cost the player dollars in the NBA. This tells us why so many players choose to leave college early and why so many players decided to skip college all together when high school players were eligible for the NBA draft. Young players—blessed with potential—often prove irresistible to NBA talent evaluators.

Let's say a young player, though, ignores these findings and decides to continue to work on his game in the college ranks. What aspects of his on-court performance should he focus on?

Most of the standard box score statistics have a statistically significant impact on where a player is selected in the draft. Players who offer more scoring, assists, blocked shots, and steals see their draft position improve. Better shooting from two-point and three-point range also helps. More personal fouls, though, cause a player to get drafted later. The only box score statistics that don't seem to matter are rebounds and turnovers. The insignificance of rebounds is especially puzzling. A variety of approaches were taken with respect to rebounds.[26] No matter the approach, though, a statistically significant relationship between a player's ability to rebound and where a player was taken in the draft was not found.

Of all the factors that are statistically significant, scoring totals have the biggest impact on where a player is drafted. Consider an NBA prospect that increased his scoring by just four points per 40 minutes played.[27] Such an improvement would improve his draft position by about six slots. Now let's imagine that such an improvement comes at the cost of less efficiency. An average player in our sample converts on 52% of his two-point field goal attempts in college. If a player saw his shooting efficiency fall to 39%—or the minimum value in the sample—he would only be drafted about four slots later. More scoring—even if it causes shooting efficiency to decline somewhat—is therefore beneficial to an NBA prospect. Just as was seen from the examinations of NBA free agents and voting for the All-Rookie team, NBA prospects have a clear incentive in college to shoot as much as possible.[28]

We have seen that a scorer blessed with youth and height will hear his name called early in the NBA draft. If he is just coming off a Final Four appearance, then his wait is even shorter. Table 6.7 reports, though, that players blessed with these characteristics are not more productive professionals. In fact, college scorers and players who won an NCAA title tend to play somewhat worse in the NBA.[29] In contrast, players who can rebound, shoot efficiently from two-point range, and generate steals in college tend to make better NBA players.

There appears to be some inconsistency between the list of factors that get a player drafted and the list of factors that impact future NBA performance. Consequently, maybe we shouldn't be surprised, as noted earlier, that where a player is taken in the draft explains less than 10% of a player's NBA performance. Much of what decision-makers focus upon on draft day is simply not related to what a player will do in the NBA.

It's possible to do better. The factors listed in Table 6.7 explain between 30% and 40% of future performance.[30] Now it's important to emphasize that just looking at what one can quantify on draft day—and ignoring all the other factors decision-makers consider—would still result in draft day mistakes.[31] However, it appears that focusing on just the factors listed in Table 6.7 would mean decision-making on draft day would be improved.

It may seem somewhat surprising to hear that decision-makers are better off considering less. This argument can be illustrated if we consider what was uncovered with respect to rebounds. Rebounds don't impact where a player is chosen on draft day but are found to be related to future productivity in the NBA. Such results suggest that decision-makers are not aware of the importance of rebounds. Such a suggestion, though, is hard to believe. Rebounds have been tracked for NBA players since 1950, and we can be fairly certain that decision-makers in the NBA understand that better rebounders help teams win games.

TABLE 6.7   What Explains a Player's Productivity in the NBA?[32]

Statistically Significant Factors...	Statistically Insignificant Factors
...that lead to more productivity in the NBA	Shooting Efficiency from Three-Point Range
Rebounds°	Free Throw Percentage
Shooting Efficiency from Two-Point Range	Turnovers°
Steals°	Assists°
...that lead to less productivity in the NBA	Blocked Shots°
Points Scored°	Personal Fouls°
Playing Center	Height, Relative to Position Played
Playing for an NCAA Champion the Year Drafted	Player's Age When Drafted
	Playing in the Final Four the Year Drafted
	Player's Race
	Playing Power Forward
	Playing Small Forward
	Playing Point Guard

° Per 40 minutes played, adjusted for position played

We also suspect, though, that decision-makers believe a vast list of factors is connected with winning basketball games. Unfortunately, the size of the list is the problem. People are taught to consider everything before making a decision. Such advice would be good to follow if the human mind had unlimited computing power. The human mind, though, has clear limits. Too much information has actually been shown by researchers to result in declines in the quality of decisions.[33]

We believe this is what's happening on draft day. Decision-makers try to consider everything, but the limits of the human mind undermine this effort. For a decision to be made, the human mind has to simplify the vast list of factors considered. The simplification process ends up emphasizing the factors that are most conspicuous. In other words, the final decision is dominated by scoring, age, height, and Final Four appearances. A list of factors, though, is not really related to future productivity in the NBA.

Catching a Baseball Draft

One might argue that NBA decision-makers do not consistently make "good" decisions on draft day. Good or bad, though, are relative terms. From 1990 to 1997, 85% of players drafted by the NBA made an appearance in the Association. Across this same time period, though, only 33% of players drafted by Major League Baseball teams made it to the big leagues, and only 8% of drafted players ever became "regular contributors" to a team.[34]

Of course, there's an important difference between baseball and basketball. In the latter, colleges and universities are primarily used to develop talent. Baseball, though, develops its talent in a number of minor league affiliates. With all these affiliates, the draft in baseball—which can include nearly 50 rounds—is not just about finding talent for the Major Leagues, but also about restocking the minor league rosters.

In these rounds, baseball teams will select some players from colleges and universities. They will also select players out of high school. For college players, more experience improves the ability of teams to gauge the player's eventual production. The players selected after high school, though, are blessed with that ephemeral quality we call potential. One wonders which source generally produces the most valuable Major League players.

A recent study by John Burger and Stephen Walters provides an answer.[35] These authors estimated the average stream of revenue a regular contributor would create. This revenue estimate was then compared to an estimate of cost, yielding the net return a regular contributor generally makes to a Major League team. The data on net returns yielded two interesting patterns. First, the expected return on players selected out of college far exceeded the return from players selected out of high school. Additionally, the expected yield on pitchers was far less than what one can expect from non-pitchers or position players.[36]

Economic theory tells us that when expected returns differ between assets, we should see people buying more of the higher earning asset (i.e., college players and position players) and buying less of the lower returning asset (i.e., high school players and pitchers). These movements would eventually lead the rates of return on all these assets to equalize.

To see if this happened, we looked at the drafts after 1997. Our examination revealed some changes in decision-making, but the movement was in the opposite direction from what was expected. In 1997, about 50% of all drafted players were taken out of high school. Across the next ten years there was a steady increase in this percentage, and in 2007 it rose to around 65%. A similar, although less dramatic story, is told for pitchers. Back in 1997, the percentage of pitchers selected from high school was a bit below 50%. Across the next ten years this percentage rose above 50%. The study of expected returns indicated that college players and positional players are the better investment, and standard investment theory tells us that decision-makers should move toward assets that generate a higher return. The data, though, tell us that Major League Baseball decision-makers are making the opposite move.

Choices on draft day are typically made by the team's general manager. These are the same people ultimately responsible for choosing free agents. We have shown that general managers in baseball, basketball, and football have problems with both sets of choices. Next we move further down the organizational chart to the coach and manager on the field. These people are responsible for making game-day decisions that allocate the talent that the general manager has hired. As will be shown, the game-day decisions of coaches—like the decisions of their bosses—are also less than perfect.

7

Inefficient on the Field

Once upon a time, the home run was a relatively rare event in a baseball game. Consequently, teams often resorted to stealing to score runs. In the early part of the 20th century, it was not uncommon for a team to attempt to steal more than 100 bases a season. The arrival of Babe Ruth and similar sluggers, though, led teams to rely more and more on home runs.[1] As a consequence, as Figure 7.1 illustrates, from 1925 to 1973 the average team never attempted to steal more than 100 bases in a single season.

In recent years, the stolen base has made a comeback.[2] With the comeback came a clear change in efficiency. Figure 7.2 illustrates the gap between the average number of stolen bases and the average number of times a team's players were caught stealing. This gap was quite narrow in the first half of the 20th century, indicating that success rates hovered around 50%. In the latter half of the century, though, this gap and the corresponding success rate increased considerably.

Such an increase suggests a change in thinking. The question to steal or not to steal is not solely decided by the base stealer. Ultimately, this is something managers decide.

To evaluate this decision one needs to think about costs and benefits. The benefit of the stolen base is obvious. Each time a runner steals second or third base, he is that much closer to scoring a run. This benefit, though, incurs a potential cost. As Hall of Fame manager Earl Weaver noted, a manager's "most precious possessions on offense are (his) twenty-seven outs."[3] Therefore, teams should think twice before risking an out just to gain one more base.

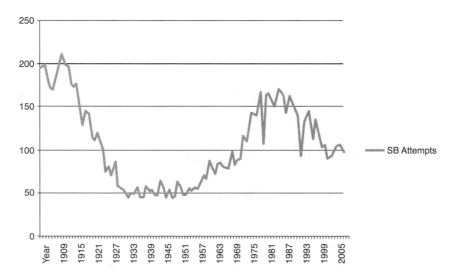

Figure 7.1   Average stolen base attempts by an MLB team (1904-2008)

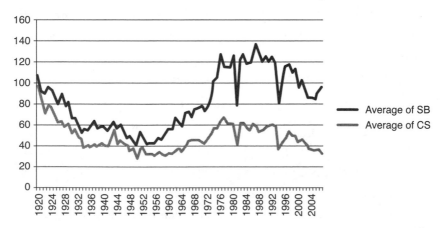

Figure 7.2   Average stolen bases and times caught stealing by an MLB team (1920-2007)

To sort through this issue, let's turn to some numbers. Researchers[4] have calculated the number of runs a team can expect given both the number of base runners and outs. For example, imagine a team has a runner on first base with nobody out. Research shows that teams can expect to score 0.90 runs in this situation. Moving that base runner to second, though, increases the expected runs to 1.14. In other words, stealing a base improves a team's expected run total by 0.24. Of course, even the best criminals get caught. If the runner is thrown out, a team will then have one out with nobody on base. In that circumstance, a team can only expect to score 0.27 runs. Therefore getting thrown out will cost a team 0.63 runs.

Given these expected benefits and expected costs one can see that a base stealer must be successful about 70% of the time just to break even.[5] Historically, though, teams have not been this successful. Figure 7.3 reports the percentage of stolen base attempts that are successful for an average baseball team from 1920 to 2007. As one can see, teams didn't reach the 70% threshold until 1987. Prior to this point—and for a number of years afterward—the costs of crime in baseball exceeded the benefits.

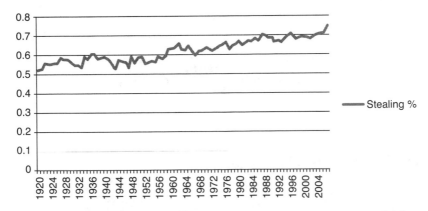

Figure 7.3   Percentage of stealing base attempts that are successful for an average MLB team (1920-2007)

The 70% mark is simply where costs equal benefits. For this strategy to truly pay off, success rates have to go beyond this break-even point. Consider, for example, the 1982 season where Rickey

Henderson stole 130 bases, setting the single-season mark. That season Henderson was also thrown out 42 times, a mark that has also not been matched in baseball history.[6] Given these numbers, Henderson attempted to steal 172 bases and was successful 75.6% of the time. Had Henderson just reached the break-even point on his attempts—in other words, had a 70% success rate—he would have stolen 120.4 bases (and still broken Lou Brock's single-season mark). This tells us that Henderson only stole 9.6 bases beyond the point where costs equal benefits.

The same year that Henderson set the record for stolen bases, he walked 116 times. Henderson later went on to break the career mark for both statistics.[7] Of the two records, which is the more impressive? Stolen bases certainly get the most attention. However, baseball research indicates that Henderson's ability to walk to first is at least twice as valuable as his ability to steal second and/or third.[8]

The Rickey Henderson story suggests that stealing bases is not a very profitable venture, but at least teams are doing this better. Prior to the 2004 season, the average success rate observed each year only reached the 70% mark on three occasions (1987, 1995, and 1996). Since 2004, though, the average rate of success has surpassed 70% in every season. Although stolen bases are not adding much to a team's level of success, at least this activity has stopped costing the average team runs.

Just Go For It!

Decision-makers in baseball—at least with respect to stealing bases—appear to be a bit reckless. Now we turn our attention to football and see just the opposite problem.

Let's go back to Super Bowl XVII. Trailing the Miami Dolphins 17-13 with just over 10 minutes left, Joe Gibbs, head coach of the Washington Redskins, faced a fourth and 1 on Miami's 43-yard line. With Mark Moseley as their kicker, trying a 60-yard field goal was out of the question,[9] leaving Gibbs with a choice between punting and going for it. Gibbs went for it, and the result was Miami's cornerback Don McNeal trying desperately to hang on to John Riggins's jersey as he turned the corner for what would end up being a 43-yard touchdown run. For NFL fans—especially for fans of Washington—this is one of the classic images in sports.

Given perfect hindsight, one might think that Gibbs's decision was obviously correct, but would anyone still believe this if McNeal had dragged Riggins to the ground before he got the first down?

Marty's oldest son, Michael, certainly thinks so. In fact, ten-year-old Michael has taken this belief to an extreme. Whenever Michael plays his favorite video game Madden NFL 2008®, he never punts. He will *go for it* on fourth and 27 on his own 9-yard line or try a 69-yard field goal from his own 48-yard line. Now his father, who has been around the block a time or two and has seen his share of football games, will punt. Nevertheless, despite the wisdom of Marty and John Madden,[10] Michael almost always wins.

Michael's approach was also employed by high school coach Kevin Kelley. Kelley is the football coach at Pulaski Academy, an Arkansas prep school. According to ESPN.com writer Gregg Easterbrook,

> Coach Kevin Kelley reports that he stopped punting in 2005.... In 2005, Pulaski reached the state quarterfinals by rarely punting. In 2006, Pulaski reached the state championship game, losing by one point—and in the state championship game, Pulaski never punted, converting nine of 10 fourth-down attempts. Since the start of the 2006 season, Pulaski has had no punting unit and never practices punts. This year, Pulaski has punted just twice, both times when leading by a large margin and trying to hold down the final score.[11]

In 2008, the Pulaski Academy finished undefeated in their conference and won their second State Championship in the past six years. Such success suggests that Coach Kelley—as well as Michael—is on to something. Then again, maybe not.[12] Kicking the ball—either via punts or field goals—has been the primary option on fourth down in football for a very long time. It seems unlikely that the experiences of a nine-year-old boy and a high school coach are enough to counter one of the key pieces of conventional wisdom in football. Fortunately, we have more than just a couple of anecdotes. Recently, David Romer set out to systematically evaluate[13] whether coaches make the *correct* choice in going for it on fourth down.

Consider the situation where a team faces a fourth down at their opponent's 2-yard line. In practical terms, the offensive team must choose between two options: kick the field goal or go for the touchdown. Which one should it choose? The obvious answer is the team should choose the option that gives them the best shot at winning the game.

Since a touchdown is worth six points (plus the shot at getting the extra point) and a successful field goal will earn three points, the offensive team should go for it, right? Well, not necessarily. A team needs to consider the probability of success. For a field goal from 19 yards, that probability is nearly 100%; so the likely, or expected, outcome of kicking is about three points. In contrast, teams only convert a fourth and goal from the 2-yard line about 40% of the time, so the expected outcome of going for it is 3.4 points.[14] These two options are quite close, so one might rationalize not going for it in this case, especially if such nuanced issues as momentum (assuming such a thing exists) or a coach's expectation that he will be ridiculed for failure are considered.

There is also a problem with leaving the analysis at this point. The potential offensive points only capture the immediate benefit. While going for it *may* maximize a team's scoring total, winning is also about being scored upon.[15] Consequently, one must go further and wonder how changing the ability of your opponent to score will impact your ability to score the next time you get the ball. Of course, changing your odds the next time you get the ball also impacts your opponent's future scoring chances, and so forth.

Following the earlier example, suppose the offensive team does go for it. If the team is successful, they receive seven points (assuming the team makes the extra point) but now must kick off from their own 35-yard line. The likely outcome of this kickoff is the opposing team starting their drive at about their own 30-yard,[16] or where teams on average begin a drive after a kickoff. If the attempt fails, the opposing team starts their next drive at about their own 2-yard line. This is another aspect to going for it—even if it fails, it forces the opponent to start very deep in their own territory. From there, it's unlikely they will score. Therefore, *going for it* yields slightly higher expected points (higher benefits) and less expected points surrendered (lower costs)—a win-win!

Obviously, not every fourth-down decision is made on the opponent's 2-yard line, but this same approach can be used at any point on the field. The trick here is to calculate the impact that "going for it" would have on the net outcome of the game—remembering that the choice not only has an impact on where the opposing team starts its impending drive (and its likelihood of scoring)—but also on your subsequent starting position.

Figure 7.4 presents the net point value associated with having the ball at any place on a football field. We are looking at net points, so the calculation includes not only the points that you might score on that drive, but also the points your opponent might score with the field position you're likely to give them if you don't score, and the points you're likely to score with the field position they give you after they do or don't score, and so on.

The shape of the curve should come as no surprise. The increase in value is consistent with what most football fans would expect. For example, having a first and 10 on your opponent's 20-yard line is 3.3 points better in terms of the final score than having a first and 10 on your own 20-yard line.

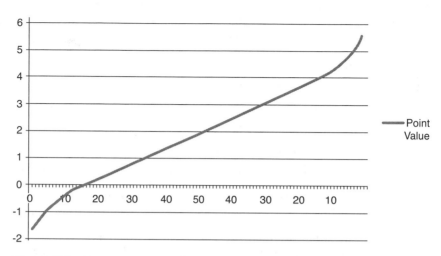

Figure 7.4   How many net points can a team expect at each place on a football field? [Source: Romer (2006), p. 346][17]

In addition to what is seen in Figure 7.4, one needs two more pieces of information to know when a team should go for it or not. First, one needs the net value of kicking (both punts and field goal attempts). Secondly, we need the net value of going for it (which includes the value of success as well as the probability a team will be successful). After that, the rest is easy. If the value of kicking is greater than the value of going for it, then the team should kick. Otherwise, the team should go for it. Determining these values is complicated, but Romer showed it can be done. His results[18] are presented in Figure 7.5.

Along the vertical axis of Figure 7.5 is the number of yards a team would need to get a new set of downs or to score. Along the horizontal axis is the field position. The line tells us when a team should go for it or not. For example, imagine a team is at midfield (i.e., the 50-yard line). The analysis suggests a team should go for it on fourth down if they have six yards or less to go for a first down.

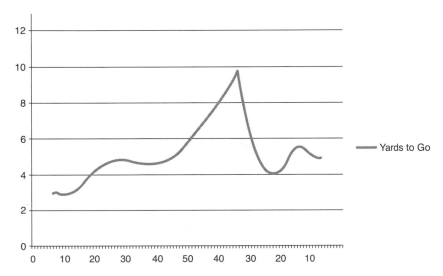

Figure 7.5   When should a team "go for it"? [Source: Romer (2006), p. 353][19]

In general, a team faced with a fourth down on its own side of the field (i.e., between their own 20-49 yard lines) is better off kicking if they have more than four or five yards to go. As a team moves into the opponent's side of the field, kicking should happen less frequently until the team reaches the opponent's 33-yard line. At this point, the decision resembles the choice on your own side of the ball, that is, a team should never kick when it has less than six yards to go. Finally, it appears that it's always optimal to go for the touchdown once you are within five yards of the opponent's end zone.

The kink around the 33-yard line stands out. Up until this point the likelihood of a field goal try being successful is quite low. In addition, as a team approaches the opponent's 33-yard line, any punt is unlikely to yield much of an advantage. Consequently, going for it on fourth and 10 may very well be the best possible expected outcome.

Let's illustrate this analysis by going back to the situation where it's fourth and goal at the 2-yard line. Having accounted for all the potential outcomes, should a team should go for it or not? Since 19-yard field goal attempts are made with near certainty, to compute the value of kicking all one needs to do is subtract the value of the subsequent kickoff. Again, that will give the opposition the ball on the own 30-yard line, and from Figure 7.4 we see that's worth about 0.8 points. So the net value of kicking a field goal—once everything is accounted for—is 2.2 (3 points from the field goal minus 0.8 points from where the opponent gets the ball on the next possession).

To compute the value of going for it, one simply determines the likelihood of the two possible outcomes: (1) the attempt is successful, which yields seven points and is followed by a kickoff, and (2) the attempt fails, and the opposition takes over somewhere around their own 2-yard line. The values of the subsequent outcomes are given in Figure 7.4. There's a 40% chance a team will score, and the net points from scoring is 6.2 (7 points from the touchdown minus 0.8 expected points the opponent receives when they start on their 30-yard line after the kickoff). If a team fails—and there is a 60% chance that this will happen—the opponent gets the ball somewhere around the 2-yard line. Such field position is worth –1.4 net points to your opponent (or 1.4 net points for you). Putting it all together, we see the expected net points from going for it is 3.3 net points (6.2 × 0.4 + 1.4 × 0.6). This is 1.1 points more than a team would expect from kicking the field goal, suggesting that going for it—even if it does risk ridicule from fans not familiar with this analysis—is the right move.

Now let's compare the actual decisions of head coaches in the NFL to the optimal decisions shown in Figure 7.5. When the optimal choice is to kick the ball, head coaches are making the right choice 99% of the time.[20] In contrast, when one turns to situations where the analysis says "go for it," the coaches only follow this advice 40% of the time.[21]

So far, there's little evidence that the behavior of coaches is changing. Prior to the 2004 season, Romer's study had already been written up in numerous newspapers, magazines, and other media outlets.[22] Before this research, teams went for it on fourth down about once a game. After 2003, though, teams still went for it about once a game.[23] This means—unlike what was seen in the discussion of stolen bases—new information has had little impact on the fourth-down decision.

Evaluating the Little Man in Football

Romer's analysis is not just about decision-making on fourth down. His work can also be used to evaluate a player often over-looked on a football roster.

Frequently, a football game proceeds as follows: For more than 59 minutes football players run and hit each other in an effort to win the contest. Then with a few seconds left, a relatively small man is invited onto the field to kick the ball through the uprights. All of the efforts of the other football players comes down to the ability of this small man—who often spends much of the game not running or hitting anyone—to complete his task.

The small man we are talking about is the kicker. Kickers are primarily known for making—and missing—field goals and extra points. Kickers, though, are also responsible for kickoffs.[24] Of these two tasks, the former is more often noted. After all, field goal attempts lead to scoring. However, as Figure 7.4 indicated, kickoffs are also about scoring. A kicker who is not very good at kickoffs can cost a team points by giving the opponent better field position. One wonders, though, if kickers are penalized for inadequate kickoffs. To address this issue, let's consider how many points a kicker—such as Neil Rackers—creates with his kickoffs.[25]

Rackers kicked off 70 times for the Arizona Cardinals in 2004. Of these kicks, 46 were returned, 23 were touchbacks, and one kick landed out-of-bounds. The average starting position on the returned kicks was the 26-yard line, or four yards better than what one would see from an average kicker. So on returned kicks, Rackers saved the Cardinals 184 yards.

Teams typically begin a drive after a kickoff at the 30 yard line; therefore a touchback, which places the opponent at the 20-yard line, saves a team 10 yards. On average, 10% of kickoffs are for touchbacks. Had Rackers been average, only seven of his kickoffs would have been touchbacks. So Rackers exceeded the average mark by 16, and consequently saved his team an additional 160 yards.

The values illustrated in Figure 7.4 allow one to convert yards into points. This conversion reveals that Rackers saved the Cardinals 19.7 points via his kickoffs in 2004.[26]

Now let's compare kickoffs to field goals and extra points. Field goal data is broken down by yardage, so one can see how an average kicker kicked from 20-29 yards, 30-39 yards, and so on. Such data allow us to calculate how many points a kicker earned from his field goals relative to what an average kicker would have done given the same kicks from the same distance. With a similar calculation for extra points, we can see that Rackers in 2004—compared to an average kicker—created 1.4 additional points from his field goals and extra points.[27]

The next two seasons, the story with respect to kickoffs stayed about the same. In both 2005 and 2006, Rackers created—relative to the average kicker—21.9 points from his kickoffs. His field goal accuracy, though, was less consistent. Rackers created 21.0 more points than an average kicker from kicking field goals and extra points in 2005. The next season, his performance on field goals plummeted; when the 2006 season was over, he had created 3.5 fewer points than the average kicker.

The Neil Rackers story illustrates two aspects of a kicker's productivity. First of all, kickoffs matter in the evaluation of kickers. In addition, compared to what we see with respect to field goals and extra points, kickers are more consistent on kickoffs. This isn't just the story when one looks at Rackers, but when all kickers are studied.[28]

So what determines a kicker's salary? Both kickoffs and field goals are statistically linked to a kicker's pay.[29] These aspects of the kicker's job, though, are not treated equally. An additional point from a kickoff is worth about $17,224. An additional point from a field goal or extra point, though, is worth $72,605. Yes, the less consistent field goal kicking is worth much more in salary, but not much more in terms of game-day outcomes. All of this suggests that the often overlooked little man in football is not being evaluated correctly by NFL decision-makers.[30]

The Hot Hand and Coaching Contradictions

In football and baseball, decision-making is relatively easy to scrutinize. The game comes to a halt after each play in these sports, so one can assess the state of the world at that point and ascertain the optimal decision. Basketball is a more fluid game. Coaches can call plays from the sidelines, but with the exception of time-outs, the players are supposed to be in constant motion. Despite these differences, it's still possible to comment on the decisions made by NBA coaches.

Our first comment will address a phenomenon felt by most everyone who has ever played basketball. When a player makes a few shots in a row, he will start to believe that he is "hot"; consequently, his teammates better start getting him the damn ball. Just because this feeling is nearly ubiquitous, though, doesn't mean it's real. In fact, numerous studies have consistently indicated that the "hot hand" is just a figment of the imagination.

The first, and now classic study by Thomas Gilovich, Robert Vallone, and Amos Tversky,[31] charted the outcome of nearly 4,000 shots taken by nine members of the Philadelphia 76ers during home games of the 1980-81 season. If the "hot hand" were real, then a player who makes a shot would be more likely to make the next. The data, though, said just the opposite. A study of free throws came to the same conclusion.[32]

This is quite provocative. Most everyone who has made consecutive shots has had the "hot hand" feeling. To date, though, no empirical evidence for this phenomenon has been uncovered.[33] In fact, a recent study[34] of NBA scorers not only failed to find evidence of the "hot hand," it also argued that belief in this "hot hand" alters behavior. When a prolific scorer makes a shot, he is more likely to take the next shot for a team. Specifically, the player making a shot takes the next shot for a team 34% of the time, as opposed to 25% of the time after a miss.

Suspending belief in the "hot hand" is difficult. Once a player makes a few shots in a row, it certainly feels like something has changed. The causality, though, is confused. People tend to think that something happens that allows them to suddenly hit their shots. However, the data show that first a player manages to hit a string of shots, and then feelings change in response. That feeling then compels a player to ask for the ball. Coaches and the player's teammates, though, should ignore these feelings. The empirical evidence suggests teams that adjust their game plan in response to the sudden appearance of a "hot hand" are not likely to find their chances of victory improving.

Of course, how teams respond to the "hot hand" is not entirely up to the coach. It may be the case that a player getting the ball after making a few shots simply reflects the decision-making of his teammates. It's a different story, though, when one considers how often a player gets to play.

Whether one looks at a player's draft position, voting for the All-Rookie team, or free agent salaries, player evaluation in the NBA is driven by a player's scoring totals. These evaluations stand in stark contrast to the rhetoric of NBA coaches. Coaches are often telling their players not to put their scoring totals ahead of team success. Although players clearly have an incentive keep shooting, the coaches have a huge weapon in this debate. It's the coach who decides who gets to play; and if a player isn't on the court, he isn't going to be able to score any points at all.

What determines the minutes the coaches allocate? One factor is where a player is taken in the draft. As noted, the link between draft position and performance is weak. Although there are many instances where a high draft pick develops into a productive NBA player, there are also many examples where this doesn't happen. How should teams react when a high draft pick fails to develop?

Basic economics says a team should regard the draft pick as a "sunk cost." In other words, the draft pick is a cost incurred in the past that cannot be changed in the present. Decisions are about the present and the future, so sunk costs should be ignored. Behavioral economists, though, have found that people tend to "double down" or more formally, escalate commitments. This means there is a tendency to keep with a project even when it's clear that project isn't working anymore. With respect to the NBA draft, if people are "escalating commitments," then there should be evidence that draft position has a persistent impact on how many minutes an NBA player plays.

This is just what we see. Studies[35] have shown that even after researchers control for the impact of player performance, where a player was taken in the draft still impacted playing time three years into a player's career. So after the coaches had already seen a player actually play in the NBA for two seasons, what was thought about a player on draft night still influenced how often that player got to be on the court. By itself, this result suggests that how coaches allocate minutes is suboptimal.

There is also an issue with the connection between a player's age and playing time.[36] At the onset of a player's career, he should get more playing time as he gains more experience. At some point, though, age takes its toll on player productivity and minutes per game should start to decline. Examining the link between age and minutes per game reveals that the specific turning point occurs at 28 years of age. In the next chapter, it's noted that a player's productivity peaks at about 24 years of age. Consequently, the allocation of minutes suggests the age profile in basketball is not well understood by NBA coaches.

And then there is the link between player performance and playing time. Positive stats—such as points scored, shooting efficiency from the field and free throw line, rebounds, steals, blocked shots, and assists—lead to an increase in minutes per game. Turnovers and personal fouls, though, cause minutes to decline.

Of these factors, personal fouls have the biggest impact on playing time. This result, though, is driven by the rules of the game. After six fouls in a game, a player is disqualified; so by rule, more fouls must lead to less playing time.

After personal fouls, points scored per minute have the largest impact on minutes per game.[37] This result directly contradicts the rhetoric from coaches. Again, coaches often tell players to focus on something besides scoring. Players, though, can see that the most effective way to get more playing time is to score more points. In essence, coaches are like the parents of a spoiled child. Although the coach might tell the player he will be sitting if he doesn't look past scoring, the player knows this is an empty threat. If the player just shows the coach he can score, he will be rewarded with more playing time. In turn, additional playing time will inflate scoring totals, which will increase a player's future salary.

All of this tells us that NBA coaches—like NBA general managers—are not making decisions efficiently. The mythology of coaching, though, is not about decisions. It's about inspiring players to greater heights. Unfortunately, as our last story illustrates, for many coaches this is just another myth.

8

Is It the Teacher or the Students?

It's said that coaches are hired to be fired. When a team fails to win as often as its fans and owner(s) would like, the coach is often asked to leave. And when a new coach is hired, he or she is often considered the potential savior of the team. Of course, as time goes by—and the team is again not as successful as people would like—yesterday's savior is asked to leave and a new savior is invited to town.

The underlying assumption that supports the ever-revolving coaching carousel is that coaches are important. If a team changes its coach it can change outcomes. Bum Phillips captured this perspective in describing the coaching abilities of Don Shula: "Don Shula can take his'n and beat your'n. Or he can take your'n and beat his'n."[1]

Phillips suggests that simply by adding a better coach, a losing team can become a winner. If the new coach simply says the right words, or devises the right strategy, then the identity of the players doesn't matter. One wonders, though, if this is true. Should we credit the success or failure of a team to the coach, or is it the players that truly matter?

As professors, we face these questions every time we step into the classroom. In any class we see students who are successful and a few—hopefully very few—who fail. We would like to think that students succeed because of our brilliant teaching, and those who fail are simply bad students. In other words, we are not responsible for the failures. Students, of course, take the opposite view.

So is it the teacher or the students? In the classroom, this might be a difficult question to answer (and we're not entirely sure we want to know the answer). In basketball, though, we think the statistics tracked by the NBA can provide an answer.

The Wealth of Coaching

An answer to this question actually existed long before the invention of basketball. Adam Smith published *An Inquiry into Nature and Causes of the Wealth of Nations* in 1776. Many people consider Smith's work to be the most important book in the history of economic thought. It certainly is considered by many to be the first book—and perhaps the best book—on the wonders of capitalism. Within this great work is a little-known discussion of the impact a manager has on a firm. According to Smith, the managers charged with supervising the daily operation of a firm are nothing more than "principal clerks."[2] Smith argued that what managers do with respect to the "inspection and direction" of a firm is essentially the same for all firms, and consequently managers can't have much impact on the success or failure of an organization.

Of course, managers and coaches in professional sports don't agree with Smith's "principal clerk" label. A number of books have been written by NBA coaches revealing their "leadership secrets" and the important role the coach plays in the success of a team. A non-random sample of coaches who have written such books includes Pat Riley, Rick Pitino, and Phil Jackson.[3] Each of these coaches offers "secrets" to better coaching, and each book argues that the secrets presented are about more than basketball. It's often argued that the methods espoused by these coaches can be applied by the leaders of any organization.

Certainly each of these coaches has led teams to success. At the time Riley's book was published in 1993—and his "formula for success" revealed—he had coached parts of nine seasons and posted a career regular season winning percentage of 0.723. This mark, back in 1993, led all NBA coaches in the history of the league. He had also led the LA Lakers to four NBA championships in the 1980s. After a few years where Riley's teams were less than successful, in 2006—as head coach of the Miami Heat—Riley won his fifth NBA title.

Pitino has also been successful, but primarily as a college coach. In 1987, he led Providence College to the NCAA Final Four. After two years with the New York Knicks, he went back to college, becoming the head coach of the University of Kentucky in 1989. Over the next eight seasons, Kentucky appeared in the Final Four three times and took the NCAA title in 1996. Pitino then left Kentucky for the Boston Celtics in 1997. After four losing seasons, though, Pitino returned to the college ranks with the University of Louisville in 2001. Under Pitino, the University of Louisville has won nearly 75% of its games and appeared in the NCAA Final Four.

Then there is Phil Jackson. At the conclusion of the 2008-09 season, Phil Jackson had coached for 18 NBA seasons. During these years, Jackson's teams have won more than 70% of their regular season contests and ten NBA titles. Both in regular season winning percentage and championships won, Jackson currently tops the charts in NBA history.

The records posted by these coaches certainly suggest that each is not a "principal clerk." A skeptic, though, might note the quality of talent each coach has led. Pat Riley won titles when he coached Magic Johnson, Shaquille O'Neal, and Dwyane Wade. When these players were not available, Riley's teams were far less successful. Similarly, Phil Jackson's title teams were led by players like Michael Jordan, Kobe Bryant, and Shaquille O'Neal. Like Riley, when Jackson didn't have such amazing talents, his teams didn't seem to win as often.[4]

Rick Pitino's experience in the NBA appears to hammer this point home. Pitino coached only six seasons in the NBA. His teams never made it out of the second round of the playoffs, and only one finished with a winning record. A quick glance at the players Pitino was given to coach suggests a reason for his lack of NBA success. While Riley and Jackson got to coach Magic, MJ, and/or Shaq,

Pitino's teams in Boston were twice led in scoring by Antoine Walker. To put this talent disparity in perspective, Walker finished his 12-year career in 2007-08 with 26.8 Wins Produced. Both Magic and Jordan eclipsed this mark in a single season on four different occasions.

It appears the talent employed by these coaches had much to do with their win-loss records. This leads one to wonder if Adam Smith was essentially correct; maybe managers and coaches are just "principal clerks." Of course, a quick look at three coaches who happened to write books on leadership does not a study make. What is needed is a study that can ascertain the impact coaches have on the performance of individual players.

"Take Your'n and Beat His'n"

Let's return to the argument put forward by Bum Phillips. The argument "Don Shula can take his'n and beat your'n. Or he can take your'n and beat his'n," suggests that coaches can change outcomes in a game. But outcomes in a game are decided entirely by the actions of the players on the field. Therefore, if coaches are crucial to outcomes, there must be evidence that a coach can actually change a player's performance.

In football, such evidence would be difficult to uncover. Player performance at every position is difficult to evaluate on the gridiron. In basketball, though, player productivity is much easier to measure; so in basketball Phillips's contention can be investigated.[5]

This investigation was conducted within a model designed to explain a player's per-minute productivity in a given season.[6] If coaches truly can change the productivity of their players, one should see player performance change when he comes to a coach.[7] For most coaches, though, this is not the story told by the data. Of the 62 coaches studied, 42—or 68%—didn't have a statistically significant positive impact on player performance. This list of 42 includes Lenny Wilkens, Pat Riley, Jerry Sloan, Bill Fitch, Dick Motta, George Karl,

K. C. Jones, Paul Westphal, and Rick Adelman. What do these coaches have in common? Each of these coaches are currently ranked in the top ten in NBA history in all-time regular season victories and/or all-time regular season winning percentage. Yet none were found to have a statistically significant impact on player performance.

It's important to emphasize that these illustrious coaches are not alone. Most coaches didn't seem to have a statistically significant impact. Of course, most is not all. Table 8.1 lists the coaches who were found to have a statistically significant impact[8] on player performance.

Topping the list is none other than Phil Jackson. Skeptics have argued that Jackson only ranks first in career winning percentage because he got to coach players like Michael Jordan, Shaquille O'Neal, and Kobe Bryant. The study of coaching, though, suggests that a team hiring Jackson could expect, after controlling for past player performance and a collection of other factors that cause player productivity to change, about 17 additional victories.[9]

For those who focus on career winning percentage, seeing Jackson leading the way is not a surprise. What will surprise are the coaches who had winning percentages below 0.500. Gene Shue, Isiah Thomas (yes, the same Isiah Thomas from Chapter 2, "Defending Isiah"), Kevin Loughery, Rick Pitino, and Chris Ford all posted career records that are below average. But all five were found to have a bigger impact on player performance than a number of coaches ranked in the top ten in career wins and/or career winning percentage.

The impacts reported in Table 8.1 are only from the first year a player is with a coach.[10] Looking at the impact of a coach in the second year he's coaching a player, one finds that only three coaches—Popovich, Jackson, and Nelson—had a statistically significant impact. In the third year, only Jackson's impact persisted. Such findings confirm the notion that Phil Jackson is a very good coach. It also suggests that the impact of a coach is generally only seen in the first year a player is with the coach.

TABLE 8.1   The Top NBA Coaches Ranked by Both Statistical Significance and Positive Impact of Coach on Player Performance[11]

Coach	Expected Wins from Adding Coach[12]	Career Record				
		Years	Games	Wins	Losses	Winning Percentage
Significant at the 1% Level						
Phil Jackson	17.1	17	1,394	976	418	0.700
Gregg Popovich	15.9	12	934	632	302	0.677
Cotton Fitzsimmons	15.8	21	1,607	832	775	0.518
Gene Shue	11.5	22	1,645	784	861	0.477
Don Nelson	11.2	29	2,234	1,280	954	0.573
Flip Saunders	10.7	13	983	587	396	0.597
Significant at the 5% Level						
Jim O'Brien	12.0	6	422	218	204	0.517
Isiah Thomas	10.6	5	410	187	223	0.456
Stan Albeck	9.7	7	574	307	267	0.535
Kevin Loughery	9.6	17	1,136	474	662	0.417
Mike Fratello	8.2	17	1,215	667	548	0.549
Significant at the 10% Level						
Rick Pitino	10.0	6	412	192	220	0.466
Chris Ford	7.7	10	699	323	376	0.462
Larry Brown	6.2	23	1,810	1,010	800	0.558
Averages	**11.1**	**14.6**	**1,105.4**	**604.9**	**500.4**	**0.536**

What about when the player leaves the coach? This question is important because it's possible that when a coach is found to have a positive impact on performance, all one is finding is the impact of whatever system(s) the coach employs. If that's the case, then the player will get worse when he departs the system(s). For O'Brien,

Nelson, and Loughery, evidence was found that supported this notion. However, for the other coaches listed in Table 8.1, there was no evidence for a corresponding negative impact when the player went to play for a different coach.[13] In other words, it doesn't appear that the impact of most of the coaches listed is about the system the coaches are using.

So what is it about? Is Phil Jackson a great coach because of his inspirational speeches? Is it the books he famously asks his players to read? Or is it an assistant coach who works for Jackson? For these questions, we don't have an answer. Players tend to get better when they come to Phil Jackson. The analysis, though, doesn't tell us why this happens.

Deck Chairs?

The study of coaches stands in stark contrast with the conventional wisdom. Coaches are often credited with the wins and losses of their respective teams. Those coaches with better records are believed to be better coaches. For most coaches, though, one can't find any statistically significant impact on player performance. This suggests that for most coaches, their win-loss record is ultimately about their players. Give the coach productive players, and he will coach a winner. Give the coach unproductive players, though, and suddenly the coach is a loser.

Does this mean the head coach in the NBA doesn't matter? Such was the reaction[14] to this research from Henry Abbott:

> All those late nights of film study. All that competition for your job. All those tricks learned at conferences. All those books by the masters you have internalized. And now there is evidence to support the notion you could be replaced by a deck chair.

Abbott's reaction is certainly understandable. When one argues that most coaches don't have a discernible impact on performance, it might sound like teams could simply replace their head coaches with "a deck chair." This, though, is not what the research is saying. The study didn't compare a team's performance with a coach to a team's performance without anyone coaching. Consequently, the research doesn't suggest teams get rid of the position of head coach, or to replace the coach with just anyone from the stands.

What was suggested was that only a few coaches could alter player performance, or on the flip side, most coaches are at the mercy of the talent on their roster. Consequently, although we are confident coaches can differentiate themselves from the "guy in the stands," most coaches don't appear different from the other coaches employed by the NBA.

Such a story tells how teams should react to losing. Before the 2008-09 NBA season was completed, eight different teams had replaced the head coach who walked the sidelines at the onset of the season. These moves were made because it was believed changing the coach would change outcomes.[15] The empirical evidence, though, suggests that changing the coach, which is often quite expensive,[16] is not likely to make much difference. What the teams should focus on instead is changing the players.

Growing Older and Diminishing Returns

To isolate the impact of coaching, a number of other factors[17] that could alter how a player performs needed to be included in the model.[18] Of these factors, listed in Table 8.2, the stories told about age and the productivity of teammates also appear to contradict conventional wisdom.

In general, athletes should get better as they gain more experience. Eventually, though, age takes its toll and performance starts to decline. The peak—where improvement tends to stop and decline begins—needs to be identified for decision-makers to correctly forecast player performance.

TABLE 8.2   What Factors Explain (Other Than Coaching) a Player's Current Performance in the NBA?

Statistically Significant and Positive Factors	Statistically Insignificant Factors
Performance Last Season	Roster Stability
Age	Moving to a New Team
Player Injury (or games played last two seasons)	

Statistically Significant and Negative Factors
Productivity of Teammates
Age Squared

The analysis of basketball requires some context. J.C. Bradbury examined 86 years of data in baseball and found that the peak performance for a hitter or pitcher occurred at about 29 years of age.[19] Although the peak for a baseball player's overall performance occurred in his late twenties, the peak with respect to specific tasks is different. A player's ability to draw a walk—or for a pitcher to prevent walks—peaks around 32 years of age. In contrast, a pitcher's ability to throw strike-outs peaks at about 24 years of age. These differences are explained by noting that the location of the peak is related to the physical skills an athlete requires. Strike-outs primarily depend on pitch speed, or the physical skills of the pitcher. In contrast, a batter needs plate discipline to draw walks, discipline that improves as a batter gains more experience.

The study of hitters and pitchers can be related to a study[20] of the age at which athletes set records in track and field, swimming, tennis, and golf. In sports that depended more on pure physical ability—such as swimming, short-distance running, and tennis—performance appears to peak in the early-to-mid twenties. When a sport depends more on experience and knowledge—such as in long-distance running and golf—the peak is closer to 30 years of age.

Is basketball like tennis or golf? In other words, does success in basketball depend more on physical skills or experience and knowledge? Although veteran players like to believe the latter, anyone watching an NBA game must be impressed by the rare physical gifts it takes to play in the Association. The study of performance and age confirms this impression. Performance in the NBA appears to hit its maximum at 24.4 years of age.[21]

Although performance peaks around 24, the drop-off in performance is not dramatic until a player approaches 30 years of age. To illustrate, let's imagine a team employs an average player at 24 years of age, or a player with a 0.100 WP48. Table 8.3 reports what one can expect will happen[22] if nothing else changes (i.e., all other factors that impact performance are unchanged) as he ages.

At the age of 25—if nothing else changes—his WP48 will be essentially the same. After this point, though, performance starts to decline. By the age of 30, our average player at 24 is now posting a 0.071 WP48. At the age of 32, this value is now down to 0.046; and at 35 his performance has dipped into the negative range.

Now let's go back to the study of how coaches allocate minutes. As noted in the previous chapter, a player's minutes will peak at about 28 years of age. This suggests that coaches not only have problems allocating minutes—remember the focus on scoring[23]—coaches in the NBA are also confusing basketball with baseball. The study of aging and performance suggests there is not much of a penalty imposed for thinking a player at 28 is close to his peak. After all, what an average player will do at 28 (WP48 of 0.088) is not far from the actual peak. However, one suspects that teams might think that the difference between 24 and 28 would be similar to the difference between 28 and 32, and that doesn't appear to be true. An average basketball player in his early 30s is well past his peak and can expect to offer much less with each passing year.

TABLE 8.3 The Impact of Age on the Performance of an Average NBA Player—Peak Age Is 24 Years

Age	WP48
18	0.061
19	0.072
20	0.081
21	0.089
22	0.095
23	0.098
24	**0.100**
25	0.100
26	0.098
27	0.094
28	0.088
29	0.080
30	0.071
31	0.059
32	0.046
33	0.030
34	0.013
35	–0.006

To drive this point home, let's compare the number of players still employed in the NBA[24] and MLB[25] after age 30. About 30% of baseball players are between 30 and 34 years of age, and 10% of baseball seasons are played by players who are 35 or older. In contrast, only 20% of basketball players are in the 30 to 34 age group. And only 4% of basketball seasons played are logged by players 35 or older. Given how quickly players exit basketball after the age of 28, it seems unlikely that this age is the peak on the hardwood.

Athletes consistently deny the powerful effects of age. Teams, though, should be very skeptical when they think of signing and playing basketball players who have passed 30 years of age. The decline at that point is steep, and the player who looked amazing when he was younger is now likely to disappoint.

Aging is not the only factor that alters performance. Teams also have to be aware of how a player's teammates impact his performance. One of the stories people tell is that great players make their teammates better. Although this is clearly part of the conventional wisdom, it defies basic economics. One of the core concepts in economics is the idea of diminishing returns. The Law of Diminishing Returns simply states that as you add a productive input (such as players), without changing anything else, the productivity of the additional inputs will eventually fall. Applied to the NBA, the Law of Diminishing Returns tells us that surrounding a player with productive teammates will cause the player to be less productive. After all, there is only one ball.

Of course, just because centuries of economic theory tell us about diminishing returns, it doesn't mean someone should abandon a cherished belief. At the very least, one should demand some empirical evidence. Fortunately, the study of player performance provides such evidence. One of the factors examined was the productivity of teammates,[26] and this study indicated that as a player's teammates become more productive, the player becomes less productive. In other words, economic theory trumps conventional basketball wisdom.

Although the diminishing returns effect is real, the size of the effect is somewhat small. To illustrate, let's consider the career of Artis Gilmore. This career began in 1971 in the American Basketball Association (ABA). When the ABA ceased to exist in 1976, Gilmore—at 28 years of age—moved on to the NBA where he primarily played for the Chicago Bulls and San Antonio Spurs.[27] The Bulls and Spurs have both won a number of NBA titles since 1988. When Gilmore played for these teams, though, neither was very successful. Gilmore only played for an NBA team that won more than half their games three times. The inability of Gilmore's teams to succeed might lead some to conclude that he wasn't a particularly effective player. The numbers, though, tell a different story.

To illustrate, let's compare Gilmore to Kareem Abdul-Jabbar. The first season one can calculate Wins Produced is 1977-78. That season, Abdul-Jabbar was 30 years of age. Across the next six seasons Abdul-Jabbar went on to produce 101.9 wins and post a 0.292 WP48. Examining Gilmore from 30 to 35 years of age reveals a player who produced 86.5 wins and posted a 0.281 WP48. All of this production, though, was provided to teams that were generally unsuccessful. In contrast, Abdul-Jabbar's NBA teams won more than half their games in all but one season in his career.

Giving the diminishing returns story, one might suspect that if Gilmore and Abdul-Jabbar switched places,[28] Gilmore's production would decline considerably. The data, though, tell a different story. The analysis suggests such a move would have caused Gilmore's WP48 to only fall from 0.281 to 0.273. Across the years discussed earlier, this decline would result in only 2.4 fewer wins. In other words, regardless of which teammates these players got to play with, both Gilmore and Abdul-Jabbar would have been very productive NBA players.

Although Gilmore's productivity rivals what we see from Abdul-Jabbar, the perception of each player is quite different. Abdul-Jabbar played on six teams that won an NBA title and is currently considered one of the greatest players to ever play the game. In contrast, Gilmore isn't in the NBA's Hall of Fame. One suspects that the quality of Gilmore's teammates has diminished people's perceptions of Gilmore's overall production, depriving one of the truly great players in NBA history his proper due.

The diminishing returns story doesn't just inform our perceptions of all-time great NBA players. It can also reinforce the story told about scoring in the NBA. One can look at diminishing returns with respect to a player's per-minute production of each of the individual box score statistics (i.e., points, rebounds, etc.). The analysis indicates that of all the box score statistics, points, and field goal attempts suffer the most from diminishing returns. After scoring, there is a smaller effect for free throw attempts and rebounds,[29] and a still smaller effect for assists and blocked shots.[30] It should make sense that diminishing returns has the biggest impact on scoring totals. The NBA has a shot clock, so shooting the ball is required. If a scorer is taken away from a team, other players will have to take those shots.[31] This finding reinforces the idea that scoring is not quite as important as people think.[32]

Putting the Picture Together

We now have a fairly complete picture of how wins are produced in the NBA. Scoring dominates perceptions. Players who score are drafted first, play more minutes, and earn more money. Wins, though, are about more than scoring. Consequently, despite the fact player performance in the NBA is relatively consistent, how much teams spend on players doesn't tell us much about how much teams win.

Of course, the conventional wisdom tells us that players don't win by themselves. Coaching is an essential ingredient in the process. As the story goes, a great coach can transform a team of losers into winners. The analysis of player productivity, though, suggests there are problems with the traditional view of coaching. Yes, there are coaches like Phil Jackson who can elicit greater productivity from his players. Yet, the majority of coaches don't have any statistical impact on player performance.

What, then, drives wins in the NBA? For the most part, winning this game is as simple as finding productive players (that is, players who shoot efficiently and help obtain and maintain possession of the ball). Despite the impact of coaching, age, and diminishing returns, in general, players are what they are.

This is not just the story told by the data. This is also the story told by coaching legend, Red Auerbach:

> These guys today want you to believe that what they're doing is some kind of science. Coaching is simple: you need good players who are good people. You have that, you win. You don't have that, you can be the greatest coach who ever lived and you aren't going to win.

We certainly like to think of ourselves as scientists, and after reviewing these studies of basketball, all we can say in response to Auerbach is "Amen."

9

Painting a Bigger Picture

Perhaps the most famous baseball statistic—batting average (or hits divided by at-bats)—was invented by H. A. Dobson in 1872.[1] Although simple to calculate, batting average treats all singles, doubles, triples, and home runs equally, and it ignores walks and stolen bases entirely. Around 1910, the flaws in batting average led Ferdinand Lane to declare that batting average is "worse than worthless."[2] Although Lane spent years as a writer and editor for *Baseball* magazine discussing the problems with how performance was measured in baseball, he was not able to convince people that batting average was inherently flawed. Consequently, batting average is still one of the most frequently cited statistics when people discuss the value of a hitter in baseball.

Decades later, another writer, Bill James, experienced the same struggles. The research on the importance of on-base percentage—and the unimportance of steals—can be traced back to work done by James in the 1980s. Yet when James introduced his findings, decision-makers in baseball didn't immediately embrace his work. James, though, continued to pound the drum, and eventually decision-makers like Billy Beane put his ideas into practice.

The Bill James story appears to illustrate how information is eventually adopted by people in an industry. However, there are two issues to consider. First, the initial reaction by people in baseball is completely consistent with a lesson taught by behavioral economics: People have trouble accepting information that contradicts their current point of view. Additionally, it's important to emphasize that James was not an employee of Major League Baseball when he first introduced his ideas. He was someone outside the industry who kept knocking on the door until people finally listened to the better ideas. It seems unlikely that an outsider would go to this much trouble in a non-sports industry. Consequently, the Bill James story doesn't illustrate the notion that people naturally learn from their own mistakes.

The way Lane's and James's insights were received also highlights how mistakes can be made year after year. The same story has been seen again and again across the North American professional sports world. Beyond what was seen with respect to on-base percentage and stolen bases in baseball, we also see

- College players and positional players generate higher returns in Major League Baseball. Teams, though, are more likely to draft high school players and pitchers, or players who have a lower expected return.
- When it comes to the NBA draft, voting for the All-Rookie team, the allocation of minutes, and the size of a player's free agent contract, the number of points scored consistently drives the evaluation of the player. Factors such as shooting efficiency, rebounds, and turnovers tend to be deemphasized, despite the fact each of these has a significant impact on wins.
- Additional factors that improve a player's draft position in the NBA, such as appearing in the Final Four and a player's relative height, are not related to future NBA performance.
- Draft position is a very weak predictor of a player's future per-minute NBA performance. Draft position supposedly takes into account all that is known about a player before draft day. Decision-makers, though, would predict future NBA performance better if they only considered the factors that can be quantified prior to draft day. Such an approach would still be flawed, but it would be better than whatever process is currently employed to make draft-day decisions.
- Escalation of commitment describes how minutes are allocated to high draft picks in the NBA. Minutes are given to high draft picks beyond what would be justified by their performance.

- An NBA player's performance peaks at 24 years of age, while his minutes per game peaks at the age of 28. Therefore, coaches are exaggerating the contribution of older players.
- Most NBA head coaches don't have a statistically significant impact on player performance.
- In the NFL, quarterbacks are primarily paid to pass. Running, though, does have a positive impact on outcomes. Consequently, part of what a quarterback does to increase wins, and this is especially true for black quarterbacks, is not fully compensated.
- The productivity of black quarterbacks, especially the very best black quarterbacks, is undervalued in the NFL's labor market.
- First-round choices in the NFL draft have a lower expected cost-benefit ratio than picks in the early second round. This tells that first-round picks are often overpaid, and teams would do better trying to trade down in the draft.
- NFL teams give up points, and wins, by kicking too often on fourth down.
- Kickers are paid more for an additional point generated by field goals than they are for an additional point from a kickoff. The latter, in addition to being undervalued, is also more predictable.

For all these examples, the decision-makers have the information, but it's not interpreted correctly. We also see instances where the predictive power of information is misunderstood.

- The factors that improve a quarterback's draft position, such as a quarterback's college performance, height, Wonderlic scores, and 40-yard dash times, don't predict his future NFL performance.
- Where a quarterback is drafted doesn't predict his per-play performance in the NFL.
- Quarterbacks are paid according to past performance, but past performance is a poor predictor of future productivity.
- There is little difference between the very best goalies and the average goalie. These differences are also very hard to predict. How goalies are paid, though, suggests that teams believe the differences are both large and predictable.

- Wins and losses in baseball, football, and hockey are assigned in each sport to a player (pitcher, quarterback, or goalie) whose performance is very dependent on his teammates. Therefore, wins and losses are assigned to a player who definitely cannot win the game by himself.

- As we have seen for more than two decades, there is no "hot hand" in basketball.

When we look over this list, we remember it was argued that the experiments of behavioral economists are flawed because how people behave in the "real world" is different from how people behave in a laboratory. Our list of sports examples, which is far from complete,[3] comes from a world that is very real to the people making these decisions. And these real world examples appear to confirm much that's been learned in the lab.

As we saw for Isiah Thomas, real world mistakes have very real consequences. The failure of the New York Knicks to win not only cost Isiah his job, but perhaps more importantly, severely damaged his reputation as a basketball expert. Yet our examination of the data suggests Isiah's only crime was implementing what every basketball expert knew to be true. Scorers are considered the most valuable players in the NBA. Therefore, a team of scorers should be the most successful team. Unfortunately, as Isiah's experience demonstrated, scorers are not nearly as important as people in the NBA believe.

We suspect Isiah's experience has been repeated throughout sports. From baseball managers who have historically relied on stealing bases to win games, to hockey teams that believe that changing the team's goalie will dramatically alter outcomes, to football teams that spend a top draft choice and millions of dollars on a "can't-miss" college quarterback, to basketball teams that invest millions in a new head coach. When these decisions don't lead to wins, the consequences to the decision-makers are indeed severe. Despite the severity of these consequences, though, learning in sports is extremely slow.

Certainly these stories inform our understanding of sports. When we think of how quickly information is understood in sports, though, we can see that these stories also inform our understanding of economics. Traditionally, economists have argued that people are fully rational, or essentially "lightning calculators," capable of adopting new information instantaneously. However, in an industry with an abundance of information, clear incentives, and severe consequences for getting it wrong, the lightning calculators don't seem to work very well. As we mentioned at the onset, we don't think such stories are a comment on the relative intellectual power of people in sports. What we do think is that people both in and outside sports don't behave consistently with the standard models in economics.

And so, at the end of our tale on sports is a message for economists. Perhaps we should stop insisting that all models have rational foundations. If our aim is to develop models that describe how actual people behave, we need to focus on how people actually make decisions. To take any other course of action in the face of all the evidence that has been presented is simply...okay, it's simply irrational.

Measuring Wins Produced in the NBA

Throughout the book, we mention Wins Produced for NBA players, a metric introduced in *The Wages of Wins* and Berri (2008). Much of the following discussion is offered for those who are interested in how this is calculated.

A Very Brief Introduction to Regression Analysis

The Wins Produced calculations are based on various regressions. For economists, regressions are often the laboratory in which we work. For many non-economists, though, the basics of regression may be unfamiliar. Fortunately, to understand our arguments one only needs to understand a few simple concepts.

Let's start with the following simple model:

$$\text{Wins} = a_1 + a_2 \times \text{Points Scored} + a_3 \times \text{Opp. Points Scored} + e \quad (1)$$

In words, this model says that wins are a function of how many points a team and the team's opponent score. The estimation of Model 1—with NBA data from 1987-88 to 2008-09—gives values for the coefficients, or a_1, a_2, and a_3 (with standard errors in parentheses):

$a_1 = 41.6 \ (2.2)$
$a_2 = 0.032 \ (0.00036)$
$a_3 = -0.032 \ (0.00038)$

These values indicate that each additional point scored is worth 0.032 wins while each point surrendered costs a team 0.032 wins.

The values of the coefficients are not the only concern. We also need to know if these coefficients are statistically significant. Statistical significance is tremendously important in evaluating regression results. Before one can discuss what the estimated values of the coefficients are saying, we first must determine if the coefficient is statistically different from zero. If the coefficient is statistically different from zero, then one moves on to the discussion of economic significance, or the importance of the variable in question. If the coefficient is not statistically different from zero, though, then this fact is reported and the discussion tends to end.

A general rule of thumb is that a coefficient has to be twice the size of the standard error (in absolute terms) for a coefficient to be considered statistically significant. When the rule of thumb is satisfied, then there is only about a 5% chance that the coefficient would be zero. Sometimes in the text, this rule was stretched a bit, and we discussed coefficients that had a 10% chance of being zero. Beyond 10%, though, one tends to always consider a coefficient statistically insignificant. With respect to the coefficient reported previously, there is a less than 1% chance the coefficient is zero.

Beyond statistical significance, there is the issue of explanatory power, or how much of the variation in the dependent variable (in this case, wins) the model explains. Explanatory power is referred to as R^2, and it's simply a ratio of the variation the model explains to the total variation that exists in the dependent variable. For Model 1, 94% of the variation in winning percentage is explained by points scored and the opponent's points scored.

Why isn't it 100%? The model examines points scored across an entire season. In any given game teams will score more points—or allow more points—than needed to decide the contest. Across an 82-game season, these excess points tend to even out, but this process isn't perfect.

The imperfection of our estimate is captured by the last term reported in Model 1. Because a regression is only an estimate, an error term—or e —is always part of the model. This term captures the difference between what the model predicts and the actual value of the dependent variable (in this case, wins).

Let's illustrate how the model works. In 2008-09, the Cleveland Cavaliers scored 8,223 points and allowed 7,491. The following prediction of wins is revealed when these values are plugged into the model:

Predicted Wins = $41.6 + 0.032 \times 8{,}223 - 0.032 \times 7{,}491$

or

Predicted Wins = 64.7

The Cavaliers actually won 66 regular season contests. A similar calculation for all teams in 2008-09, reveals that the difference between predicted and actual wins—in absolute terms—was only 1.8. Not surprisingly, points scored and surrendered do a very good job of predicting a team's winning percentage.

Modeling Wins in the NBA

Now that we see the basics of regression analysis, let's move on to how we measure player productivity in the NBA.

That discussion starts with the data. The NBA tracks the measures reported in Table A.1 for its players and teams.

Each of these statistics is tracked for the team and the team's opponent. The objective is to connect the statistics tracked for the players being evaluated to wins achieved by the player's team. Given this objective, one should try and avoid using statistics tracked for the player's opponents. However, there is a serious constraint. The validity of an empirical model depends on how well it is specified. In other words, if one ignores all statistics tracked for a team's opponent, the model would be improperly specified. Consequently, one must employ some factors that are only tracked for a team's opponent, although it's a good idea to minimize this practice as much as possible.

TABLE A.1   The Box Score Data of the NBA

Statistic	Label	Statistic	Label
Points	PTS	Offensive Rebounds	ORB
Field Goals Made	FGM	Defensive Rebounds	DRB
Free Throws Made	FTM	Steals	STL
Field Goals Attempted	FGA	Turnovers	TO
Free Throws Attempted	FTA	Blocked Shots	BLK
Assists	AST	Personal Fouls	PF

Before arriving at the specific model employed, a number of steps were taken. Repeating these steps, which are detailed in previously published work, can be confined to stumblingonwins.com. For our purposes, let's just discuss what is learned from the final model.

The final model that we employed is actually familiar to anyone who has studied basketball statistics. Both the writings of John Hollinger (2002) and Dean Oliver (2004) argue that the number of wins a team has in a season is determined by the team's offensive efficiency and defensive efficiency, where efficiency is calculated by dividing points scored (or allowed) by the number of possessions in a game.

Both Hollinger and Oliver essentially define possessions as follows:

$$\text{Possessions Employed (PE)} = \text{FGA} + 0.45 \times \text{FTA} + \text{TO} - \text{ORB}$$

This definition tells us how a team can employ a possession. Once a team acquires the ball it can take a field goal attempt and/or a number of free throw attempts, or the team can turn the ball back over to its opponent. Additional offensive rebounds can allow a team to keep the ball after an errant shot and take additional field goal attempts or free throw attempts (or turn the ball over).

The term "Possessions Employed" is not employed by Hollinger or Oliver. For these writers, there is only one definition of possessions. To measure Wins Produced, though, a second definition is utilized:

Possessions Acquired (PA) = Opp.TO + DRB + TMRB + Opp.FGM + 0.45 × Opp.FTM

Possessions Acquired focuses on how a team acquires the ball. A team gains possession of the ball each time it forces a turnover or rebounds an errant shot by the opponent. One should note the difference between a defensive rebound and a team rebound (TMRB). A defensive rebound is a rebound of an opponent's missed shot that can be credited to a specific individual player. If a rebound cannot be credited to an individual player, a team rebound is recorded.

If a team fails to force a turnover or rebounds a missed shot, the opponent will eventually make a shot. By rule, a team will acquire possession of the ball each time an opponent makes a field goal attempt. The team also acquires possession after an opponent makes a free throw, but since players are often awarded more than one free throw at a time, only a fraction of made free throws result in a change in possession.

Given the definitions of Possessions Employed and Possessions Acquired, wins can now be modeled as follows:

Winning Percentage = $b_1 + b_2 \times$ PTS/PE $- b_3 \times$ Opp.PTS/PA + e   (2)

Model 2 argues that wins are determined by offensive efficiency and defensive efficiency, which is the same approach advocated by Hollinger and Oliver. By utilizing Possessions Employed and Possessions Acquired, though, one can now connect much of what a player does on the court to wins.

Utilizing NBA data from the 1987-88 to 2008-09 seasons, the estimation of Model 2 gives us the following values (with standard errors in parentheses):

$$b_1 = 0.481 \ (0.057)$$
$$b_2 = 3.15 \ (0.040)$$
$$b_3 = -3.13 \ (0.045)$$

By themselves, these values are hard to interpret. As detailed at stumblingonwins.com, though, from these coefficients one can determine the value of points scored, field goal attempts, free throw attempts, turnovers (which includes team turnovers or TMTO), offensive rebounds, opponent's points scored, opponent's turnovers (which includes steals), defensive rebounds, team rebounds, opponent's field goals made, and opponent's free throws made. And from the value of the opponent's free throws made—again, as detailed at stumblingonwins.com—one can ascertain the impact of a player's personal fouls.

From these values, one learns something important about how wins are produced in the NBA. With the exception of factors associated with free throws and personal fouls, most factors listed in Table A.2 have the same impact—in absolute terms—on wins. Although this is what the regression reports, it's important to emphasize the intuition behind this result. From 1987-88 to 2008-09, teams averaged 1.02 points per possession. Consequently, the value of anything that gets—or loses—possession of the ball is worth about one point.

The results also indicate that each time a team acquires the ball it has acquired the right to take one field goal attempt. This observation is illustrated by Model 3:

$$\text{FGA} = c_1 + c_2 \times \text{Opp.TO} + c_3 \times \text{DRB} + c_4 \times \text{Opp.FTM} + c_5$$
$$\times \text{Opp.FTM} + c_6 \times \text{TO} + c_7 \times \text{ORB} + c_8 \times \text{FTA} + e \qquad (3)$$

TABLE A.2   The Impact of Various Player and Team Factors on Wins in the NBA

Player Factors	Impact on Wins
PTS	0.033
FGA	–0.033
FTA	–0.015
ORB	0.033
TO	–0.033
DRB	0.033
Opp.FTM	–0.017
STL	0.033
Team Factors	**Impact on Wins**
Opp.PTS from Opp.FGA	–0.032
Opp.FGM	0.033
Opp.TO (that are not STL)	0.033
TMTO	–0.033
TMRB	0.033

Estimating Model 3 with data from 1987-88 to 2008-09 reveals that the coefficients for the opponent's turnovers, defensive rebounds, opponent's field goals made, turnovers, and offensive rebounds range (in absolute terms) from 0.95 to 1.08. So, each of these factors is worth essentially one field goal attempt. From 1987-88 to 2008-09, teams scored 0.97 points per field goal attempt, so once again, one sees that these factors are each worth about one point.

Model 3 explains 98% of the variation in field goal attempts. What's missing from this model is team rebounds that change possession. Such a factor is not provided in a box score, but it can be estimated (as detailed at stumblingonwins.com).

Looking back on Table A.2, one sees values for almost every factor tracked for individual players in the box score. The lone exceptions are blocked shots and assists. Neither of these factors is a part of Possessions Employed or Possessions Acquired, and consequently, neither blocked shots nor assists directly impacts wins. Yet one can utilize the results reported, as noted at stumblingonwins.com, to derive the impact blocked shots and assists have on wins. Such analysis indicates that each blocked shot is worth about 0.019 wins. An additional assist adds about 0.022 wins.

Calculating Wins Produced in the NBA

With values in hand, let's illustrate this methodology by calculating the Wins Produced of Chris Paul in 2008-09.

Step One: Calculate the Value of a Player's Production

$PROD = 0.033 \times PTS - 0.033 \times FGA - 0.015 \times FTA + 0.033 \times ORB + 0.033 \times DRB - 0.033 \times TO + 0.033 \times STL - 0.017 \times Opp.FTM + 0.019 \times BLK + 0.022 \times AST$

For Chris Paul in 2008-09, the calculation would be as follows:

Paul's PROD $= 0.033 \times 1{,}781 - 0.033 \times 1{,}255 + -0.015 \times 524 + 0.033 \times 69 + 0.033 \times 363 - 0.033 \times 231 + 0.033 \times 216 - 0.017 \times 185.0 + 0.019 \times 10 + 0.022 \times 861 =$ **38.0**

In addition to total production, one also needs to consider production per 48 minutes (PROD48). This is calculated as follows:

Paul's PROD48 $= [(PROD / \text{Minutes Played}) \times 48] = (38.0 / 3{,}002) \times 48 = 0.608$

Step Two: Adjust for Production of Teammates

Two adjustments need to be made. The first, MATE48, adjusts a player's value for his teammates' production of blocked shots and assists. The second, TMDEF48, adjusts for team defense.

The calculation of each adjustment is detailed at stumblingon wins.com. For here, it should be noted that TMDEF48 incorporates the five factors reported in Table A.2 that are tracked for the team, but not tracked for individual players. These include opponent's points scored, opponent's made field goals, opponent's turnovers that are not steals, team turnovers, and team rebounds. These statistics are allocated across players according to the minutes each player plays. This approach essentially follows from Scott, Long, and Somppi (1985); Berri (1999); and Oliver (2004).

Such an approach assumes that defense is essentially a team activity. The validity of this assumption is bolstered by the fact that teams typically play defense together. This is especially true in the NBA today, where zone defenses are legal. This approach allows one to differentiate players who play on good and bad defensive teams. However, it fails to differentiate between players who are relatively better or worse on an individual team.

An alternative approach was suggested by Ty Willihnganz of Bucks Diary (mvn.com/bucksdiary). Willihnganz has augmented Win Score (a simplified version of Wins Produced discussed below) by incorporating defensive data from 82games.com. This is a Web site—primarily known for plus-minus data—that reports how well a player's supposed defensive assignment performs. As noted in Chapter 3, "The Search for Useful Stats"—and at stumblingonwins.com—we question the ability of a plus-minus measure (and adjusted plus-minus) to completely and accurately capture a player's value. It does seem possible, though, that such data could better capture a player's defensive ability. In other words, perhaps plus-minus data—as Willihnganz attempts— could supplement what we learn from the standard box score data.

It appears that the player evaluations offered by Willihnganz are quite consistent with what we see from our calculations (which are based solely on box score data). In considering the few differences that exist, though, it's important to remember the primary problem with plus-minus data. A player's plus-minus value, as we observed in

Chapter 3, appears to depend on his teammates. This feature is illustrated by the inconsistency of these measures. Willihnganz has noted that such inconsistency also plagues the data he employed on the performance of each player's opponent. Such inconsistency suggests that the data he utilizes is not fully capturing a player's defensive ability. Consequently, although we find Willihnganz's approach interesting, we are not convinced it's necessarily an improvement over our approach to capturing defense.

To illustrate our approach, we turn back to Chris Paul and the Hornets. For the Hornets in 2008-09, MATE48 was -0.008 while TMDEF48 was 0.002. With these values in hand, one can calculate a player's Adjusted P48 (AdjP48). This is illustrated for Chris Paul below.

Paul's AdjP48 = PROD48 – MATE48 + TMDEF84 = 0.608 – (–0.008) + 0.002 = **0.618**

Across the league in 2008-09, the average value of PROD48 was 0.311. The average value of MATE48—in absolute terms—was only 0.006. TMDEF48—in absolute terms—had an average value of 0.011. So these two adjustments are small and have very little impact on the assessment of an individual player's per-minute performance. To illustrate, the correlation coefficient between PROD48 and AdjP48 in 2008-09 was 0.999.

Step Three: Adjust for Position Played

The average value for AdjP48 is not the same across all positions. Centers and power forwards tend to get rebounds and tend not to commit turnovers. Guards are the opposite. The nature of basketball is that teams need little men and big men. Given that teams appear to require all five positions, players should be evaluated relative to their position averages. These are reported in Table A.3.

To incorporate the position averages one needs to identify the position each player plays. Although this process is imperfect for all players, Chris Paul is clearly a point guard. Consequently, one can evaluate Paul's performance relative to the average point guard.

Paul's Relative AdjP48 = AdjP48 − League Average AdjP48
= 0.618 − 0.266 = **0.352**

TABLE A.3   Value of AdjP48 Across Positions

Position	Average AdjP48
Centers and Power Forwards	0.432
Power Forwards	0.353
Small Forwards	0.276
Shooting Guards	0.228
Points Guards	0.266

So, per 48 minutes, Paul produced 0.352 more wins than an average point guard. Given that he played 3,002 minutes, Paul produced 22.0 wins (or 0.352/48 × 3,002) beyond what a team would get from an average point guard.

Step Four: Calculate WP48 and Wins Produced

After Step Three, one has a player's production relative to the position average. To move from relative wins to absolute wins, one needs the average number of wins produced by a player per 48 minutes. This is easy to calculate.

The average team will win half its games, or have 0.500 wins per 48 minutes played. Since a team employs five players per 48 minutes, the average player must produce 0.100 wins per 48 minutes played. Because teams do play overtime games once in awhile, the actual average production of wins per 48 minutes is 0.099.

Given what we know about an average player, Wins Per 48 minutes (WP48) is calculated as follows:

WP48 = Relative AdjP48 + 0.099

For Paul, the calculation is as follows:

Paul WP48 = 0.352 + 0.099 = **0.451**

Given how many minutes Paul played, if he produced 0.451 wins per 48 minutes, he must have produced 28.2 wins for the season:

Paul's Wins Produced = WP48 / 48 × Minutes Played = 0.451/48 × 3,002 = **28.2**

Paul's production, as noted in Chapter 3, led all players in 2008-09. Unfortunately, Paul's teammates were not quite as helpful. Table A.4 reports the Wins Produced calculation for each player the Hornets employed in 2008-09. An average player will post a WP48 of 0.100. As one can see, after Paul the Hornets employed only two above average performers; and David West and James Posey were only slightly above average. Consequently, despite the productivity of Paul, the summation of Wins Produced for the Hornets was not far beyond average.

TABLE A.4   The New Orleans Hornets in 2008-09

Hornets	Minutes Played	Position	AdjP48	WP48	Wins Produced
Chris Paul	3,002	PG	0.618	0.451	28.2
David West	2,982	PF	0.364	0.105	6.5
James Posey	2,140	SG-SF	0.286	0.111	5.0
Rasual Butler	2,614	SG	0.205	0.077	4.2
Tyson Chandler	1,445	C	0.411	0.078	2.4
Peja Stojakovic	2,089	SF-PF	0.235	0.044	1.9
Morris Peterson	515	SG	0.217	0.089	1.0
Antonio Daniels	733	PG	0.228	0.061	0.9
Julian Wright	772	PF	0.308	0.054	0.9
Ryan Bowen	219	SF-PF	0.233	0.057	0.3

TABLE A.4   The New Orleans Hornets in 2008-09

Hornets	Minutes Played	Position	AdjP48	WP48	Wins Produced
Mike James	74	PG	0.046	−0.120	−0.2
Devin Brown	869	PG-SG	0.119	−0.015	−0.3
Sean Marks	838	C	0.266	−0.067	−1.2
Melvin Ely	373	C	0.082	−0.251	−1.9
Hilton Armstrong	1,092	C	0.218	−0.115	−2.6
			Summation of Wins Produced		**44.9**

The Hornets actually won 49 games in 2008-09, so the summation of Wins Produced is off by 4.1. As Table A.5 reveals, that's the largest difference, in absolute terms, for any team in 2008-09. The average difference between a team's Wins Produced and actual wins is only 1.7, indicating that this approach does accurately connect team wins to the performance of individual players.

TABLE A.5   Evaluating the Accuracy of Wins Produced: 2008-09

Team	Summation of Wins Produced	Wins	Difference in Absolute Terms
Cleveland	64.6	66	1.4
Los Angeles Lakers	61.2	65	3.8
Boston	61.1	62	0.9
Orlando	58.6	59	0.4
Portland	55.2	54	1.2
Denver	51.8	54	2.2
Houston	51.5	53	1.5
San Antonio	51.1	54	2.9
Utah	48.1	48	0.1
Dallas	46.2	50	3.8

TABLE A.5   Evaluating the Accuracy of Wins Produced: 2008-09

Team	Summation of Wins Produced	Wins	Difference in Absolute Terms
Phoenix	46.0	46	0.0
New Orleans	44.9	49	4.1
Atlanta	44.9	47	2.1
Miami	42.1	43	0.9
Philadelphia	41.0	41	0.0
Chicago	40.4	41	0.6
Detroit	39.8	39	0.8
Indiana	38.1	36	2.1
Milwaukee	38.0	34	4.0
Charlotte	37.8	35	2.8
New Jersey	34.5	34	0.5
Toronto	33.5	33	0.5
New York	33.3	32	1.3
Golden State	31.2	29	2.2
Minnesota	27.6	24	3.6
Memphis	26.4	24	2.4
Oklahoma	24.7	23	1.7
Washington	20.9	19	1.9
Sacramento	17.9	17	0.9
Los Angeles Clippers	17.7	19	1.3
Average Error in Absolute Terms			**1.7**

Win Score and PAWS48

Wins Produced appears to provide an accurate assessment of a player's contribution to success (or failure) on a basketball court, but it lacks the simplicity of baseball measures like OPS. Fortunately, one can take what was learned about the value of the NBA's statistics and calculate a simple measure.

Looking back at Table A.2, we see that points, rebounds, steals, field goal attempts, and turnovers have essentially the same impact in absolute terms on wins. Meanwhile, blocked shots, assists, free throw attempts, and personal fouls have a smaller impact on outcomes. For the sake of simplicity, let's set the value of each of these last four factors equal to ½ (again, in absolute terms). Such a step gives the following metric, which we have labeled Win Score:

$$\text{Win Score} = \text{PTS} + \text{REB} + \text{STL} + \tfrac{1}{2} \times \text{BLK} + \tfrac{1}{2} \times \text{AST} - \text{FGA} - \tfrac{1}{2} \times \text{FTA} - \text{TO} - \tfrac{1}{2} \times \text{PF}$$

Win Score is certainly far simpler to calculate than PROD48. And the cost of this simplicity is low. There is a 0.998 correlation between Win Score per 48 minutes (WS48) and PROD48. On a per-minute basis, the simple approach is about as good as the more complex approach detailed above.

As Tables A.3 and A.6 illustrate, position played matters. So to compare players at different positions, one must turn to Position Adjusted Win Score per 48 minutes (PAWS48):

PAWS48 = Win Score per 48 minutes – Average Win Score per 48 minutes at position played

TABLE A.6   Average WS48 at Each Position: 1977-78 to 2007-08

Position	Average WS48
Centers	11.36
Power Forwards	10.47
Small Forwards	7.87
Shooting Guards	6.08
Point Guards	6.54

PAWS48 has a 0.99 correlation with WP48. This result suggests that a player's performance in the NBA is primarily about the statistics the player generates relative to the position played.

A Comment on Alternatives

Relative to baseball, the statistics tabulated for basketball players have a stronger link to current wins. Basketball players are also more consistent across time, suggesting that the statistics tracked for basketball players are more often about the player being examined (and not the player's teammates or luck).

Despite better data, research in basketball has one serious handicap. A researcher in need of a performance measure for a baseball player can turn to an established measure, such as OPS or other more complex statistics. When we first started conducting research in basketball, though, it became clear that existing metrics didn't capture productivity very accurately.

Consider the two most commonly cited measures: NBA Efficiency and Game Score. The former is similar to Dave Heeran's TENDEX model, a model originally developed by Heeran in 1959. The latter is the simplified version of John Hollinger's Player Efficiency Rating (PER). Although PER makes a number of adjustments beyond the Game Score formulation seen below, the end results are essentially the same. For the 2008-09 season, PER and Game Score per 48 minutes had a 0.99 correlation for the 445 NBA players employed by the league:

NBA Efficiency = PTS + ORB + DRB + STL + BLK + AST – TO – All Missed Shots

Game Score = PTS + 0.4 × FGM - 0.7 × FGA – 0.4 × (FTA – FTM) + 0.7 × ORB + 0.3 × DRB + STL + 0.7 × AST + 0.7 × BLK – 0.4 × PF – TO

A similar story is told about NBA Efficiency and Game Score. These measures look different, but for 2008-09 season, there was a 0.99 correlation between a player's NBA Efficiency and Game Score.

As Berri and Bradbury (2010) note, these measures all align because each tells a similar story about player scoring. For example, imagine a player who takes 12 shots from two-point range. If he makes four shots, his NBA Efficiency will rise by eight. The eight misses, though, will cause his value to decline by eight. So a player breaks even with respect to NBA Efficiency by converting on 33% of his shots from two-point range. From three-point range, a player only needs to makes 25% of his shots to break even.

Most NBA players can exceed these thresholds. Therefore, the more shots most NBA players take the higher will be his NBA Efficiency total. As a consequence, players who take a large number of shots tend to dominate the player rankings produced by this measure.

For Game Score, the same problem exists, only the problem is a bit worse. As detailed at stumblingonwins.com, the break-even point on two-point shots for Game Score is 29.2%. From three-point range a player breaks even if he hits 20.6% of his shots. If a player surpasses these break-even points—and again, most players can do this—then the more shots he takes the higher will be his value.

Because these measures reward a player for just taking shots, they don't tend to explain wins very well. As detailed at stumblingonwins.com and in Berri and Bradbury (2010), a team's NBA Efficiency only explains 32% of the variation in team wins. A team's Game Score and PER explains 31% and 33% of the variation in wins, respectively. One might note, though, that these measures don't include the team defensive adjustment employed in the calculation of Wins Produced. Unfortunately, if you add the team defensive adjustment to NBA Efficiency, Game Score, and PERs, explanatory power only rises to 58%, 60%, and 56%, respectively.

Three Objections to Wins Produced for the NBA

Wins Produced was introduced in 2006. In the past few years, three objections have been raised to this methodology:

1. The ranking of players by Wins Produced is inconsistent with what people "know" about basketball.

This is by far the most common complaint. Chapter 3 reports the leaders in Wins Produced from the 2008-09 season. This list reports a few names, such as Chris Paul, LeBron James, Dwyane Wade, and Dwight Howard, that people generally believe are among the best. But how many NBA fans would rank Troy Murphy, David Lee, and Antonio McDyess among the best players in the game?

Our response to this complaint is that it's essentially true. Wins Produced is inconsistent with common perceptions of player performance. Common perceptions are driven by points scored. Non-scoring factors tend to be minimized or ignored. Given this disconnect between how the factors are perceived and the impact these factors have on wins, it's not surprising that a model that measures wins would give results that differ with how people perceive the game. Or to put it another way, both PERs and NBA Efficiency are consistent with perceptions of performance, but neither is very consistent with wins.

2. The box score statistics in basketball do not take into account the impact of teammates.

Statistics from football tend to be inconsistent. This suggests a player's numbers are influenced by his teammates. Although it's suspected this is true in the NBA, the consistency of performance across time suggests that teammates don't have much impact on an individual player's productivity. Consequently, it seems safe to assume that the statistics tracked for an individual player represent that player's contribution to team success.

3. Because of diminishing returns, the model overrates certain players.

The existence of diminishing returns leads some to suspect that the impact of productive players is inflated by Wins Produced. In Chapter 8, "Is It the Teacher or the Students?," this concern was addressed when it was noted that although diminishing returns exist, the effect is quite small.

When one looks at specific statistics, one does see large effects with respect to points scored and field goal attempts. One also sees an effect with respect to defensive rebounds (although it's only about half of what we see with respect to scoring). People tend not to be troubled by the possibility the value of scorers is overstated. When people see a player like Ben Wallace (a player known for rebounding) lead the league in Wins Produced in 2001-02, then questions are raised.

To address these concerns, two versions of Position Adjusted Win Score (PAWS) were constructed. The first only counted half of a player's rebounds. Re-ranking the players with this adjusted version of PAWS revealed that Ben Wallace was still the top ranked player in the game in 2001-02. This is because the revised version of PAWS per minute and WP48 have a 0.95 correlation. One can also construct PAWS by giving offensive rebounds a weight of 0.7 and defensive rebounds a weight of 0.3 (following Hollinger's lead). With these values, Ben Wallace was still the top ranked player in 2001-02. Again, this is not surprising since this version of PAWS per minute and WP48 also has a 0.95 correlation.

In sum, Wins Produced appears to be—at a minimum—a reasonable approximation of an NBA player's productivity. We would argue the model is both theoretically and empirically sound, and superior—for the reasons stated—to a number of popular alternatives. Once again, though, Wins Produced is not consistent with popular perceptions. Given the problems with popular perceptions, though, this result shouldn't be a surprise.

B

Measuring Wins Produced in the NFL

The NFL's Quarterback Rating is often mentioned by NFL announcers, but we suspect most football fans don't fully understand how it's computed. In fact, most announcers probably don't understand how this measure is calculated. These suspicions are grounded in the steps one has to take to calculate a player's Quarterback Rating (we are not making this up):

> First, one takes a quarterback's completion percentage, then subtracts 0.3 from this number and divides by 0.2. You then take yards per attempt, subtract 3 and divide by 4. After that, you divide touchdowns per attempt by .05. For interceptions per attempt, you start with .095, subtract from this number interceptions per attempt, and then divide this result by .04. To get the Quarterback Rating, you add the values created from your first four steps, multiply this sum by 100, and divide the result by 6. Oh, and by the way, the sum from each of your first four steps cannot exceed 2.375 or be less than zero.

Yes, this is how the NFL's Quarterback Rating—often seen during the broadcast of each game   is calculated. There are three issues with this metric. First, all else being equal, we tend to prefer simplicity to complexity, and obviously the Quarterback Rating is not simple. Second, it's not clear that the assigned value of each statistic (i.e., passing yards, interceptions, etc.) actually represents the impact the statistic has on outcomes (i.e., points and/or wins). Finally, the NFL's measure only considers passing. Sacks, fumbles, and rushing are completely ignored.

To overcome these problems, we turn to a quarterback's production of Net Points and Wins Produced, measures that were discussed in *The Wages of Wins* and Berri (2007). This approach begins by connecting points scored and points surrendered to wins.

$$\text{Wins} = d_1 + d_2 \times \text{Points Scored} + d_3 \times \text{Points Surrendered} + e \quad (1)$$

Model 1 was estimated with data from the 1995 to 2005 NFL seasons. This estimation gives the following values (with standard errors in parentheses):

$d_1 = 9.1 \ (0.52)$
$d_2 = 0.027 \ (0.001)$
$d_3 = -0.030 \ (0.001)$

The model has an R^2 of 0.84. In other words, the model explains 84% of the variation in wins. These results also tell us that each additional point scored is worth 0.027 wins, while each point surrendered costs a team 0.030 wins.

The next step is to develop models that explain how many points a team's offense scores and a team's defense allows. A team's offensive ability is influenced by four factors: Acquisition of the Ball, Moving the Ball, Maintaining Possession, and Scoring. These four factors are then captured by the variables listed in Table B.1.

A team's offensive point production—or the number of points a team scores that can be attributed to a team's offense—were regressed on the factors listed in Table B.1. The results are reported in Table B.2.

A similar model was estimated to explain the number of points the opponent's offense scores. With these two models one can estimate the value of the statistics tabulated for a quarterback. For example, Table B.2 reports that each yard gained by a team (rushing yards or passing yards) gains 0.080 points. Each play (i.e., rushing attempt, passing attempt, sack), though, costs a team -0.214 points. This means a team needs to gain nearly 2.7 yards on a play just to break even.

TABLE B.1   Factors Explaining the Points Scored by a Team's Offense

Actions	Variables
Acquisition of the Ball	Opponent's Kickoffs
	Opponent's Punts
	Opponent's Missed Field Goals
	Opponent's Interceptions Thrown
	Opponent's Fumbles Lost
Moving the Ball	Average Starting Position of Drives
	Offensive yards = Rushing yards + Passing yards
	Penalty Yards
	Opponent's Penalty Yards
Maintaining Possession	Plays = Rushing attempts + Passing attempts + Sacks
	Third Down Conversion Rate
	Field Goals Missed
	Interceptions Thrown
	Fumbles Lost
Scoring	Percentage of Scores That are Touchdowns
	= OFFTD / (OFFTD + FGMADE)
	Where OFFTD = Touchdowns scored by a team's offense
	and FGMADE = Field goals made
	Extra Points Conversion Rate = OFFXP / OFFTD
	Where OFFXP = Extra points earned on offensive touchdowns

Source: Berri (2007), p. 240.

Note: The data utilized to estimate the model of offensive points, as well as the model for the opponent's offensive points, came from various issues of the *Official National Football League Record & Fact Book*. The lone exception is Average Starting Position of Drives, which was taken from Football Outsiders.com.

**TABLE B.2   Modeling Offensive Scoring
Dependent Variable: Offensive Point Production
Team Fixed Effects and Dummy Variables for Each Season Employed**

Variable	Coefficient	Standard Errors
Opponent's Kickoffs°	0.909	0.254
Opponent's Punts°°	0.448	0.203
Opponent's Missed Field Goals	0.465	0.579
Opponent's Interceptions Thrown°	1.272	0.293
Opponent's Fumbles Lost°°	1.033	0.401
Average Starting Position of Drives°	10.069	0.902
Yards Gained, Offense°	0.080	0.004
Penalty Yards	−0.015	0.012
Opponent's Penalty Yards°	0.055	0.011
Plays°	−0.214	0.051
Third Down Conversion Rate°	1.927	0.483
Field Goals Missed°	−2.986	0.557
Interceptions Thrown°	−1.337	0.365
Fumbles Lost°	−1.481	0.418
Percentage of Scores That Are Touchdowns°	102.831	22.557
Extra Point Conversion Rate	45.626	27.781
Adjusted R-squared	0.91	
Observations	251	

Source: Berri (2007), p. 243.

°Denotes significance at the 1% level.

°°Denotes significance at the 5% level.

In addition to yards and plays, one can also see the impact of turnovers. For that story, one needs to look at both Tables B.2 and B.3. An interception reduces a team's scoring by 1.337 points. Turning to Table B.3, each interception also adds 1.408 points to the opponent's scoring. Putting these values together, each interception costs a team 2.745 Net Points. Similar calculations reveal that a lost fumble costs a team 2.899 Net Points.

**TABLE B.3 Modeling Opponent's Offensive Scoring
Dependent Variable: Opponent's Offensive Point Production
Team Fixed Effects and Dummy Variables for Each Season Employed**

Variable	Coefficient	Standard Errors
Kickoffs°	0.923	0.267
Punts°	0.764	0.224
Missed Field Goals	1.008	0.590
Interceptions Thrown°	1.408	0.297
Fumbles Lost°	1.418	0.424
Opponent's Average Starting Position of Drives°	9.094	0.915
Opponent's Yards Gained, Offense°	0.078	0.005
Opponent's Penalty Yards°	−0.022	0.013
Penalty Yards°	0.043	0.011
Opponent's Plays°	−0.143	0.052
Opponent's Third Down Conversion Rate°	1.848	0.533
Opponent's Field Goals Missed°	−3.425	0.543
Opponent's Interceptions Thrown°	−1.559	0.250
Opponent's Fumbles Lost°	−1.630	0.359
Opponent's Percentage of Scores That Are Touchdowns°	122.152	20.583
Opponent's Extra Point Conversion Rate	45.404	23.161
Adjusted R-squared	0.88	
Observations	251	

Source: Berri (2007), p. 245.
°Denotes significance at the 1% level.

The results of these calculations are reported in Table B.4. This table also reports the value of yards, plays, and turnovers in terms of wins. For example, each yard gained is worth 0.080 points. From the estimation of Model 1 it was learned that each point scored is worth 0.027 wins. Putting these two results together reveals that each yard gained is worth 0.002 wins. Similar calculations were completed for plays, fumbles, and interceptions.

TABLE B.4   Value in Net Points and Wins of Various Performance Statistics Tabulated for NFL Quarterbacks

Variable	Net Points	Wins
Every Yard (either from Passing or Rushing) is worth...	0.080	0.002
Every Play (where Plays = Passing Attempts + Rushing Attempts + Sacks) is worth...	0.214	–0.006
Every Interception is worth...	–2.745	–0.078
Every Fumbles Lost is worth ...	–2.899	–0.082

Source: Berri (2007), p. 246.

The numbers reported in Table B.4 indicate that each play, in absolute terms, is worth 2.7 yards (0.214 divided by 0.080). In addition, the value of an interception is worth 34.5 yards (2.745 divided by 0.080), while a fumble lost costs a team 36.4 yards (2.899 divided by 0.080). One can simplify these values and argue that each play is worth about 3 yards and each turnover costs a team about 30 yards. We should note that Brian Burke at Advanced NFL Stats (www.advancednflstats.com) argues that turnovers are worth more than 30 yards. And in the original version of QB Score presented in *The Wages of Wins*, a value of 50 was employed. Berri (2007), though, reports values ranging from 30 to 50 will produce similar rankings of quarterbacks. Consequently, for the sake of simplicity, we have chosen—as illustrated next—to employ the value of 30 in calculating QB Score.

QB Score = All Yards – 3 × All Plays – 30 × All Turnovers

Looking at all quarterbacks from 1994 to 2008, the correlation coefficient between QB Score and Wins Produced is 0.99.

Although QB Score tells essentially the same story, we tended to focus on Wins Produced in our discussion of quarterbacks. Given this focus, an illustration of how Wins Produced is calculated would be helpful. Table B.5 reports the 2008 regular season production of Ben Roethlisberger, starting quarterback for the Super Bowl Champion Pittsburgh Steelers.

TABLE B.5   The Production of Ben Roethlisberger in 2008

Statistic	Totals	Net Points	Wins Produced
Passing Yards	3,301	262.7	6.99
Rushing Yards	101	8.0	0.21
Yards Lost from Sacks	284	22.6	−0.60
Passing Attempts	469	−100.4	−2.67
Rushing Attempts	34	−7.3	−0.19
Sacks	46	−9.8	−0.26
Interceptions	15	−41.2	−1.17
Fumbles Lost	7	−20.3	−0.57
Totals	—	**114.3**	**1.73**
Net Points per Play	—	**0.208**	—
Wins Produced per 100 Plays (WP100)	—	—	**0.316**

Table B.4 reports—in terms of Net Points and Wins Produced—the value of the various box score statistics tracked for quarterbacks. With these values and Roethlisberger's statistics in hand, one can calculate Roethlisberger's Net Points and Wins Produced. For example, Roethlisberger threw 3,301 passing yards in 2008. Table B.4 reports that each passing yard creates 0.08 Net Points. Consequently, Roethlisberger's passing yards produced 262.7 Net Points (3,301 × 0.080). When we turn to Wins Produced, we see these same passing yards were worth 6.99 wins.

Applying this approach to each statistic reveals—as noted in Table B.5—that all of Roethlisberger's box score numbers were worth 114.3 Net Points and 1.73 Wins Produced, or 0.208 Net Points per Play and 0.316 Wins Produced per 100 plays (WP100). An average quarterback in 2008 posted a Net Points per Play of 0.175 and a WP100 of 0.450. So Roethlisberger was below average in 2008. Such results suggest that the Steelers' success in 2008 (the team won 12 games in the regular season) was primarily about something else besides the numbers associated with the team's starting quarterback.

Such analysis can be applied to all quarterbacks, although one has to note that the performance of an average quarterback changes over time. Consequently, to compare quarterbacks across time one needs to calculate Relative Wins Produced per 100 plays (RELWP100). This simply involves subtracting the average performance seen in each season from a quarterback's WP100. Then 0.377, or the average WP100 mark observed from 1970 to 2008, is added back. A similar calculation was completed anytime we reported a "relative" value for a quarterback (for example, Relative QB Rating).

Table B.6 reports the top 50 quarterbacks from 1970 to 2008. According to RELWP100, the best quarterback performance since 1970 was offered by Roger Staubach in 1971. Although Staubach was amazing that season, he actually split time with Craig Morton. Consequently, Staubach doesn't rank as high in Relative Wins Produced.

TABLE B.6   The Top 50 Quarterbacks from 1970 to 2008 Ranked in Terms of Relative WP100

Rank	Quarterback	Year	Team	Relative Wins Produced	Relative WP100
1	Roger Staubach	1971	Dallas	2.95	1.073
2	Bert Jones	1976	Baltimore Colts	4.04	0.984
3	Peyton Manning	2004	Indianapolis	5.15	0.963
4	Dan Marino	1984	Miami	5.73	0.948
5	Steve Young	1992	San Francisco	4.77	0.941
6	John Brodie	1970	San Francisco	3.67	0.930
7	Dan Fouts	1982	San Diego	3.19	0.910

**TABLE B.6   The Top 50 Quarterbacks from 1970 to 2008
Ranked in Terms of Relative WP100**

Rank	Quarterback	Year	Team	Relative Wins Produced	Relative WP100
8	Steve Young	1991	San Francisco	3.21	0.896
9	Mark Rypien	1991	Washington	3.84	0.867
10	Ken Stabler	1976	Oakland	2.73	0.862
11	Randall Cunningham	1998	Minnesota	4.11	0.862
12	Kurt Warner	2000	St. Louis Rams	3.27	0.850
13	Tom Brady	2007	New England	5.38	0.846
14	Ken Anderson	1975	Cincinnati	3.87	0.845
15	Joe Montana	1989	San Francisco	3.95	0.844
16	Kurt Warner	1999	St. Louis Rams	4.65	0.843
17	Joe Montana	1984	San Francisco	4.06	0.824
18	Boomer Esiason	1988	Cincinnati	3.79	0.823
19	Craig Morton	1970	Dallas	1.99	0.819
20	Ken Anderson	1974	Cincinnati	3.32	0.817
21	Steve Young	1994	San Francisco	4.41	0.801
22	Greg Landry	1971	Detroit	2.92	0.798
23	Ken Anderson	1981	Cincinnati	4.38	0.797
24	Donovan McNabb	2006	Philadelphia	2.93	0.795
25	Peyton Manning	2006	Indianapolis	4.71	0.793
26	Jim Hart	1976	St. Louis Cardinals	3.26	0.790
27	Steve Young	1993	San Francisco	4.44	0.789
28	Ken Stabler	1974	Oakland	2.66	0.783
29	Steve McNair	2003	Tennessee	3.57	0.782
30	Peyton Manning	2005	Indianapolis	3.93	0.781
31	Fran Tarkenton	1974	Minnesota	3.00	0.771

**TABLE B.6   The Top 50 Quarterbacks from 1970 to 2008
Ranked in Terms of Relative WP100**

Rank	Quarterback	Year	Team	Relative Wins Produced	Relative WP100
32	Brian Griese	2000	Denver	2.94	0.770
33	Dan Fouts	1983	San Diego	2.81	0.769
34	Dan Fouts	1981	San Diego	4.93	0.759
35	Joe Namath	1972	New York Jets	2.57	0.754
36	Roger Staubach	1977	Dallas	3.33	0.753
37	Joe Theismann	1983	Washington	3.98	0.750
38	Steve Young	1997	San Francisco	3.28	0.745
39	Troy Aikman	1993	Dallas	3.35	0.744
40	Donovan McNabb	2004	Philadelphia	4.01	0.740
41	Damon Huard	2006	Kansas City	1.97	0.734
42	Vinny Testaverde	1998	New York Jets	3.40	0.733
43	Billy Kilmer	1974	Washington	1.85	0.733
44	James Harris	1974	Los Angeles Rams	1.84	0.730
45	Dan Fouts	1985	San Diego	3.35	0.730
46	Virgil Carter	1971	Cincinnati	1.77	0.730
47	Roger Staubach	1979	Dallas	3.89	0.729
48	Trent Green	2000	St. Louis Rams	2.06	0.726
49	Jeff Garcia	2000	San Francisco	4.77	0.726
50	Fran Tarkenton	1976	Minnesota	3.36	0.725

From 1970 to 1977, minimum 196 pass attempts needed to qualify for ranking.

From 1978 to 2008, minimum 224 pass attempts needed to qualify for ranking.

Note: One should note in looking at these results that the data we employed to measure a quarterback's performance did not report fumbles lost prior to 1994. Consequently, this one statistic was omitted from our evaluation of all quarterbacks reported.

The top spot in Relative Wins Produced is held by Dan Marino, who offered 5.73 Relative Wins Produced for the Miami Dolphins in 1984. That season Miami won 14 games. Even if one ignores the contributions of Miami's receivers, offensive line, running backs, and so on, and argues that Marino's stats are strictly about Marino, one still couldn't credit half of this team's wins to the amazing performance of its quarterback. In sum—as we argue in Chapter 3, "The Search for Useful Stats"—although wins are often assigned to this position, much of an NFL team's success (or failure) is not about the quarterback.

Endnotes

Chapter 1

[1] The quotes from Seinfeld were found at www.seinfeldscripts.com.

[2] The quote is from Veblen [(1898): p. 389]: "In all the received formulations of economic theory...the human material with which the inquiry is concerned is conceived in hedonistic terms; ... The hedonistic conception of man is that of *a lightning calculator of pleasures and pains* who oscillates like a homogeneous globule of desire of happiness under the impulse of stimuli that shift him about the area, but leave him intact." (Italics added to the original.)

[3] Thaler and Sunstein (2008): p. 6.

[4] This definition is more precisely referred to as "instrumental rationality," and it comes from Etzioni (1988, p. 136). Instrumental rationality was also described by Douglass North (1994). Finally, a more recent definition of rationality was offered by Dan Ariely [(2008), p. 239]: "Standard economics assumes that we are rational—that we know all the pertinent information about our decisions, that we can calculate the value of different options that we face, and that we are cognitively unhindered in weighing the ramifications of each potential choice." We apply this definition to the study of the real world of sports. For a nonsports discussion of irrationality, refer to Bryan Caplan's (2007) discussion of how irrational voters impact politics.

[5] For a wonderful review of such experiments one is referred to *Predictably Irrational* (2008) by Dan Ariely.

[6] Dan Ariely, author of *Predictably Irrational* (2008), highlighted the skepticism people have of experiments on his blog: "After I gave a presentation at a conference, a fellow I'll call Mr. Logic (a composite of many people I have debated with over the years) buttonholed me. 'I enjoy hearing about all the different kinds of

small-scale irrationalities that you demonstrate in your experiments,' he told me, handing me his card. 'They're quite interesting—great stories for cocktail parties.' He paused. 'But you don't understand how things work in the real world. Clearly, when it comes to making important decisions, all of these irrationalities disappear, because when it truly matters, people think carefully about their options before they act. And certainly when it comes to the stock market, where the decisions are critically important, all these irrationalities go away and rationality prevails.'" [www.predictablyirrational.com/?p=409; posted May 20, 2009]. Levitt and List (2006, 2007) have also questioned how much laboratory experiments apply to the real world.

[7] Steve Walters described the market for sports executives as follows: "The pool of talent attracted to the sports business is incredibly rich and deep. Clawing your way to the top of any team's organizational chart must be an epic struggle involving long days, endless study, and relentless pressure for results. It's reasonable to assume that those who survive this brutal competition are the best and brightest, their big brains crammed with relevant knowledge and experience and their motivation levels off the charts. If there's an efficient market for executive talent anywhere, it must be in sports." [dberri.wordpress.com/2009/08/02/why-smart-gms-do-stupid-things]. We would also like to thank Walters for alerting us to the Costanza quotes from *Seinfeld*.

[8] Brad Humphreys and Jane Ruseski (2009) estimate that the economic value generated by sports ranged from $44 billion to $60 billion in 2005. To put that number in perspective, in September 2008 the United States government seized control of American International Group, Inc., in a deal worth $85 billion [Karnitschnig, Solomon, Pleven, and Hilsenrath (2008)]. In sum, one troubled insurance company is worth more than the entire sports industry.

[9] This study was cited by Thaler and Sunstein [(2008): p. 32]. The study was also cited by Paul Price (2006). The original study is by P. Cross (1977).

[10] Thaler and Sunstein (2008): p. 32.

[11] Thaler and Sunstein (2008): p. 33.

[12] According to ESPN.com, out of 147 hitters who had enough at-bats to qualify for the season ending rankings, Francoeur ranked 137th in batting average, 146th in on-base percentage, 137th in slugging percentage, and 142nd in OPS (on-base percentage + slugging percentage). Meanwhile, Jones ranked 1st in batting average and on-base percentage, 4th in slugging percentage, and 2nd in OPS.

[13] Ian Ayres [(2007): pp. 1-6] detailed the work of economist Orley Ashenfelter. Ashenfelter developed a statistical model that linked the quality of a wine to winter rainfall, average growing season, and harvest rainfall. This model has been shown to predict the quality of a vintage the day the wine is made, something "experts" are not able to do with the same level of accuracy.

[14] Ian Ayres [(2007): pp. 104-108] reported that Andrew Martin and Kevin Quinn developed a simple empirical model designed to predict how Supreme Court justices would vote on a case. For the 2002 term, Martin and Quinn used their model to predict the outcome of each case. At the same time, legal experts from the specific research area related to the case also predicted the votes of the Supreme

Court justices. The simple model was correct 75% of the time. The "experts"—who considered far more than the factors employed in the empirical model—were only correct in 59.1% of the cases.

[15] The following story was detailed by Malcolm Gladwell [(2005): pp. 125-136]. In the early 1980s, a cardiologist named Lee Goldman constructed a statistical model to evaluate whether a person complaining of chest pains was having a heart attack. Relying on their own expertise, doctors were able to make this determination correctly between 75% and 89% of the time. Goldman's model, though, was correct more than 95% of the time. For more on Goldman's work see Goldman et al. (1982) and Goldman et al. (1996).

[16] Paul Meehl and William Grove looked at 136 studies where statistical models were pitted against the "experts." In these studies the statistical models were found to be right 73.2% of the time. In contrast, human experts only got it right, on average, 66.5% of the time. Overall, in only 8 of the 136 studies examined, did the "human experts" do better than the statistical models. The Meehl and Grove study was cited by Ayres [(2007): p. 111].

[17] Miller, George (1956).

[18] Ayres (2007), along with many people who look at data, also trumpets the importance of confidence intervals.

[19] Diaconis, Holmes, and Montgomery (2009) have demonstrated that coin tossing is not entirely random. There is actually a 51% chance that a coin will come up as it started.

[20] This argument was made by Michael Lewis (2003), and it builds on the work that Bill James did in the 1980s.

[21] Bill Gerrard (2007) investigated the size of Oakland's advantage. Gerrard's study suggested that the Oakland A's from 1998 to 2006 won 144 more regular season games than their payroll would indicate. No other team in baseball managed to exceed the wins forecast from their payroll by more than 70 victories.

[22] Hakes and Sauer (2006): p. 173.

[23] On-base percentage = (Hits + Walks + Hit-by-pitch) / (At-bats + Walks + Hit-by-pitch + Sacrifice flies).

[24] Slugging percentage is simply total bases divided by at-bats.

[25] Appendix A, "Measuring Wins Produced in the NBA," offers a brief review of the basics of regression analysis.

[26] The importance of economic significance is often noted by Deirdre McCloskey (1996, 1998, and 2002).

[27] Hakes and Sauer (2006) argue that baseball's labor market was changing before the publication of *Moneyball*. In other words, the market correction was not caused by *Moneyball* but rather by other teams noticing the success of the Oakland A's.

[28] The market correction appears to coincide with the declining fortunes of the Oakland A's. After winning their division in 2006, the A's finished 2007, 2008, and 2009 with a losing record.

Chapter 2

[1] Throughout the book, we report various statistical examinations. The details of these examinations are noted in the endnotes, as well as at stumblingonwins.com.

[2] The results reported in Table 2.1 are based on a regression of team winning percentage on a team's relative payroll (a model first introduced by Szymanski [2003]). Payroll data for each league was taken from USAToday.com. The years examined are as follows: the NHL from 2000-01 to 2007-08, MLB from 2000 to 2008, the NBA from 2001-02 to 2008-09, and the NFL from 2000 to 2008. Further details can be found at stumblingonwins.com.

[3] Another name for "variation in winning percentage" would be the R^2 of the model used to predict winning percentage. R^2 is calculated by dividing Total Sum of Squares by Explained Sum of Squares (i.e. ESS/TSS). Explained Sum of Squares is the variation in the dependent variable (in this case, winning percentage) that we explained. Total Sum of Squares is the total variation that exists in the dependent variable.

[4] Rhoden, William (2003).

[5] A complete review of Isiah's career can be found at Basketball-Reference.com: www.basketball-reference.com/players/t/thomais01.html.

[6] Isiah was also the owner of the Continental Basketball Association from 1999 to 2000. Under Isiah's leadership, the CBA went from the primary minor league of the NBA to bankruptcy. This disaster took less than two years to achieve. For more on this era, see www.cbamuseum.com/cbaisiah.html.

[7] Adjusted field goal percentage—or effective field goal percentage—is simply [total field goals made + ½ three point field goals made] / total field goal attempts. Another measure of shooting efficiency is Points-Per-Shot (PPS). PPS is calculated as follows: [points – free throws made] / field goals attempted. Given these two calculations one should see that adjusted field goal percentage is simply PPS divided by two. Effective field goal percentage is mentioned in Oliver (2004). PPS comes from the work of Rob Neyer (1996).

[8] Possessions, as John Hollinger notes (2002, p.1), are the currency of basketball. Appendix A notes two measures of possessions, Possessions Employed and Possessions Acquired. Each of these equations notes that each time a team turns the ball over it loses possession. Each time the opponent commits a turnover the team gains possession. A similar story can be told about rebounds. Because rebounds and turnovers are worth one possession, the equations for Possessions Employed and Possessions Acquired are essentially identities. Kubatko et al. (2007) actually collected data on possessions and attempted to derive the value of the various factors that comprise possessions via a regression. Their model, though, omitted team rebounds that change possessions; a factor included in the definition of Possessions Acquired. Consequently, the Kubatko et al. (2007) model was mis-specified and erroneously concluded that each rebound was actually worth less than one possession. Had it been properly specified the authors would have seen that the only unknown coefficients in possessions are connected to free throws, and therefore, regression analysis is not necessary to determine the value of the other factors that comprise possessions.

[9] This label is taken from Price and Wolfers (2006). Price and Wolfers reported the Win Score calculation as follows: Win Score = Points + Possession gained (rebounds, steals) – Possession lost (turnovers, field goal shots, ½ free throws) + ½ Offensive help (assists) + ½ Defensive help (blocks) – ½ Help opponent (fouls).

[10] These are the averages for an average point guard in the NBA from 1977-78 to 2007-08. As noted at stumblingonwins.com, the averages for the first and second half of this time period are similar.

[11] Much of the discussion of Wins Produced and Win Score is taken from *The Wages of Wins* and Berri, David J. (2008). The Wins Produced and/or Win Score models were also employed and briefly discussed in numerous peer-reviewed academic articles. More information on this approach is provided in Appendix A and at stumblingonwins.com.

[12] Our list of factors that determine wins in the NBA is hardly unique. Dean Oliver (2004) focuses on the following four factors: shooting efficiency from the field, rebounds, turnovers, and getting to the free throw line. There is an important difference between the approach taken by Oliver and Wins Produced. To calculate the latter one needs to determine the value of a point scored, rebound, turnover, and so on. To calculate these values one begins with the model connecting winning percentage to offensive and defensive efficiency (see Appendix A), and then one takes the derivative of winning percentage with respect to points, possessions employed, points surrendered, and possessions acquired. If one wants to compare players across teams one should utilize league averages for points scored and possessions employed to calculate marginal values. Oliver utilizes team values in his analysis, which allows him to analyze the value of a player in the context of his team. Such an approach, though, makes comparisons of players on different teams more difficult.

[13] The Pistons of 1988-89 and 1989-90 were led in Wins Produced by Dennis Rodman and Bill Laimbeer. This was detailed at dberri.wordpress.com/2007/06/20/looking-back-at-the-bad-boys.

[14] The leaders in games played in the Isiah era were Jamal Crawford (288 games), Stephon Marbury (240 games), Eddy Curry (212 games), and Quentin Richardson (169 games). These four players, along with Zach Randolph, were also the only veteran acquisitions to average more than 29 minutes per game.

[15] The average shooting guard from 1990-91 to 2007-08 posted the following numbers: 20.8 points per 48 minutes, 2.8 turnovers per 48 minutes, and an adjusted field goal percentage of 48.1%. In Crawford's last season in Chicago, he scored 23.6 points per 48 minutes, committed 3.3 turnovers per 48 minutes, and had an adjusted field goal percentage of 44.9%.

[16] Richardson posted the following career numbers prior to coming to New York: 21.7 points scored per 48 minutes and an adjusted field goal percentage of 47.7%. Richardson plays both shooting guard and small forward. An average shooting guard (from 1990-91 to 2007-08) scored 20.8 points per 48 minutes with a 48.1% adjusted field goal percentage. The numbers for a small forward are 19.9 points per 48 minutes and a 48.2% adjusted field goal percentage.

[17] The average power forward from 1990-91 to 2007-08 posted the following numbers: 19.3 points per 48 minutes, 11.4 rebound per 48 minutes, 2.8 turnovers per 48 minutes, and an adjusted field goal percentage of 48.4%. As a Knick, Frye posted the following numbers per 48 minutes: 20.6 points scored, 10.6 rebounds, and 2.7 turnovers. He also had a 45.6% adjusted field goal percentage. In Randolph's last year in Portland, he scored 31.8 points and grabbed 13.6 rebounds per 48 minutes. He also committed 4.3 turnovers per 48 minutes while posting a 47.2% adjusted field goal percentage.

[18] The average center from 1990-91 to 2007-08 posted the following numbers: 48.8% adjusted field goal percentage, 17.7 points scored per 48 minutes, 12.4 rebounds per 48 minutes, and 2.8 turnovers per 48 minutes. Curry posted the following numbers his last season in Chicago: 53.8% adjusted field goal percentage, 26.9 points per 48 minutes, 9.0 rebounds per 48 minutes, and 4.3 turnovers per 48 minutes.

[19] This mark is broken down as follows: Marbury, Crawford, Curry, and Richardson cost the Knicks $37.3 million. Another $33.7 million was spent on players who retired or were released (Allan Houston, Shandon Anderson, and Jerome Williams). The remainder of the roster cost the team $55.7 million. Most of this was paid out to Anfernee Hardaway, Antonio Davis, Maurice Taylor, Malik Rose, and Jerome James. Of this group, Taylor—an above average scorer—played the most, logging 1,210 minutes. Hardaway was traded at midseason to the Orlando Magic—along with Trevor Ariza—for Steve Francis. Francis—a.k.a. Stevie Franchise—was yet another All-Star point guard who was primarily known for his scoring.

[20] See Coplon (2008) and Lee (2008).

[21] The discussion of NBA salaries is based on Berri, David J., Stacey L. Brook, and Martin B. Schmidt (2007).

[22] The salary model is an updated version of what was reported in Berri, Brook, and Schmidt (2007). The model specifically examined 337 free agents who signed multiyear contracts from 2001 to 2008. Salary data was taken from both USA Today.com and the Web site of Patricia Bender. Details of this model can be found at www.stumblingonwins.com.

[23] Following Jenkins (1996), only players who recently signed a contract were examined. Lewin and Rosenbaum (2007) recently illustrated why the Jenkins approach is necessary. These authors examined a data set that included all NBA players. The results reported by these authors indicated that scoring totals were the primary determinants of player salary. The results also indicated, though, that shooting efficiency and steals had a negative—and statistically significant—impact on player salaries. Such a result suggests that players who miss more shots get paid more. Before anyone believes such analysis, though, it's important to note that the data set included players who signed contracts years before the performance data was generated. Furthermore, it appears players were evaluated who were still playing under their rookie contract. The failure to restrict the salary data might explain such odd findings.

[24] The model considered both turnovers per minute and turnover percentage. Turnover percentage—as detailed at Basketball-reference.com—is calculated by dividing turnovers by field goal attempts + 0.44 × free throw attempts + turnovers. This numbers is then multiplied by 100. Turnover percentage is essentially an estimate of turnovers per possession. The advantage of using this measure is that it is not highly correlated with points scored per game. The inclusion of turnover percentage, though, still indicated that turnovers and free agent salaries are not statistically related.

[25] The average free agent in our sample scored 18.7 points per 48 minutes played and was paid $5.9 million per season.

[26] Standard deviation for a sample is the square root of the sample variance. Sample variance is the average of the squared deviations of each observation in a sample around the mean in the sample. In more simple words, standard deviation tells us how much variation there is in a series of numbers. The practice of utilizing a one standard deviation change to evaluate the economic impact of a variable was employed by Hakes and Sauer (2007).

[27] Rebounds do come close, but a one standard deviation increase in rebounds only leads to about $950,000 in additional salary.

[28] Dean Oliver (2004) also looked at the relationship between possessions utilized and efficiency. Oliver created what he called "skill curves" to illustrate the relationship. A skill curve is downward sloping, which tells us that a player who uses more possessions is less efficient. One should note, though, that Oliver does not explain exactly how the skill curves were calculated. He does state the following: "Skill curves are neat to look at, but you probably don't want to know the details about how to make them. Generally, they come from looking at box scores and general trends that players show when using a lot of possessions. How much better do players seem to get if they use fewer possessions? If they seem to get worse when they use fewer possessions, I say, 'That's not right.' It's just not a sustainable trend.....*Effectively, I force the curves to be declining.* The details of how I do that would scare someone who doesn't know formal statistics. They would scare someone who did know formal statistics for different reasons" (p. 239; italics added to original). We are not sure we would be scared by Oliver's unexplained methods, but we are somewhat troubled by his statement that he "forced the curves to be declining."

[29] Typically one argues that a coefficient that is significant at the 5% level is statistically significant. Except for shooting efficiency, the player statistics reported as statistically significant in Table 2.3 met the 5% threshold. Shooting efficiency, though, was only significant at the 10% level; if one only considers what a player did last year—as was done in *The Wages of Wins*—shooting efficiency becomes insignificant.

[30] Craggs, Tommy (2007).

[31] This story of how Red Auerbach viewed scoring can be found at [espn.go.com/classic/biography/s/auerbach_red.html]. It was also noted at The Wages of Wins Journal [dberri.wordpress.com/2006/11/13/the-wisdom-of-red-auerbach] and in the paperback version of *The Wages of Wins*.

[32] In an interview broadcast on ESPN Classic, Auerbach argued that today's player focuses more on statistics than they do on winning. This interview was also noted at The Wages of Wins Journal [dberri.wordpress.com/2006/11/13/the-wisdom-of-red-auerbach] and in the paperback version of *The Wages of Wins*.

[33] This quote appeared in Chuck Klosterman (2008).

[34] Sloan's displeasure was noted by Russ Siler and Steve Luhm of the *Salt Lake City Tribune*. Part of this story was also noted by Henry Abbott at ESPN's True Hoop (myespn.go.com/nba/truehoop) and at The Wages of Wins Journal (dberri. wordpress.com/2008/10/14/jerry-sloan-repeats-himself). The Morris Almond story by Siler and Luhm can be found at blogs.sltrib.com/jazz/2008/10/jazz-96-suns-89. htm.

[35] This article "Bobcats guard going beyond the score" can be found at www. charlotteobserver.com/sports/story/296078.html.

[36] Per 48 minutes, Morrison lost 2.7 turnovers and committed 3.7 personal fouls. An average small forward—from 1991-92 to 2007-08—commits 2.8 turnovers per 48 minutes while being charged with 4.2 personal fouls. So even here he was only slightly better.

[37] Morrison received 35 points, just two points behind LaMarcus Aldridge and Jorge Garbajosa (the last two players named to the first team). Some details on this vote: Each NBA head coach is asked to vote for the All-Rookie team. Each rookie who receives a first team vote is given two points. A second team selection is worth one point. A coach cannot vote for players on his team, so the maximum voting points a player could receive in the 30-team NBA is 58. From 1995-96 to 2003-04 only 29 teams played in the NBA, so the maximum points was only 56. Prior to 1995-96 only 27 teams played, so maximum points was only 52. The voting data was taken from the Web site of Patricia Bender.

[38] The All-Rookie voting model is an updated version of what was reported in Berri, Brook, and Schmidt (2007). The model examined rookie data from 1995 to 2009. Details of this model can be found at www.stumblingonwins.com.

[39] A one standard deviation increasing in per-minute scoring is associated with 7.1 additional voting points. A one standard deviation increase in per-minute rebounds leads to only 1.1 additional voting points. For per-minute steals and per-minute assists, a one standard deviation increase leads to 0.7 and 1.1 additional voting points, respectively.

[40] The NBA has a salary cap so one might wonder why Isiah was less constrained. The NBA's salary cap is more precisely a cap on payrolls. But a team can exceed this cap under the Larry Bird exemption. Red Auerbach lobbied for this exemption so the Celtics could re-sign Larry Bird in the 1980s. As a consequence, teams can exceed the cap to sign their own players. If a team is over the cap it can still acquire new players, as long as the salaries of the new players match the salaries of the players the team is letting go. The NBA does impose a luxury tax —or a tax on payrolls that exceed a designated threshold—if a team is too far over the cap on payroll. If a team is willing to pay the luxury tax—and the Knicks under Isiah seemed quite willing—then the luxury tax will not prevent a team from assembling a very expensive roster.

Chapter 3

[1] Alan Schwartz (2004).

[2] J.C. Bradbury (2007).

[3] This discussion was taken from Berri and Bradbury (2010). The data used to examine this relationship came from Baseball–Reference.com. The years considered began with the 1996 season and ended in 2008. The specific dependent variable employed was runs scored per game. The independent variable was a team's batting average. The same regression was also run with OPS as the independent variable.

[4] The approach taken to differentiate batting average and OPS looks at how each factor explains current outcomes. The measure that explains current outcomes better is considered the superior measure. This is the same approach noted in Appendix A to differentiate Wins Produced, NBA Efficiency, Player Efficiency Rating (PER), and Game Score. Berri and Bradbury (2010) critiqued an alternative approach advocated by Lewin and Rosenbaum (2007). These authors were examining a variety of measures used to evaluate NBA players (Wins Produced, PER, etc.). They begin by regressing a team's efficiency differential (points scored per possession minus points surrendered per possession) on a team's PER (or whatever metric was being examined). The result of this regression, plus the regression's residual (or error term), was then used to evaluate players. This evaluation was then used to predict a team's efficiency differential for the next season. The results indicated that the models could explain between 75% and 77% of future wins, suggesting that all models were the same. Of course, as any student of econometrics would know, any model plus the error term (as Lewin and Rosenbaum actually noted) would explain 100% of current wins. Appendix A notes that when one does not include the error term in the evaluation of a model, it's clear Wins Produced does a better job of explaining wins than PERs or NBA Efficiency.

[5] One can do an even better job if runs scored are regressed on all the individual statistics (i.e. singles, double, triples, home runs, stolen bases, etc.). Such a model explains 93% of the variation in runs. The specific regression is derived from the work of Asher Blass (1992) and employed team data from 1996 to 2008 (taken from Baseball-Reference.com).

[6] Here is how Bradbury explains the importance of consistency: "One method researchers can use for separating skill from luck is to look at repeat performance of players. If performance is a product of skill, then the athlete in question ought to be able to replicate that skill. If other factors, such as random chance or teammate spillovers are responsible for the performance, then we ought not observe players performing consistently in these areas over time. A common way to gauge the degree of skill contained in a performance metric is to observe its correlation year to year. If metrics for individual players do not vary much from year to year, then it is likely that players have a skill in that area. If there is no correlation, then it is likely that other factors are heavily influencing the metric. In the latter case, even if a particular metric appears to have a powerful influence on the overall performance of the team, its utility as a measure of quality is quite limited." [Bradbury (2008): p. 48]

[7] From 1996 to 2008, 97% of the variation in a team's runs allowed per game was explained by a team's ERA. Data for this regression was taken from Baseball-Reference.com.

[8] Bradbury's analysis of hitters and pitchers employed data from 1980 to 2005.

[9] Bradbury also considered Linear Weights. This is a model that employs play-by-play data to weight the run-generating probabilities for individual events. This metric was originally developed by operations research analyst George Lindsey (1963) and updated by sabermetricians John Thorn and Pete Palmer (1984). Bradbury (2008) reports that 49% of a player's Linear Weights in the current season was explained by what he did last year.

[10] Bradbury (2008, p.53) notes that the DIPs concept was originally introduced by Voros McCracken in 2001.

[11] The consistency of numbers in football was addressed in Berri (2007). This work also noted that the measures presented in Appendix B, "Measuring Wins Produced in the NFL," and at Football Outsiders.com are just as inconsistent as the box score statistics presented in Table 3.2.

[12] Data on quarterbacks and running backs was taken from Yahoo.com (sports.yahoo.com/nfl/stats/byposition). This site only reports fumbles lost back to 1994; hence, this is where the analysis begins. The data set for quarterbacks included 399 passers with consecutive seasons of at least 100 pass attempts. The data set for running backs included 348 players with consecutive seasons of at least 100 rushing attempts. The last year in the data set was 2007.

[13] Data on hockey skaters was taken from Hockey-Reference.com. The data set consisted of 2,729 skaters who logged at least 500 minutes on the ice in consecutive seasons from the 2000-01 to 2007-08 seasons. Plus-minus was adjusted for time on the ice. This result is also noted in Berri and Bradbury (2010).

[14] Data on basketball players can be found at Basketball-Reference.com. The data set consisted of 6,766 players who logged at least 500 minutes in consecutive seasons from 1977-78 to 2007-08.

[15] The discussion of plus–minus in basketball follows from Berri and Bradbury (2010).

[16] For hockey, the plus-minus statistic is "calculated by subtracting the total number of goals allowed by a player's team while the player is on the ice (at even strength or on the power play) from the total number of goals scored by the player's team while the player is on the ice (at even strength or short-handed)" (Hockey-Reference.com).

For basketball, 82games.com reports a player's Net48, which is defined as "the team net points per 48 minutes of playing time for the player." "Net points" is the plus-minus statistic for basketball, or the difference between the points a team scores and allows when a player is on the court. The consistency of Net48 was established with data on 364 players from the 2006-07 to 2008-09 seasons. The player had to play at least 1,000 minutes in consecutive seasons to be included in the data set. 82games.com also reports Net On Court/Off Court. A player's off-court performance is the net points a team realizes when the player is not in the game. On court is simply Net48. So Net On Court/Off Court is intended to capture how well a team performs with and without the player. Only 12% of a player's Net On Court/Off Court is explained by what the player did last year.

[17] Because a player's plus-minus depends on his teammates, people have turned to a measure called adjusted plus–minus. This approach involves employing a regression that is designed to control for the impact of a player's teammates. Although an attempt is made to control for player interactions, as Berri and Bradbury noted, an examination of 239 players revealed that only 7% of the variation in a player's adjusted plus–minus value in 2008-09 was explained by what he did in 2007-08. And if we turn to a sample of 87 players who switched teams in these years, only 1% of the variation in adjusted plus–minus in 2008-09 was explained by the player's adjusted plus–minus in 2007–08. Furthermore, the relationship between performances in each of these seasons—for the players who switched teams—was statistically insignificant. So if we change all of a player's teammates, his adjusted plus–minus appears to change as well.

There is another issue with adjusted plus–minus noted by Berri and Bradbury (2010). For each player, a coefficient is estimated that represents a player's value, theoretically holding all else constant. Each coefficient comes with a standard error, and the size of these errors suggests that for the vast majority of players, one cannot differentiate his adjusted plus–minus coefficient from zero. In general, if a coefficient is twice the size of the standard error, then one is 95% confident that the coefficient is actually different from zero (i.e. there is only a 5% chance that the coefficient is zero). Of the 666 player observations from the 2007-08 and 2008-09 season, only 10% had a coefficient that was twice the value of the standard error. Only 20% of coefficients were at least 1.5 times the value of the standard errors. In sum, for most players it appears the results are not statistically significant and therefore one cannot say if most players—according to adjusted plus–minus—have any impact on team outcomes at all.

Proponents of adjusted plus–minus have argued that increasing the amount of data results in smaller standard errors. This is true. BasketballValue.com reports coefficients for 292 players who played in both 2007–08 and 2008-09. For this data set, 15% of players had a coefficient that was twice the value of a standard error. Looking at the 1.5 threshold, 26.0% of coefficients surpass this mark. An even greater gain is seen if five years of player data is examined. Examining the results for 373 players who played for five seasons, one sees that 39% of coefficients are at least twice the value of the standard error. And 50% surpass the 1.5 threshold. Although more data does increase the level of statistical significance, it's still the case that most players—even when five years of data is employed—are not found by this method to have a statistically significant impact on outcomes.

Adjusted plus-minus is designed to account for everything a player does on the court, including on-the-ball defense. The box score data—as proponents of adjusted plus-minus note—does not fully measure a player's contribution to defense. Consequently, when a disparity between a box score measure and adjusted plus-minus is uncovered, one might conclude that the disparity reflects the inability of the box score data to capture on-the-ball defense. Unfortunately, such differences might also reflect the substantial noise in adjusted plus-minus. And it is simply not clear how one could tell the difference between the ability to capture defense and the noise in the adjusted plus-minus system.

The data on adjusted plus–minus comes from BasketballValue.com. This data was compiled by Aaron Barzilai. According to BasketballValue.com, the calculations were done in the spirit of the work of Dan Rosenbaum. Rosenbaum's work, in turn, is based on the work of Wayne Winston and Jeff Sagarin. We do not have access to the original work of Winston-Sagarin so we cannot say the issues raised apply to the work of Winston-Sagarin. Winston (2009)—in discussing his work—does note that there is "... a lot of noise in the system. It takes many minutes to get an accurate player rating" (p. 215).

[18] The phrase "variation that is explained" refers to R^2. Since the models used to examine consistency are univariate models (i.e., only one independent variable), one can also look at r, or the correlation coefficient. A correlation coefficient is a measure of the strength of a linear relationship between two variables. The value ranges from 0 to 1, with a value of 1 telling us that two variable are perfectly correlated.

With respect to rebounds per minute, the correlation coefficient between current and past performance is 0.95. Part of this very high correlation is due to the nature of basketball. Bigger players tend to get more rebounds, while smaller players accumulate more assists and turnovers. If one adjusts a player's per-minute production for position played, though, one still sees a great deal of consistency. With respect to rebounds, blocked shots, assists, and turnovers, we see correlation coefficients—after adjusting for position played—of 0.83, 0.88, 0.82, and 0.77. The imperfection of the position adjustments likely reduces the size of these correlation coefficients. Nevertheless, there are no statistics tracked for quarterbacks and running backs that show this much consistency. Only strike-outs for pitchers in baseball are this consistent. In sum, it looks like much of what a player does in basketball is not dependent on his teammates.

[19] Appendix A discusses NBA Efficiency, the Player Efficiency Rating, and Game Score; three alternatives to Wins Produced that do not explain outcomes in basketball very well. *The Wages of Wins* also noted that Dean Oliver (2004) offered yet another approach. Oliver employs "my personal Difficulty Theory for Distributing Credit in Basketball: The more difficult the contribution, the more credit it gets." (p. 145). *The Wages of Wins* argued that statistics should be valued in terms of the impact the statistic has on wins, not on the difficulty a player has getting the statistic. In other words, we disagree with a fundamental premise employed by Oliver. That being said, we have not looked at Oliver's work with respect to the two issues raised by Bradbury.

[20] The following study of goalies is based on Berri and Brook (2009).

[21] Diaccord (1998): p. vi.

[22] Currently, a team gets two points for a win and one point for losing in overtime. In the past, it was two points for a win and one point for a tie.

[23] The outcome in hockey—or standing points—was regressed on goals scored and goals allowed. This simple regression reveals that each goal scored is worth 0.31 standing points. A goal allowed is worth -0.31 standing points. This model was estimated with team data that began with the 1983-83 season and ended in the 2007-08 campaign. Complete details on this regression can be found in Berri and Brook (2009) and at stumblingonwins.com.

[24] According to Hockey-Reference.com, this is the first season save percentage is recorded.

[25] One can also compare the variation in NBA and NHL performance by looking at the coefficient of variation, which is calculated by dividing the standard deviation by the mean. For example, the average NBA player from 1977-78 to 2007-08 with a minimum of 1,000 minutes played posted a 0.102 WP48. The standard deviation of WP48 for this sample was 0.101. Consequently, the coefficient of variation was 0.989. Looking at all goalies who logged at least 1,000 minutes from 1983-84 to 2007-08, one sees an average save percentage of 89.5%. The standard deviation of save percentage, though, is only 0.018. Hence the coefficient of variation of save percentage is only 0.02. In sum, there simply is very little difference in the performance of most NHL goalies.

[26] Goalie statistics are adjusted for time on the ice and were taken from the 2000-01 to 2007-08 season. We also looked at consistency from 1983-84 to 2007-08 and discovered a much higher correlation across time. But if we segmented this time period into smaller segments we found the same weak correlation we observe from 2000-01 to 2007-08. Berri discussed this issue with Kim Craft, a fellow economics professor at Southern Utah University, and after some thought he (Craft) offered an explanation. Craft argued that there was a significant time trend in the data. Hence the stronger correlation across the entire time period did not reflect actual consistency, just a general trend in the performance of goalies.

[27] According to Hockey-Reference.com, Goals Against Average are calculated by dividing goals against by minutes played, and then multiplying by 60 (the length of a regulation game).

[28] The goalies had to play 1,000 minutes in a season to be ranked.

[29] The examination of regular season and postseason performance consisted of 125 goalies who logged at least 1,000 minutes in the regular season and 100 minutes in the corresponding playoffs from 2000-01 to 2007-08.

[30] From 2000-01 to 2007-08, 42 goalies managed to accumulate at least 100 minutes in two consecutive playoffs. One can also consider the link between a goalie's performance in a postseason and what he did in his most recent appearance. The results, though, were identical.

[31] A study of unrestricted free agent goalies is challenging. There simply are not many goalies each year who sign a new free agent contract. Plus, the data on these free agents (as Stacey Brook discovered, the co-author of the study our discussion is based on) is not particularly easy to find. Given these limitations, the sample consisted of 33 unrestricted free agents at the goalie position from 2004 to 2008. To qualify for the sample a goalie had to have played at least two seasons prior to signing the contract (if one only focused on a single lag the sample would have increased to 40). Salary data came from USAToday.com (content.usatoday.com/sports/hockey/nhl/salaries/default.aspx). For details on the specific model employed, one is referred to Berri and Brook (2009) and stumblingonwins.com.

[32] Salary data was also collected from USA Today on goalies who played at least 2,500 minutes in a single season from 2000-01 to 2007-08. Across 181 goalie observations there was no statistical relationship between current pay and current save percentage. This larger data set didn't consider when the goalie signed his contract or his free agent status when he signed the contract.

[33] Further evidence can be seen if one looks at the variation in what these goalies are paid. For the goalies considered in the study of salaries one finds that save percentage has a 0.01 coefficient of variation. Player salary, though, has a 0.74 coefficient of variation. A similar result can be seen if one looks at 181 goalies who played 2,500 minutes from 2000-01 to 2007-08. Our results are similar. The coefficient of variation for player salary was 0.672. For save percentage the coefficient of variation was 0.011. In simple words, the variation in pay suggests that decision-makers think there are substantial differences in the contribution of individual goalies. The variation in performance, though, suggests otherwise.

Chapter 4

[1] This statement is not entirely true. As Charles Ross (1999) notes, J.W. Fowler, Moses Fleetwood Walker, and Weldy Walker played in the American Association in the 1880s. At the time, the American Association was considered a Major League. By 1889, though, black participation in both Major and Minor League Baseball had ended [Ross (1999): p. 4].

[2] Earl Lloyd, Nat Clifton, and Chuck Cooper were the first African-Americans to play in the NBA. Their careers began in 1950.

[3] Goff, Brian, Robert McCormick, and Robert Tollison (2002).

[4] Goff et al. (2002) examined the average slugging percentage of black and white players across time. It was not until the 1980s that the averages from each group were the same. These authors also note that in the National League black players won eight of the ten MVP awards from the 1950s and nine out of thirteen Rookie of the Year awards from 1947 to 1959.

[5] Goff et al. (2002).

[6] Ross (1999): p. 10.

[7] Ross (1999): p. 5.

[8] Ross (1999): p. 46.

[9] The Cleveland Rams had just moved to Los Angeles in 1946. Part of their lease agreement with the L.A. Coliseum required that the Rams field an integrated team [Ross (1999): p. 82].

[10] Ross (1999): p. 82-85.

[11] Ross (1999) observed: "The AFL did not have the luxury to be as selective as the NFL in choosing its players. And many black players who would have found themselves bypassed by the NFL, entered professional football via the AFL." (p. 140-141).

[12] Levy (2003): p. 149.

[13] Ross (1999): p. 160.

[14] Ross (1999): p. 130. Alexander Wolff (2009) notes "In 1920, the Akron Pros' black quarterback, Fritz Pollard, was the first great star of the league that would two

years later rename itself the NFL, and he even served as his team's player-coach. (Not just a black NFL quarterback, not just a black NFL coach, but *both at the same time!*)" The Pro Football Hall of Fame, though, lists Pollard as a halfback and makes no mention of him playing quarterback.

(See www.profootballhof.com/hof/member.aspx?PlayerId=242)

[15] Although Briscoe finished second in the voting for the AFL's Rookie of the Year, he was cut from the team before the start of the 1969 season. Briscoe did enjoy a career as an NFL wide receiver, but he never played quarterback again. (Associated Press: February 22, 2005).

[16] The restriction of the sample to quarterbacks with 100 pass attempts follows from the work of Leeds and Kowalewski (2001).

[17] Harris attempted 100 passes in a season four times during the 1970s. Joe Gilliam, the first black quarterback to be named a team's starter at the onset of a season, did this in 1974. Dave Mays, in a backup role, attempted 121 passes for the Cleveland Browns in 1977. Doug Williams, a first-round draft choice for the Tampa Bay Buccaneers in 1978, attempted more than 100 passes in both 1978 and 1979.

[18] Namath started the first four games of the 1977 season for the Rams. He was then replaced by Pat Haden. When the season ended, Namath retired from pro football. Details on the careers of Namath and Haden can be found at Pro-Football-Reference.com.

[19] Ross [1999: p. 161] reports that Gilliam left football in 1975 because of an addiction to cocaine. According to Gilliam, this developed because of the pressure to succeed as a black quarterback.

[20] It's interesting to note that a team that contributed to the efforts to integrate the quarterback position in the NFL utilizes a racial epithet as its name. George Preston Marshall, longtime owner of the Redskins, was also reportedly the person behind the ban on black players instituted in 1933. And Marshall's Redskins were the last team in the NFL to integrate. It took until 1962 for the Redskins to employ a black player. [Levy (2003)].

[21] The two exceptions for the white quarterbacks were Joe Montana and Steve Young. Steve Young began his NFL career with the Tampa Bay Buccaneers in 1985. After two below average seasons, though, Young was traded to the 49ers to serve as Montana's backup in 1987. Young served as the backup for four seasons, and only after Montana was severely injured in a 1991 playoff game did Young become the starter. Young played so well as the starter that Montana was traded to the Kansas City Chiefs in 1993. One suspects that if Young hadn't come along it is less likely that Montana would have ever left San Francisco.

[22] The discussion of the role race plays in the pay of NFL quarterbacks is derived from an article by David Berri and Rob Simmons (2009a).

[23] Berri and Simmons (2009a) utilized salary data for each veteran quarterback (i.e., non-rookies) who played from 1995 to 2006. Across this time period there were 435 season observations for white quarterbacks, with an average quarterback in this grouping earning $2.62 million. There were also 85 observations for black signal callers, who were paid an average wage of $2.54 million. The richest white quarterbacks (top 10% of the income distribution) earned an average salary of

$6.05 million while the richest black quarterbacks—again, on average—earned only $5.46 million. The salary data was taken from www.rodneyfort.com/SportsData/BizFrame.htm.

[24] The model reported in Berri and Simmons (2009a) was estimated with a quantile regression. With a quantile regression, one can estimate a statistical model at different points in the distribution of the dependent variable. In other words, one could see how the determinants of salary changed as one considered the richest or poorest quarterbacks (and those in between).

[25] Berri and Simmons (2009a) report that first and second round draft choices do see higher pay, even after controlling for performance. Such a result suggests, as the study of the NFL draft will also indicate, that draft day evaluations have persistence even if player performance suggests the initial evaluation was incorrect.

[26] Berri and Simmons (2009a) considered both experience and experience squared, finding that increases in experience caused pay to increase until a quarterback is between the ages of 28 and 32. After 32 years of age, salary tends to decline (holding all else constant). Experience was also examined by looking at career pass attempts. Increases in career pass attempts were also found to have a positive impact on salaries.

[27] Berri and Simmons (2009a) reported that market size did not impact player pay. This is due to both the extensive revenue sharing observed in the NFL and the league salary cap.

[28] Berri and Simmons (2009a) also considered the impact of having quality skill players around the quarterback. This was captured by considering the salaries paid to skill players on a team. The results indicated that the higher the salaries of the skill players the greater the quarterback's pay.

[29] In the discussion of the NFL draft, it will be noted that interceptions are not ignored when it comes to drafting quarterbacks.

[30] This is the example employed by Berri and Simmons (2009a) to explain how differently the top black and white quarterbacks were treated (p. 39): "As an example, Donovan McNabb is a Black quarterback located at the top decile of the salary distribution with an average per season pass yards figure of 2,500 up to [the year] 2005. At 2,000 yards, his salary differential, compared to a white quarterback of similar experience and career pass attempts, is estimated at 0.72, with a confidence interval of 0.54 to 0.96. At 3,000 yards, McNabb's salary differential falls further to 0.61, within a confidence interval of 0.39 to 0.94."

[31] Don Banks and Peter King of *Sports Illustrated* in separate articles explicitly made this argument. (See sportsillustrated.cnn.com/2008/writers/don_banks/04/18/mcnair/index.html and also sportsillustrated.cnn.com/2008/writers/peter_king/04/20/mmqb/3.html.) James Walker at ESPN.com also made a similar argument: "Favre is a lock for Canton, but McNair's candidacy will be a subject of debate in the coming years." (See sports.espn.go.com/nfl/columns/story?columnist=walker_james&id=3351356.)

[32] In contrast, there is a statistically significant relationship between current salary and current performance in the NBA.

Chapter 5

[1] Berri—who spent his teenage years in Lincoln, Nebraska—remembers the *Journal-Star* fondly. That being said, one suspects most journalists would prefer to work for the *New York Times*.

[2] The story of the birth of the NFL draft is reported in Quirk and Fort (1992, pp. 187-188). This story was also noted in Leeds and Von Allmen (2008, p. 163), Fort (2006, p. 258), and Quinn (2008). Bert Bell was not only the founder of the NFL draft; he also served as NFL commissioner from 1946 to 1959 and was elected to the Hall of Fame in 1963 (www.profootballhof.com/hof/member.aspx?PLAYER_ID=23).

[3] *Time* magazine published an article titled "Football" on November 2, 1934. This article describes the Minnesota Golden Gophers in 1934. The team was better known as the "Hook 'Em Cows," and the "hero" of this team was Kostka. The article goes on to note that Kostka's hero was Bronco Nagurski. The author of the article is not identified, but it can be found online at www.time.com/time/magazine/article/0,9171,882323-1,00.html.

[4] See www.bls.gov/data/inflation_calculator.htm. This Web site was accessed on May 20, 2009.

[5] The minimum rookie salary for 2008 in the NFL was reported by proathletesonly.com (proathletesonly.com/news/tag/nfl-minimum-salaries).

[6] This definition of competitive balance comes from Leeds and Von Allmen [(2008), p. 147].

[7] The reverse-order draft is but one example of an institution in North American sports that prevents a player from selling his services on a free market. Simon Rottenberg argued in 1956 that labor market restrictions should not impact the level of competitive balance in a league. His arguments have been summarized by the Rottenberg Invariance Principle. This has been restated by Rodney Fort (2006) as follows: "The distribution of talent in a league is invariant to who gets the revenues generated by the players; talent moves to its highest valued use in the league whether player or owners receive [the revenues the player generates]" [Fort (2006): p. 272]. For more on this topic one is referred to *The Wages of Wins*.

[8] Schmidt and Berri (2003) failed to find a statistical link between competitive balance and the reverse order draft in Major League Baseball. Quinn (2008) reviewed research on how the draft impacts competitive balance across a variety of sports. This review noted that there is little evidence that a draft impacts the level of competitive balance.

[9] The lack of an economically significant link between competitive balance and league attendance was discussed in *The Wages of Wins*.

[10] Anthony Krautmann, Peter Von Allmen, and David Berri (2009) examined the determination of free agent salaries in the MLB, NFL, and NBA. Models were estimated linking the salaries paid to free agents to past performance (and other explanatory variables). The coefficients from these models were used to estimate the value of non-free agents. In addition to the reported results for the NFL, the

analysis indicates that Major League Baseball players are paid only 19% of their marginal revenue product (MRP) prior to arbitration and free agency rights. In the NBA, players are paid 66% of their MRP before gaining free agency rights.

[11] Massey, C., and R. Thaler (2005).

[12] Utilizing data from 1991 to 2002, Massey and Thaler (2005) found that "surplus value increases at the top of the order, rising to its maximum of $750,000 in the top half of the second round before declining through the rest of the draft. The treasured first pick in the draft is, according to this analysis, actually the least valuable pick in the first round! To be clear, the player taken with the first pick does have the highest expected performance (that is, the performance curve is monotonically decreasing), but he also has the highest salary, and in terms of performance per dollar, is less valuable than players taken in the second round" (p. 25).

[13] This example was cited in Massey and Thaler (2005).

[14] Wayne Winston (2009) and Phil Birnbaum (2006) noted that the approach taken by Massey and Thaler failed to account for actual performance differences. In other words, if two players played the same number of games (with the same number of starts and Pro Bowl appearances) at the same position, then Massey and Thaler treated the two players as equally valuable. To illustrate the problem with this approach, consider the performances of Jon Kitna and David Garrard in 2007. Kitna started 16 games and produced 0.376 Relative WP100. Garrard only played 12 games, but produced 0.685 Relative WP100. The Massey and Thaler approach would treat Kitna as the better quarterback, when the performance data suggests otherwise. Despite this critique, we find the essential point Massey and Thaler made held up when we considered productivity data. As we will show, we find that first round picks for quarterbacks are indeed overvalued.

[15] Much of the analysis of the NFL's drafting of quarterbacks is based on a paper by David Berri and Rob Simmons (2009b).

[16] To be ranked in terms of Relative Wins Produced, the quarterback had to play in five seasons. Order taken in the draft, though, includes all quarterbacks who were selected in the draft.

[17] Data on first year contract terms can be found for most players at USAToday.com (content.usatoday.com/sports/football/nfl/salaries/default.aspx). Wes Pate's contract terms were found at ESPN.com (espn.go.com/nfl/afc/draftsignings2002.html).

[18] The analysis examined quarterbacks drafted between 1970 and 2007 who participated in at least 500 plays in their first five seasons. A simple regression was run connecting a quarterback's Relative Wins Production after five years in the league to his draft position. Similar results were obtained from an examination of quarterbacks after two, three, four, six, seven, and eight years in the league.

[19] The number of plays an average quarterback participated in changed across the years examined. Consequently, the Relative Plays for each quarterback were calculated. Relative Plays is the number of plays a quarterback ran, adjusted for the average number of plays by a quarterback in the year the quarterback played. Looking at quarterbacks after five years in the league, draft position explained 16% of the variation in Relative Plays. This link was examined after two, three, four, six,

seven, and eight years in the league, and the analysis always uncovered a statistically significant relationship.

[20] A quarterback's Relative WP100 was also examined at other points in his career. Whether one looks at what a quarterback did after two, three, four, six, seven, or eight years, a statistically significant relationship was never uncovered. Other performance indicators were also considered. Examinations of the link between draft position and such factors as the NFL's QB Rating, interceptions per pass attempt, touchdowns per pass attempt, passing yards per pass attempt, or completion percentage failed to unearth a statistically significant link. There simply does not appear to be a statistical relationship between where a quarterback is taken in the draft and his per play production in the NFL.

[21] Berri and Simmons (2009b) repeated this analysis for QB Score, Net Points, completion percentage, passing yards per attempts, touchdowns per attempt, and interceptions per attempt. With respect to each measure, quarterbacks taken from picks 11 to 50 outperformed the quarterbacks taken from picks 1 to 10.

[22] Clayton, John. (2009).

[23] Seifert, Kevin (2009).

[24] Berri is a fan of the Lions, so he really hopes this investment proves to be wise.

[25] The telecast of the NFL draft draws a bigger audience than playoff games in the NBA and NHL, as well as regular season games in Major League Baseball. One is refereed to sportsmediawatch.blogspot.com for more information on these ratings.

[26] Table 5.4 is adapted from Berri and Simmons (2009b). From 1970 to 2007, there were 1,943 season observations from quarterbacks taken between the 1st pick and the 250th slot in the draft. These observations were divided into five segments, each consisting of roughly 400 observations. The first segment consists of quarterbacks taken in the first 10 slots, the next grouping consists of quarterbacks taken between picks 11 and 50, and so on.

[27] The NFL Scouting Combine (specifically called the National Invitational Camp) began in 1982 in Tampa, Florida. Since 1987 it has been held in Indianapolis, Indiana. The history of the NFL's National Invitational Camp can be found at http://www.nflcombine.net/?q=node/9. Combine data from 1999 to 2008 can be found at nfldraftscout.com.

[28] According to the Centers for Disease Control and Prevention (cdc.gov), the Body Mass Index is calculated by first dividing weight (in pounds) by height (in inches) squared. This number is then multiplied by 703. A score of 18.5 indicates that a person's weight is below normal. A score between 18.5 and 24.9 is considered normal. A BMI from 25.0 to 29.9 indicates a person is overweight, and scores above 30.0 are indicative of an obese person. In our sample of NFL quarterbacks, the average BMI score was 27.8, with a range from 24.4 to 31.5. The CDC notes that "highly trained athletes may have a high BMI because of increased muscularity rather than increased body fatness." (http://www.cdc.gov/nccdphp/dnpa/healthyweight/assessing/bmi/adult_BMI/about_adult_BMI.htm#Interpreted).

[29] The Wonderlic test —according to Wonderlic.com—was developed by industrial psychologist Eldon F. Wonderlic in 1937. According to Mike Chappell of USA Today, the test utilized by the NFL consists of 50 questions and must be answered

in 12 minutes. The average score of all people who take the test (it is not just taken by NFL prospects) is 21. For the NFL quarterbacks examined with respect to the draft, the average score was 26.1 (with a range from 10 to 42). The study utilized data from NFL Quarterback Wonderlic Scores (http://www.macmirabile.com/wonderlic.htm). This is a Web site maintained by Mac Mirabile. As Mirabile notes, "these results represent research and generally come from reliable sources, i.e., notes from NFL scouts, newspaper articles. It is important to understand that scores cannot by 'verified' since they are not released by the NFL, but rather leaked by teams or scouts."

[30] The model considered a player's height, BMI, BMI squared, Wonderlic score, 40-yard dash time, dummy variables for each year our model considered (except one), a dummy variable for a player who played for a Football Championship Subdivision team, the number of wins a quarterback's team achieved his last year in college, and the quarterback's performance his last year in college. Berri and Simmons (2009b) considered a linear specification, as well as a model where the dependent variable was logged. In addition, a negative binomial specification was estimated. In general, the results reported were similar for all specifications. The data set Berri and Simmons (2009b) examined began in 1999 and concluded in 2008. The sample consisted of 121 quarterbacks. Performance data on college quarterbacks since 2000 was taken from the NCAA's Web site reporting Division I Football Statistics (http://web1.ncaa.org/d1mfb/mainpage.jsp?site=org). College data for quarterbacks selected in the 1999 and 2000 drafts was taken from CNNSI.com. The complete estimation results are reported in Berri and Simmons (2009b) and at stumblingonwins.com.

[31] Specific statistics such as completion percentage, touchdowns per pass attempt, yards per attempt, and rushing yards per rushing attempt were not found to statistically impact draft position. Interceptions per attempt, though, were statistically connected to draft position.

[32] For example, one can explain 20% of draft position with a model that doesn't include any performance measure. Adding Wins Produced to this model increases explanatory power to 24%. In contrast, removing the Combine factors (Wonderlic score, 40-yard dash time, height, and BMI) but including Wins Produced, results in a model that only explains 10% of the variation in draft position.

[33] When one logs the dependent variable the estimated coefficient is not the slope. Specifically the slope, or the impact of a one-unit change in the independent variable, will vary across the distribution. To find the value at a specific point, one multiplies the coefficient by a specific value of the dependent variable. At the mean value of draft position, each inch of height improves draft position by 50 spots. When one looks at a linear model where draft position is not logged, then the coefficient is the slope. The linear model indicates that each additional inch of height improves draft position by about 21 spots. Looking at 40-yard dash times one sees a standard deviation of 0.18. According to the logged model, such an improvement would improve draft position by 49.9 slots. In a linear model, though, a similar improvement is only worth 19 slots. The MacKinnon-White-Davidson test for functional form [detailed in Gujarati (1995)] was conducted, and the results were inconclusive.

[34] This is what is reported for a logged model. The linear model indicates that a player needs to improve his test score by about 12 points to improve his draft position by 30 slots.

[35] The statistical significance of the Wonderlic score depended on how one estimates the model. In a linear model it was significant at the 5% level. If one logs the dependent variable, or employed a negative binomial model, the Wonderlic score was only significant at the 10% level. The significance of this factor was also impacted by the choice of independent variables.

[36] The NCAA used to divide its members into Division I-A, Division I-AA, Division II, and Division III. Today, though, Division I-A is known as the Football Bowl Subdivision (FBS) while Division I-AA is known as the Football Championship Subdivision (FCS). The analysis indicates that playing for an FCS school generally costs a player between two to four rounds in draft position (depending on whether one looks at a linear or logged model). Six of the FBS conferences—Atlantic Coast Conference, Big 12, Big East, Big 10, Pacific-10, and Southeastern Conference— are referred to as the Bowl Championship Series (BCS) conferences. One might expect that a quarterback from a BCS conference would have a higher profile— and thus be drafted earlier—than a quarterback from a lesser conference. The analysis, though, didn't find any conference that consistently had a statistically significant impact on draft position. Additionally, playing in a generic BCS conference was also not found to matter.

[37] The data set for draft position and performance extended for at least 25 years. For the factors that explain draft position, though, data was only found for about 10 years.

[38] David Lewin posted an article on the NFL draft at ESPN.com ("College Stats Don't Lie," (April 17, 2008): http://sports.espn.go.com/nfl/news/story?id= 3350135). Lewin argued in this article that NFL performance was influenced by only two statistics: games started in college and completion percentage. Lewin's full results were not published, but he did indicate that his sample consisted of "highly drafted quarterbacks since 1996." We did not have data on games started for all the quarterbacks selected since 1999, but the analysis did look at the number of career plays (and one should expect a high correlation between number of games started and career plays). Nevertheless, career plays in college were not found to explain much of a quarterback's performance in the NFL.

[39] One could also look at the other components of the NFL's Quarterback Rating. Such an examination failed to unearth any statistically significant explanatory variables for yards per attempt or TD per attempt. Interceptions per attempt were positively impacted by being a non-FBS player in the first year of a player's career. Also in the first year, a higher BMI was found to reduce interceptions per attempt; but no other factor had a statically significant impact on interceptions per attempt, and even the two factors that were statistically significant didn't explain much. NFL career performance after three years (to hold experience constant) was also considered. Furthermore, college career plays were also included as an explanatory variable. The results of these latter estimations were little different.

Chapter 6

[1] Justin Fox in *The Myth of the Rational Market* (2009) referred to the Pareto Principle as "a standby of pop sociology and business advice" (p. 350). Fox also noted that Fred Macaulay failed to find a similar pattern in data from the United States in the 1920s.

[2] NBA teams from 1977-78 to 2007-08 employed an average of 16.1 players per season. So 20% of the average roster is 3.2 players.

[3] The players in Table 6.1 are listed in terms of their production of wins. The first name listed led the team in Wins Produced.

[4] Prior to 1966, teams could forfeit their first round pick and make what was called a territorial pick. This involved selecting a player from the immediate geographic area of the team. See *Evolution of the Draft and Lottery* (www.nba.com/history/draft_evolution.html) for more information on the history of the NBA draft.

[5] Beck Taylor and Justin Trogdon (2002) presented evidence that NBA teams did intentionally lose to improve their draft position prior to the institution of the lottery in 1985. When the unweighted lottery was put into place from 1985 to 1989 this tendency vanished, only to return when the weighted lottery was put into place. Price, Soebbing, Berri, and Humphreys (2009) offer evidence that the Taylor and Trogdon story is not entirely correct. There is only weak evidence of "tanking" (i.e., losing intentionally) prior to 1985. It was not until the 1990s, when the NBA turned to a weighted lottery system, that stronger evidence of tanking is uncovered.

[6] Five seasons was chosen because the player taken with the second pick in the draft from 1997 to 2004 tended to play, on average, 4.5 seasons with the team that chose him on draft day.

[7] In Bowie's rookie season, he produced 10.1 wins and posted a 0.218 WP48; Michael Jordan, the third choice in the draft, produced 23.3 wins and posted a 0.355 WP48; Charles Barkley, the fifth choice, produced 13.2 wins with a 0.270 WP48; and Olajuwon produced 15.0 wins with a 0.247 WP48. Just focusing on what these players did as rookies illustrates why Portland—a team that already had Clyde Drexler at shooting guard (14.5 Wins Produced and a 0.272 WP48 in 1984-85)—passed on Jordan. Unfortunately, Bowie's injuries limited him to only 21.6 additional wins across the remainder of his career. For more details on this story, see dberri.wordpress.com/2008/09/11/a-little-bit-of-hindsight-bias-reviewing-the-drafting-of-sam-bowie/.

[8] We first began examining this issue in May 2007. At that time, Darren Rovell wrote a post for his SportsBiz blog at CNBC.com. In Rovell's post, he examined the economic impact of Portland's first pick in the 2007 NBA draft. In response to Rovell's post, Stephen Dubner of Freakonomics.com stated: "I don't know what the *Wages of Wins* boys would make of Rovell's analysis, but it's well worth a look." A day after Dubner issued his assignment, Berri made an effort to answer the question (see dberri.wordpress.com/2007/05/25/the-value-of-winning-the-lottery-in-the-nba). This effort was expanded on in Price, Soebbing, Berri, and Humphreys (2009); it's this expanded effort that serves as the foundation of the discussion offered here.

[9] Iverson's lack of production was not just seen at the beginning of his career. At the conclusion of the 2008-09 season Iverson had posted a career WP48 of 0.080. His very best seasons were in 1997-98 (8.8 Wins Produced and a 0.135 WP48) and 2007-08 (9.3 Wins Produced and a 0.130 WP48). In sum, Iverson has generally been slightly below average, although he was capable of exceeding the average mark of 0.100 in a few seasons. The disconnect between perceptions of Iverson's ability and his production of wins was detailed in *The Wages of Wins*. It has also been a frequent topic at The Wages of Wins Journal (dberri.wordpress.com).

[10] According to Forbes.com, the 30 teams that comprise the NBA earned $3.765 billion in revenue for the 2007-08 season. Gate revenue, which is calculated with team attendance and weighted ticket prices, only sum to $1.064 billion in 2007-08. In other words, the study only considers the impact these rookies have on about 28% of the average team's revenue.

[11] Star power is measured by adding together the number of fan votes a team's players received for the midseason All-Star game. Data was taken from the Web site of Patricia Bender.

[12] On the road, it's a different story. Berri and Schmidt (2006)—and also *The Wages of Wins*—presented evidence that star power does have a substantial impact on a team's road attendance. However, the home team in the NBA keeps all the gate revenue. So the benefit of star power on the road is entirely realized by the star's opponent, not the team that signs his checks.

[13] The gate revenue model estimated is based on Berri, Schmidt, and Brook (2004) as well as the model reported *The Wages of Wins*. The data employed begins with the 1992-93 season and ends with the 2007-08 season. Due to the lockout, there was no All-Star game for the 1998–99 campaign. Consequently, the measure of star power could not be calculated for this season, and it was omitted from the study. Further details on the data utilized, estimation techniques employed, and complete results can be found at stumblingonwins.com.

[14] The value of the number one pick reported is for an average NBA team. The average overstates the impact for teams with lower levels of gate revenue and understates the impact for teams with higher levels of gate revenue.

[15] Data on the rookie salary scale comes from NBA.com.

[16] According to Patricia Bender's payroll data, NBA teams in 2005-06 paid their players $1.89 billion. The NBA employed 458 players that season, so the average wage was $4.13 million. Bogut was paid $3.6 million that season while M. Williams was paid $3.2 million. If one argues that players are primarily paid to produce wins, then the payroll numbers from 2005-06 suggest that each win would cost a team $1.5 million in salaries ($1.89 billion divided by the 1,230 regular season wins from 2005-06). Bogut produced 5.9 wins during his first season. Given the cost of a win, such production would have cost his team more than $9 million. In sum, Bogut's production came at a substantial discount. The argument that players under a rookie contract are paid less than their economic value to a team is also consistent with what is reported in Krautmann, Von Allmen, and Berri (2009).

[17] The analysis of the draft begins with players drafted in 1995. Performance after two, three, and five years was also examined. The results for other years were similar to what is reported. Complete results can be found at stumblingonwins.com.

[18] The analysis probably overstates explanatory power. The data set only includes players who logged an average of 500 minutes per season. A player like Jerome Moiso, selected with the 11th pick of the 2000 draft, never averaged 500 minutes in his career. So this lottery pick is not included in our data set. If such picks were included the link between draft position and performance might be even weaker.

[19] Studies by Staw, B. M., and Ha Hoang (1995) and Colin Camerer and Roberto Weber (1999) found that minutes-per-game was linked to draft position after a player's first NBA season. This link was uncovered even after each set of authors controlled for performance. This result will be touched on again in the next chapter.

[20] David Robinson began playing in 1989. The top producer of wins after four seasons from the 1987 draft (among those who actually began playing that year) was Kevin Johnson.

[21] If one looks at career performance after two, three, and five seasons the results are similar. In every instance, less than 8% of career Wins Produced—and less than 3% of WP48—is explained by where a player is taken in the draft. One could also look at the link between draft position and NBA Efficiency (a measure described in Appendix A). Between 33% and 36% of the variation in NBA Efficiency—and between 12% and 20% of NBA Efficiency per minute—is explained by draft position. Similar results are uncovered for Game Score and Game Score per minute (also described in Appendix A). As Appendix A notes, NBA Efficiency and Game Score are not highly correlated with wins in the NBA. These measures, though, do capture perceptions of performance better than Wins Produced. Complete details on these estimations are reported at stumblingonwins.com.

[22] The study of the NBA draft looked at the population of players that were selected from 1995 to 2008 and asked what factors influenced their location in the draft. A different question is what factors cause a player to be selected in the first place. This question is certainly a good subject for future research. The complete results of the study of the draft reported here can be found at Berri, Brook, and Fenn (2007) and at stumblingonwins.com.

[23] Relative height refers to a player's height relative to the average height at the position the player plays. A point guard that is 6'6" is relatively tall. A power forward of the same height, though, is relatively small.

[24] The examination of free agent NBA players revealed that shooting guards are discounted. This is the same story with respect to the NBA draft. All else being equal, a shooting guard is taken later in the draft.

[25] Performance was measured relative to the average production seen at a player's position. For example, to calculate relative points per 40 minutes, one subtracts from each player the average number of points a player at his position would score per 40 minutes. Then to this value, the average number of points scored per 40 minutes at all positions was added. This was done for points, rebounds, assists, steals, blocked shots, and personal fouls. For turnovers, both turnovers per 40 minutes and turnover percentage were considered, and each was adjusted for position played. The results are essentially the same regardless of how turnovers are measured.

[26] Rebounds per game, rebounds per minutes, and rebound percentage were all examined, and none of these had a statistical link to draft position. Rebound percentage is calculated according to Basketball Reference.com as follows: $100 \times$ (total rebounds $\times$ (team minutes played/5)) / (Minutes played $\times$ (team total rebounds + opponents total rebounds)). We want to thank Dean Oliver for providing us with data on rebound percentage.

[27] The standard deviation of scoring per minute is 4.07 in the sample considered.

[28] Young (2008) provides a study of both the NBA draft and how coaches allocate minutes. Similar to the findings reported here, Young reports that scoring is the primary determinant of a player's draft position. As for minutes, Young finds that coaches consider a wider array of factors (wider relative to the draft-day decision). Scoring, though, is still the best predictor of minutes played. Young's results with respect to minutes played are similar to what is reported in Chapter 8, "Is It the Teacher or the Students?"

[29] An NBA roster is divided into two groups: scorers and role players. Of these two groups, the latter is the larger. In other words, most NBA players cannot be major scorers, but to get drafted in the NBA it helps tremendously to be a scorer in college. Those who score the most in college, though, probably have the hardest time adjusting to an NBA life where they are not asked to be the primary option on offense. This might be why college scorers tend to perform worse in the NBA.

[30] The model designed to predict where a player is drafted does not explain everything (something that can be said about all econometric models). The residual—or what is not explained with the model—could be thought of as a variable that captures everything about a player's draft position not explicitly captured by the list of independent variables. Given this reasoning, it would be interesting to see if the residual from the draft pick model could predict future NBA performance. When one looks at WP48, this residual is not statistically significant. This residual, though, is consistently significant when one looks at NBA Efficiency per minute and Game Score per minute.

[31] The approach reported involves regressing NBA performance on the list of factors, including both college performance numbers and nonperformance characteristics, that are known on draft day. One can also do a direct comparison of college and professional productivity. For each player drafted out of college from 1995 to 2008 one can calculate Position Adjusted Win Score per 40 minutes (PAWS40), with the adjustments based on the average college performance of each drafted player at each position. Comparing college PAWS40 to NBA WP48 revealed that more than 80% of the drafted college players who posted a PAWS40 that was one standard deviation below the mean managed to post a career NBA WP48 that was below the mean (this was true whether you looked at players after three or five seasons). If you look at players with a PAWS40 that was one standard deviation above the mean, though, between 60% to 65% went on to post a career WP48 that was above average. These results suggest that identifying poor NBA performers with college data is easier than identifying outstanding NBA performers. Or in other words, if you play poorly in college, it's likely that you will play poorly in the NBA. Excelling in college, though, is not a guarantee of future success.

[32] The model connects the factors examined with respect to draft position (reported in Table 6.6) to career performance. Career performance is measured via WP48, and players were examined after two, three, four, and five years in the league. For a factor to be reported as "statistically significant," it had to be statistically connected to NBA performance at each career juncture we considered. One can also measure career performance with NBA Efficiency per minute and Game Score per minute. The results with respect to the Final Four, relative height, and rebounds are the same regardless of performance measure chosen. College scoring was not found to be statistically related to NBA Efficiency or Game Score. Meanwhile, younger players did perform better with respect to these latter two measures. Complete results can be found at stumblingonwins.com.

[33] Jonah Lehrer (2009) made the following observation: "If the mind were an infinitely powerful organ, a limitless supercomputer without constraints, then rational analysis would always be the ideal decision-making strategy" (p. 150). Lehrer then proceeded to detail experimental results that demonstrated the limitations of the processing power of the human mind.

[34] Burger and Walters (2009) report that more than two-thirds of the players drafted by Major League Baseball from 1990 to 1997 never made it to a Major League roster. Another 25% of players made it the big leagues, but never became regular players. This leaves about 8% of players who were drafted and became regular contributors.

[35] John D. Burger and Stephen J.K. Walters (2009).

[36] Burger and Walters (2009) state that, "the estimated 57 percent annual return on college selections far exceeds the 36 percent yield on high school draftees," and that "the yield on pitchers is 34 percent versus 52 percent for position players."

Chapter 7

[1] This is a point made by Bursick and Quinn (2009) and Bill James (September 6, 1982).

[2] Bill James (1982) explains why stolen bases returned. "Why did the stolen base come back to the game in the late '50s? The way was opened for its return, in a sense, by its mere absence: More and more teams were ignoring the stolen base as something that had to be defended against. Since no one was stealing, throwing ability at the catching position became secondary to getting another big bat in the lineup. It would be silly to give up offense for a good throwing arm if nobody was going to steal any bases on you anyway....There is another critical point to consider here, of course. Before 1947, major league baseball was played exclusively by white Americans in bandbox parks, in which their style of play—dominated as it was by the long ball—was becoming increasingly narrow and stultified. In the meantime, their black and Latin American counterparts were playing in environments which were, to put it mildly, diverse: one day a major league stadium, the next day a cow pasture. They played, by all accounts, a wide-open, aggressive game in which the stolen base was a prominent feature. When Jackie Robinson finally led these players to the majors, they found a game which was ill equipped to defend against many of the things that they could do—most of all, steal bases."

3 Pluto and Weaver (1984).

4 The numbers reported come from Albert and Bennett [(2003): p. 245]. These authors report that their numbers come from the 2002 season and were originally reported by Zumsteg (2002). Albert and Bennett also report similar numbers from George Lindsey (1963). Additionally, Dan Levitt (2006) also conducted such analysis.

5 As noted by Albert and Bennett [(2003): p. 250], the Run Potential of a stolen base attempt is calculated as follows: Run Potential = [p × (run potential if attempt is successful)] + [(1-p) × (run potential if he fails)]; where p is the probability a base runner is successful. To determine the break-even point one sets the above equation equal to the number of expected runs a team has if the base runner doesn't make the attempt. One can look at the benefit of stealing second or third, with none out, one out, or two outs. All of these calculations reveal that the break-even point ranges from 0.696 to 0.749. Albert and Bennett [(2003): p. 251] also note that this analysis focuses on maximizing runs. In a late inning situation, though, a team might only want to score one run. In such a circumstance, Albert and Bennett show that a team can expect to benefit from an attempted steal if the probability of success is only 0.55.

6 The all-time marks for stolen bases and caught stealing can be found at Baseball-Reference.com. One should note that caught stealing data has not been kept as consistently as data on stolen bases. So we cannot be sure that no one topped Henderson's mark for caught stealing. The fact that caught stealing data was not always kept highlights the point that teams did not always properly evaluate the costs and benefits of stealing bases. After all, you can't be fully considering costs if you are not even tracking cost data.

7 Barry Bonds went on to break Henderson's record for walks.

8 There are a number of ways one can value a walk. One approach is to follow the lead of Blass (1992). This involves regressing runs scored on singles, doubles, triples, home runs, walks, hit-by-pitch, grounded into double plays + caught stealing, sacrifice flies, and outs. Utilizing data from 1996 to 2008, this regression reveals that a walk is worth 0.358 runs, a stolen base is worth 0.136 runs, and being caught stealing is worth -0.279. Using Henderson's numbers from 1982 (116 walks, 130 stolen bases, 42 caught stealing), Henderson produced 5.9 runs with his stolen bases and 41.5 runs with his walks. Another approach is the Thorn and Palmer (1984) linear weights model. This model says a stolen base is worth 0.3 runs, being caught stealing is worth –0.6, and a walk is worth 0.33. These weights tell us that Henderson's walks are worth 38.3 runs while his stolen bases added 13.8 runs.

9 During his entire career, Moseley converted only 12 field goals from over 50 yards. The longest was from 54 yards, some six years earlier.

10 In a commercial for Madden NFL, John Madden notes that the game now penalizes people for doing "stupid" stuff, like going for it on fourth and forever.

11 Easterbrook, Gregg (November 15, 2007).

12 For example Michael's ability to wax his father likely has more to do with dexterity, interest, and practice than with strategy. As for Pulaski Academy, the school's record was every bit as good and perhaps better before Coach Kelley "stopped punting in 2005"—even to the point of winning the State Championship in 2003.

[13] Romer, David (2006).

[14] Expected points in this circumstance is simply 40% of seven points since teams connect on nearly 100% of extra point attempts.

[15] In Romer's words: "The choice between kicking and going for it leads to an immediate payoff (which may be zero) and to one team having a first down somewhere on the field. That first down leads to additional scoring (which again maybe zero) and to another possession and first down. And so on." (p. 342)

[16] Romer noted in his article that average starting position is the 27-yard line. We found in our sample, though, that the average was the 30-yard line. So this is the figure we used in explaining Romer's results.

[17] Romer's picture has been simplified by omitting the two-standard-error bands.

[18] Suppose your team faces a fourth down at its opponent's 22-yard line. The net value of kicking would be the difference between the average points scored when a field goal is attempted (around 2.4), and the value of the average subsequent starting position (around 0.2). To determine the value of kicking, Romer turned to a sample that had more than 2,500 kicking observations. These occur all over the field, and therefore he could calculate the success rates of punting and/or field goal attempts from all possible situations on the field with relative certainty.

Determining the value of going for it is more complicated. Unlike punts and field goals, which occur many times over a season and over all possible situations on the field, going for it on fourth down happens infrequently in the NFL, and such attempts generally occur at only a few spots on the field. In addition, the success of a fourth-down attempt is influenced by how many yards are left to reach the first-down marker or the end zone line. To get around the first problem, Romer uses third down success rates as a proxy for the success or failure of any fourth-down attempt. The second complication makes it necessary to talk about the choice of going for it or kicking in terms of different scenarios during the same state. In other words, the choice of going for it from your opponent's 30-yard line might change depending on whether it is fourth and 8 or fourth and 1. All of this needed to be mapped out. As before, if the attempt on fourth down is successful, then the offensive team gets a new set of downs or scores a touchdown. If it fails, the opposing team takes possession of the ball and the game moves to the new state. The net value of going for it is then simply the difference between the two. With everything mapped out, Romer was able to determine where and when a team would be better off kicking and where and when the team would be better off going for it.

[19] We have simplified Romer's figure by omitting the two-standard-error bands.

[20] Across 1,604 fourth downs in Romer's sample where the analysis suggests teams should be kicking, coaches only went for it nine times.

[21] Romer's data set has 1,608 fourth downs where the analysis suggests teams were better off going for it. In these circumstances, though, teams kicked it 959 times.

[22] For example, see Leonhardt, David (February 1, 2004). One of the very early readers of Romer's study was New England football coach Bill Belichick. When asked about Romer's working paper, Belichick responded, "I read it. I don't know much of the math involved, but I think I understand the conclusions and he has some valid points" (p.199).

[23] In 2003, the average NFL team attempted 15.7 fourth-down attempts per season. The next season, average attempts fell to 14.2. In 2007 the average had risen to 16.7, but the next season the mark fell to 15.3. In sum, there is no evidence that Romer's paper changed the behavior of NFL coaches. Even getting *Moneyball* author Michael Lewis into the act hasn't helped. Lewis (December 18, 2006) wrote an article in *ESPN the Magazine* describing the reaction, or lack of reaction, to Romer's study. Lewis finds the response to Romer's study to be consistent with the initial response of MLB decision-makers to *Moneyball*. In other words, decision-makers tended to react with some hostility.

Failing to learn from this research is not the only odd aspect of how NFL coaches make decisions on fourth down. Brian Burke (2009)—at Advanced NFL stats (advancednflstats.com)—presented evidence that how far a team had to go for a first down impacted the decision to kick a field goal or punt. Specifically, Burke notes, "On 4th down from identical field positions, coaches tend to attempt FGs more often with shorter distances to go and punt more often with longer distances to go. For example, when kicking on 4th and 1 from the 32, coaches went for the FG 100% of the time. But when kicking on 4th and long (7+ yds) from the 32, coaches went for the FG less often—80% of the time."

[24] Although most teams give these two jobs to one player, some teams actually hire two kickers. The Denver Broncos, for example, used Matt Prater for kickoffs and Jason Elam for field goal attempts in 2007.

[25] Data on kickers comes from NFL.com. The performance of the average kicker was determined with data from 2003 to 2007.

[26] Rackers's kickoffs were returned 46 times. These kicks traveled 66.2 yards, or about 4.7 yards farther than the average returned kickoff from 2003 to 2007. Moving the opponent from a starting position at the 30 yard line to the 26 yard line—according to Romer's calculations—is worth 0.233 points. Therefore Rackers saved 10.97 points on his returned kickoffs. According to Romer's calculations, a touchback (moving a team from the 30 yard line to the 20 yard line) is worth 0.556 points. Rackers had 15.8 more touchbacks than the average kicker, so these were worth 8.8 additional points. An out-of-bounds kick costs a team 0.604 points. Rackers had one out-of-bounds kick while the average kicker would have had 1.22 in the same number of kickoffs. Relative to the average kicker, Rackers in 2004 saved 0.13 points on out-of-bounds kicks.

[27] In 2004, Rackers was perfect on 28 extra point attempts, 6 of 6 on field goals from 20-29 yards, 5 of 7 from 30 to 39 yards, 6 of 7 from 40-49 yards, and 5 of 9 from beyond 50 yards. From these distances an average field goal kicker would have made 27.72 extra points out of 28 attempts, 5.76 of 6 on field goals from 20-29 yards, 6.04 of 7 from 30 to 39 yards, 5.10 of 7 from 40-49 yards, and 4.71 of 9 from beyond 50 yards. Given all this, an average kicker would have scored 92.55 points on all these attempts while Rackers scored 94 points.

[28] Looking at a sample of 87 kickers from 2003 to 2007 who had consecutive seasons of at least 16 kickoffs and 16 field goal attempts, one sees a 0.47 correlation coefficient for current and lagged points from kickoffs. A similar calculation with respect to points from field goals and extra points gave a correlation coefficient of 0.08.

[29] The study of kickers' salaries employed data on 128 kickers from 2004 to 2008. Complete results are reported at stumblingonwins.com.

[30] Aaron Schatz (2006) also observed that kickers are inconsistent with respect to field goals, and it would be better for teams to focus on kickoffs.

[31] Gilovich, T., R. Vallone, and A. Tversky (1985).

[32] The study of free throws involved an examination of the free throws attempted by nine members of the Boston Celtics over two seasons: 1981-82 and 1982-83. Gilovich, et. al. calculated the probability that a shooter makes the second free throw given that he made or missed the first and found "(t)he data provide no evidence that the outcome of the second free throw is influenced by the outcome of the first free throw" (p. 304). This would seem to be a more accurate test of the "hot hand," since free throw attempts remove the complicating factor of defense.

[33] Thaler and Sunstein note (2009, p. 30) "many researchers have been so sure that the original Gilovich results were wrong that they set out to find the hot hand. To date, no one has found it."

[34] John Huizinga and Sandy Weil (2009). This working paper looked at a data set consisting of 49 prolific scorers from four NBA seasons (2002-03 to 2005-06).

[35] The studies include Colin F. Camerer and Roberto A. Weber (1999) and B. M. Staw and Ha Hoang (1995).

[36] The study of minutes per game employed a data set that began with the 1977-78 season and ends in 2007-08. Details on this model are reported at stumblingonwins. com.

[37] The model indicates an increase in points scored per minute of 0.117—or a one standard deviation increase—will cause a 2.8 increase in minutes per game. A one standard deviation increase in assists leads to 1.6 additional minutes per game, while a similar increase in rebounds leads to a 1.0 increase. At the bottom of the list we see turnovers, steals, and free throw percentage. A one standard deviation in each of these factors will cause minutes per game to change by less than 0.3. One can also re-estimate the minutes-per-game model by removing points scored per minute, and instead employing shot attempts per minute (both field goal attempts and free throw attempts). Focusing again on the impact of a one standard deviation change, field goal attempts per minute have the second largest impact (second to personal fouls). Independent of shooting efficiency, more shot attempts lead to more playing time for a player.

Chapter 8

[1] This quote is taken from a *New York Times* article written by Dave Anderson (November 1, 1992). Others have argued that Bum Phillips borrowed the quote. The original quote may have been about Bear Bryant, the legendary football coach of the University of Alabama. It has also been attributed to other coaches.

[2] The "principal clerk" observation was taken from Chapter VI of *The Wealth of Nations* [Of the Component Parts of the Price of Commodities, pp. 54-55 (1976 edition)]. The "principal clerk" argument was also noted by Ira Horowitz (1994).

³ Pat Riley wrote *The Winner Within: A Life Plan for Team Players* (1993); Rick Pitino wrote two books: *Success Is a Choice: Ten Steps to Overachieving in Business and Life* (1998) and *Lead to Succeed: 10 Great Traits of Leadership in Business and Life* (2002); and Phil Jackson published *Sacred Hoops* in 2006.

⁴ Jordan retired in 1993 and then returned with 17 games remaining in the 1994-95 season. Across the 147 games MJ was playing baseball, Jackson's teams only won 60.5% of their games. A similar story played out with the Lakers. With Shaq, the Lakers won three titles and lost in the NBA Finals in 2004. After the 2003-04 season, Phil Jackson retired and Shaquille O'Neal was traded to the Miami Heat. Jackson returned to the Lakers for the 2005-06 season, and although the Lakers were still above average, the team's winning percentage from 2005-06 to the middle of the 2007-08 season was only 57.7%. In the midst of the 2007-08 season, though, the team acquired Pau Gasol, and after that the Lakers were again an elite NBA team. Overall, Phil Jackson's teams in the years without Jordan and Shaq only won 62.7% of their games. When these two superstars were available, though, Jackson's teams won 74.4% of their games.

⁵ The investigation of coaches reported is taken from Berri, M. Leeds, E. Leeds, and Mondello (2009). The study considered player data from 1977-78 to 2007-08 (such data can be found at Basketball-Reference.com). Additional details can be found in the published article and at stumblingonwins.com. An alternative approach to the study of coaching was offered in Lee and Berri (2008) and Fort, Lee, and Berri (2008). These two papers examined the link between a team's current wins and the past performance of the team's players across three years of data. These works indicated that between 65% and 75% of current wins can be explained by what a team's players did in the prior season, a result that provides further evidence that NBA players are consistent across time.

⁶ The metric employed to measure performance was Adjusted Production per 48 minutes played (AdjP48). As detailed in Appendix A, AdjP48 measures the value of a player's statistical production. This value is then adjusted for team defense and the teammates' production of assists and blocked shots. To get to Wins Produced and WP48, one adjusts for position played. The position adjustment, though, is not exact. Furthermore, because the coaching study looked at how each player's performance changed over time, the position adjustment is not necessary. In other words, position adjustments are only needed when you compare a player to a different player, not when a player is compared to himself.

The coaching study also looked at three decades of data. Because teams generally played at a faster pace in the earlier years in the sample, an adjustment for the average pace in the season the player played was made. This was done by subtracting the average AdjP48 in a given season from each player's AdjP48. Then the average AdjP48 across all 31 seasons was added. So if a player played in a year with an above average pace, his AdjP48 would be lowered. If a player appeared in a slower year, his AdjP48 would be raised. The model was estimated without this adjustment, and the story was essentially the same. One can also consider WP48, Win Score per minute, and NBA Efficiency per minute, and again the story told about coaches was essentially the same. How productivity is measured does not change the result that most coaches do not have a statistically significant impact on player performance.

[7] To measure the impact of coaching one needs an adequate sample of productivity data from the season before and after the move to the new coach. Consequently, only players who played at least 20 games and 12 minutes per game in both the prior and subsequent seasons were included. Across the 30 seasons investigated, there were 3,595 observations of a player getting a new coach. To be included in the study, a coach needed to have at least 15 new players who played enough to qualify as a member of the player sample. In addition, the coach had to have at least 15 qualifying players depart for another coach. In all, 62 coaches met these requirements. Given all the coaches examined, as well as the non-coaching variables considered, the model included 189 independent variables. This model was then estimated across 973 specific players and 5,211 player season observations.

[8] The estimation of a regression gives a coefficient—or the impact of the independent variable on the dependent variable—and a corresponding standard error. The standard error is important because it tells us how confident we should be in the estimates of our coefficients. Most coaches were not found to have a statistically significant impact. When one says "statistically insignificant impact" this means that the standard error is so large that one can't differentiate the estimated coefficient from zero. How large does a standard error have to be for one to reach this conclusion? A standard rule of thumb is that the estimate coefficient has to be twice the size—in absolute terms—of the standard error. This rule of thumb can be explained by thinking about confidence intervals. The confidence interval for a coefficient can be found by subtracting and adding two standard errors to a coefficient. For example, Don Nelson has an estimated coefficient of 0.030 and a corresponding standard error of .012. This means that the confidence interval—at the 95% level—for Nelson's impact ranges from .006 to .054. Using the rule of thumb, only 11 coaches have a positive impact on performance. We weakened these standards somewhat, though, and reported the three coaches that had an impact at the 10% level of significance. If we weakened our standards even further we would note that we find George Karl and Mike Dunleavy have an impact at the 15% level. At the 20% level, we would add the name of Bill Fitch, and at the 30% level we can add Del Harris, Alvin Gentry, Rick Carlisle, and Eddie Jordan. After these names, the coefficient for all other coaches is actually less than the corresponding standard error. In sum, for 41 coaches the corresponding standard error is bigger—in absolute terms—than the coefficient.

[9] Although Jackson tops the list, the list is misleading. One can argue that Jackson's impact—and the impact of other coaches listed—is different from zero. One cannot argue, though, that these coaches are statistically different from each other. So there really are two groupings. In one group are 14 coaches who have a positive impact that is different from zero. In another grouping are coaches who were not found to have a positive and significant impact on performance.

[10] Players and coaches tend to come and go frequently, so the sample for the second and third year only included twenty and five coaches, respectively. In other words, given the desire to only consider coaches with at least 15 players fitting a specific situation, the number of coaches one could look at beyond the first year was limited.

[11] There is one coach—Matt Goukas—who had a statistically significant and negative impact on player performance when the player came to the coach.

[12] Players who come to Phil Jackson see their AdjP48 increase by 0.045. An average NBA team plays 19,826 minutes in an entire season, with 91% on average played by NBA veterans. Given the minutes played by veterans—and Jackson's impact on a veteran player's performance—the analysis indicates that hiring Jackson as your head coach will cause an estimated 17.1 increase in wins. A similar calculation was done for each coach listed in Table 8.1.

[13] There was a statistically significant decline in player performance when players left the following coaches: Doug Collins, Bernie Bickerstaff, Jim O'Brien, Paul Silas, Jack Ramsay, Doug Moe, Kevin Loughery, Rick Carlisle, Don Nelson, and Paul Westhead. Player performance had a statistically significant increase when they left Isiah Thomas and Chris Ford.

[14] The research on coaching was discussed by Ryan McCarthy (November 18, 2008). Henry Abbott (November 18, 2008) responded to McCarthy's article.

[15] Of these eight teams, only one—the Philadelphia 76ers —went on to make the playoffs, and the Sixers were eliminated in the first round.

[16] Coaching contracts tend to be guaranteed. If you fire a coach before his contract expires a team is then forced to pay the salaries of two head coaches.

[17] The primary factor that impacts current performance is what a player did in the previous season. The correlation coefficient, or r, between current and past performance is 0.83. Therefore, past performance explains 69% of the variation in current performance (or the R^2 is 0.69). Consistency is still high when one examines players who switch teams. For these players, the correlation coefficient between current and past performance is 0.76 (so R^2 is 0.58).

[18] In looking at specific statistics (such as points scored, rebounds, steals, etc.) roster stability and coming to a new team or new coach had a statistically significant impact. At least with respect to certain statistics an effect was found. When you look at AdjP48, though, these factors were not statistically significant.

[19] Bradbury, John Charles (2009). Other studies by Albert (2002) and Fair (2007) found the peak varied in baseball between the ages of 27 and 30.

[20] Schulz, R. and C. Curnow (1988).

[21] The model included both a player's age and age squared. To get the expected relationship between age and performance (i.e., players initially improve and eventually get worse as they age) the impact of age has to be positive while age squared must have the opposite sign. Changing performance metrics does not appear to alter the results. When per-minute NBA Efficiency is used, the model indicates that performance peaks at 23.8 years of age.

[22] The study of performance looked at AdjP48. WP48 is simply AdjP48 adjusted for position played. Table 8.3 reports WP48 because the average performance of 0.100 makes the discussion easier.

[23] Although most coaches cannot inspire greater production from a specific player, people have argued that the coach can increase wins by making sure the most productive players are playing. As reported in Chapter 7, "Inefficient on the Field," minutes are primarily influenced by points scored per minute. Since wins are about more than scoring, this suggests coaches on average are not allocating

minutes optimally. An examination of specific coaches with respect to the optimal allocation of minutes, though, is going to have to be a subject of future research.

[24] The numbers come from the 1977-78 to 2007-08 NBA season.

[25] We wish to thank J.C. Bradbury for providing numbers from Major League Baseball. Bradbury provided percentages for the 1980s, 1990s, and 2000s. The numbers we report are the average across these three percentages.

[26] To measure the performance of teammates, for each player in the study the WP48 of the player's teammates was calculated.

[27] Career information on Artis Gilmore and Kareem Abdul-Jabbar can be found at Basketball-Reference.com.

[28] Abdul-Jabbar's teams averaged 53.5 wins per season from 1977-78 to 1982-83 (the years where he was 30 to 35 years old). Across these years, the average WP48 of Abdul-Jabbar's teammates was 0.101. Gilmore's teams averaged 40 wins per season, and his teammates posted a 0.076 WP48. On average, such a difference in the productivity of a player's teammates would cause a player's WP48 to change by 0.007.

[29] With respect to rebounds, the effect is mostly centered on defensive rebounds. The number of offensive rebounds a player gets per minute is not statistically related to the offensive rebounds of his teammates.

[30] Diminishing returns are not seen with respect to turnovers and personal fouls. As for steals, as a player's teammates get more steals a player's per-minute steals production will increase. Although the effect is statistically significant, the link between a player's per-minute steals and the per-minute production of his teammates is small.

[31] To illustrate the impact of requiring shots in the NBA, consider the case of Allen Iverson and the Philadelphia 76ers. In 2006 the 76ers traded Iverson to the Denver Nuggets. Prior to the trade, the Sixers averaged about 78 shots per game, with Iverson taking about 30% of the team's field goal attempts per game. After the trade, with Iverson taking shots in Denver, the Sixers still averaged about 78 shots per game.

[32] The key issue in looking at scoring is not shots taken but shooting efficiency. It's thought that a player who takes more shots will see his shooting efficiency decline. If you regress shooting efficiency—measured with points per shot or adjusted field goal percentage—on shot attempts you do not see this relationship. However, if you look at the link between the change in a player's shooting efficiency from season to season and the change in his per-minute shot attempts, the expected link is seen. The effect, though, is small. To see how small, imagine a player who takes 16.3 shots per 48 minutes and has an adjusted field goal percentage of 48.4% (these are the league average marks). If that player increased his shots per 48 minutes to 25.3 (a two standard deviation increase), his adjusted field goal percentage would be expected to decline to 47.1%. This is a very large increase in shot attempts, but it only appears to reduce shooting efficiency by about 1%. Consequently, players have a clear incentive to shoot as much as they can. Even large increases in shot attempts don't diminish efficiency very much. But such increases do add to scoring totals, and more scoring will lead to more minutes, money, and fame. One should

note that there is no statistical link between a player's shooting efficiency and the shooting efficiency of his teammates. In other words, playing with teammates who tend to hit their shots will not make a player a more efficient shooter.

Chapter 9

[1] Alan Schwartz (2004): p. 11.

[2] Alan Schwartz (2004): p. 33-36. Lane went on to develop a measure of performance that was similar to the Linear Weights metric offered by Pete Palmer in the 1980s.

[3] Our focus has been on North American professional sports, and even with this limited focus, our list is incomplete. For example, Kovash and Levitt (2009) presented evidence that suggests pitchers in baseball throw too many fastballs. In addition, these same authors offered evidence that suggests football teams pass too often. In each case, teams would win more with an alternative set of choices. Wayne Winston, in *Mathletics*, also presents an abundance of evidence that decision-makers—in baseball, football, and basketball—are imperfect. Moving past North American sports, Simon Kuper and Stefan Szymanski (2009) in *Soccernomics* provide a number of examples of suboptimal decision-making in soccer. A sample would include a tendency for stars of the World Cup or European Championships to be overvalued, a player's nationality tends to inflate his value (being Dutch or Brazilian is apparently a positive), and blond players tend to get paid more. We thank Stefan for letting us see an advance copy of his book.

References

Books and Articles

Abbott, Henry. (2008). "Stat Geeks and Coaches." Posted November 18, 2008. myespn.go.com/blogs/truehoop/0-36-67/Stat-Geeks-and-Coaches.html.

Albert, J. (2002). Smoothing career trajectories of baseball hitters. Manuscript, Bowling Green State University.

Albert, James and J. Bennett. (2003). *Curve Ball: Baseball, Statistics, and the Role of Chance in the Game*. Springer.

Anderson, Dave. (1992). "Sports of The Times; At Age 62, Don Shula Is Still Going Strong." *New York Times*. (November 1).

Ariely, Dan. (2008). *Predictably Irrational: The Hidden Forces that Shape Our Decisions*. Harper Collins.

Ayres, Ian. (2007). *Super Crunchers: Why Thinking-By-Numbers Is the New Way to Be Smart*. Bantam Books.

Banks, Don. (2008). "Snap Judgements: McNair's HOF chances and pre-draft rumblings." (April 18). sportsillustrated.cnn.com/2008/writers/don_banks/04/18/mcnair/index.html.

Berri, David J. (2008). "A Simple Measure of Worker Productivity in the National Basketball Association." In *The Business of Sport*, eds. Brad Humphreys and Dennis Howard, 3 volumes, Westport, Conn.: Praeger: 1-40.

Berri, David J. (2007). "Back to Back Evaluation on the Gridiron." In *Statistical Thinking in Sport*, eds. James H. Albert and Ruud H. Koning, Chapman & Hall/CRC: 235-256.

Berri, David J. (1999). "Who is Most Valuable? Measuring the Player's Production of Wins in the National Basketball Association." *Managerial and Decision Economics*, 20(8):411-27.

Berri, David J. and J. C. Bradbury. (2010). "Working in the Land of Metricians." *Journal of Sports Economics*, 11(1).

Berri, David J. and Stacey L. Brook. (2009). "On the Evaluation of Goalies in the National Hockey League." Presented at the 2009 Western Economic Association meetings, Vancouver, British Colombia, June.

Berri, David J., Stacey L. Brook, and Aju Fenn. (2007). "From College to the Pros: Predicting the NBA Amateur Player Draft." Working paper.

Berri, David J., Stacey L. Brook, and Martin B. Schmidt. (2006). *The Wages of Wins: Taking Measure of the Many Myths in Modern Sport*. Stanford University Press.

Berri, David J., Stacey L. Brook, and Martin B. Schmidt. (2007). "Does One Need to Score to Score?" *International Journal of Sports Finance*, 2: 190-205.

Berri, David J., Michael Leeds, Eva Marikova Leeds, and Michael Mondello. (2009)."The Role of Managers in Team Performance." *International Journal of Sport Finance*, 4, n2; (May): 75-93.

Berri, David J. and Martin B. Schmidt. (2006). "On the Road with the National Basketball's Superstar Externality." *Journal of Sports Economics*, 7:347-58.

Berri, David J. and Martin B. Schmidt. (2002). "Instrumental vs. Bounded Rationality: The Case of Major League Baseball and the National Basketball Association." *Journal of Socio-Economics* (formerly the *Journal of Behavioral Economics*), 31(3):191-214.

Berri, David J. and Robert Simmons. (2009a). "Race and the Evaluation of Signal Callers in the National Football League." *The Journal of Sports Economics*, 10: 23-43.

Berri, David J. and Rob Simmons. (2009b). "Catching a Draft: On the Process of Selecting Quarterbacks in the National Football League Amateur Draft." *Journal of Productivity Analysis*. On-line citation: DOI 10.1007/s11123-009-0154-6 (available in print in 2011).

Birnbaum, Phil. (2006). "Do NFL Teams Overvalue High Draft Picks?" (December 5). sabermetricresearch.blogspot.com/2006/12/do-nfl-teams-overvalue-high-draft-picks.html.

Blass, Asher. (1992). "Does the Baseball Labor Market Contradict the Human Capital Model?" *Review of Economics and Statistics*, 74: 261-268.

Bonnell, Rick. (2008). "Bobcats guard going beyond the score." *Charlotte Observer* (November 9). www.charlotteobserver.com/sports/story/296078.html.

Bradbury, John Charles. (2009). "Peak Athletic Performance and Ageing: Evidence from Baseball." *Journal of Sports Sciences*, 27(6): 599-610.

Bradbury, John C. (2008). "Statistical Performance Analysis in Sport." In *The Business of Sport*, eds. Brad Humphreys and Dennis Howard, 3 volumes, Westport, Conn.: Praeger: 41-56.

Bradbury, John C. (2007). *The Baseball Economist: The Real Game Exposed*. Plume Publishing.

Burger, John D. and Stephen J. K. Walters. (2009). "Uncertain Prospects: Rates of Return in the Baseball Draft." *Journal of Sports Economics*, 10(5):485-501.

Burke, Brian. (2009). "Irrational Play Calling." October 8, 2009. advancednflstats.com/2009/10/irrational-play-calling.html.

Bursik, P. B. and K. G. Quinn. (2009). "Whither or Whether the Stolen Base." *NINE: A Journal of Baseball History and Culture*, 17(2).

Camerer, Colin and Roberto A. Weber. (1999). "The econometrics and behavioral economics of escalation of commitment in NBA draft choices." *Journal of Economic Behavior & Organization*, 39:59-82.

Caplan, Bryan. (2007). *The Myth of the Rational Voter: Why Democracies Choose Bad Policies*. Princeton: Princeton University Press.

Chan, David, Neal Schmitt, Richard P. DeShon, Cathy S. Clause, and Kerry Delbridge. (1997). "Reactions to cognitive ability tests: The Relationships between race, test performance, face validity perceptions, and test-taking motivation." *Journal of Applied Psychology*, 82:300-310.

Chung, Jason. (2005). "Racial Discrimination and African-American Quarterbacks in the National Football League, 1968-1999," Working paper. http://papers.ssrn.com/sol3/papers.cfm?abstract_id=835204.

Clayton, John. (2009). "Lions Secure QB Stafford." (April 25). sports.espn.go.com/nfl/draft09/news/story?id=4097641.

Coplon, Jeff. (2008). "Absolutely, Positively the Worst Team in the History of Professional Sports: A Eulogy for Isiah Thomas's New York Knickerbockers." *New York Magazine* (April 6).

Craggs, Tommy. (2007). "What Happened to the Pride of Coney Island?" *New York Magazine* (November 19).

Cross, P. (1977). "Not Can But Will College Teaching Be Improved?" *New Directions for Higher Education*, 17:1-15.

Diaccord, Brian. (1998). *Hockey Goaltending: Skills for Ice and In-Line Hockey*. Human Kinetics.

Easterbrook, Gregg. (2007). "New annual feature! State of high school nation." (November 15). sports.espn.go.com/espn/page2/story?page=easterbrook/071113.

Etzioni, Amitai. (1998). *The Moral Dimension: Toward a New Economics*. New York: Free Press.

Evolution of the Draft and Lottery. www.nba.com/history/draft_evolution.html.

Fair, R. (2007). "Estimated Age Effects in Baseball." Cowles Foundation Discussion Paper No. 1536, Yale University.

Farkes, George. (2003). "Cognitive skills and noncognitive traits and behaviors in stratification processes." *Annual Review of Sociology*, 29: 541-62.

Fort, Rodney. (2006). *Sports Economics*. Prentice Hall Publishing, 2nd ed.

Fort, Rodney, Young Hoon Lee, and David J. Berri. (2008). "Race and Coaching Efficiency in the NBA." *International Journal of Sport Finance*, 3, n2; (May): 84-96.

Fox, Justin. (2009). *The Myth of the Rational Market: A History of Risk, Reward, and Delusion on Wall Street*. Harper Business.

Gerrard, Bill. (2007). "Is the Moneyball Approach Transferable to Complex Invasion Team Sports?" *International Journal of Sports Finance*, Vol. 2; 214-28.

Gilbert, Daniel. (2006). *Stumbling on Happiness*. Alfred A. Knopf, a division of Random House, Inc.

Gilovich, Thomas, Robert Vallone, and Amos Tversky. (1985). "The Hot Hand in Basketball: On the Misperception of Random Sequences." *Cognitive Psychology*, 17: 295-314.

Gladwell, Malcolm. (2005). *Blink: The Power of Thinking Without Thinking*. Little, Brown, and Company.

Goff, Brian, Robert McCormick, and Robert Tollison. (2002). "Racial Integration as an Innovation: Empirical Evidence from Sports Leagues." *American Economic Review*, 92:16-26.

Goldman L., M. Weinberg, M. Weisberg, R. Olshen, E.F. Cook, R.K. Sargent, et. al. (1982). "A Computer-Derived Protocol to Aid in the Diagnosis of Emergency Room Patients with Acute Chest Pain." *New England Journal of Medicine*, 307: 588-596.

Goldman, L., E.F. Cook, P.A. Johnson, D.A. Brand, G.W. Rouan, and T.H. Lee. (1996). "Prediction of the Need for Intensive Care in Patients Who Come to Emergency Departments with Acute Chest Pain." *New England Journal of Medicine*, 334: 1498-1504.

Gujarati, Damodar N. (1995). *Introductory Econometrics: A Modern Approach*. McGraw Hill Publishing, 3rd ed.

Hakes, Jahn K. and Raymond D. Sauer. (2006). "An Economic Evaluation of the Moneyball Hypothesis." *Journal of Economic Perspectives*, 20: 173–186.

Heeren, Dave. (1994). *Basketball Abstract 1994–95 Edition*. Indianapolis: Masters Press.

Hollinger, John. (2002). *Pro Basketball Prospectus 2002*. Washington D.C.: Brassey's Sports.

Horowitz, Ira. (1994). "On the Manager as Principal Clerk." *Managerial and Decision Economics*, 15: 187-194.

Huizinger, John and Sandy Weil. (2009). "Hot Hand or Hot Head: Overconfidence in Shot-Making Ability in the NBA." Working paper.

Humphreys, Brad R. and Jane E. Ruseski. (2009). "Estimates of the Dimensions of the Sports Market in the US." *International Journal of Sport Finance*, 4, pp. 94-113.

Jackson, Phil. (2006). *Sacred Hoops: Spiritual Lessons of a Hardwood Warrior*. Hyperion Books.

James, Bill. (1982). "So What's All the Fuss? Rickey Henderson may be the man of the hour but, argues the author, base stealing has never really amounted to very much." *Sports Illustrated* (September 6).

Jenkins, Jeffery. (1996). "A Reexamination of Salary Discrimination in Professional Basketball." *Social Science Quarterly* 77, no. 3 (September), 594–608.

Karnitschnig, M., D. Solomon, L. Pleven, and J. Hilsenrath. (2008). "U.S. to take over AIG in $85 billion bailout; central banks inject cash as credit dries up." *Wall Street Journal* (September 16).

King, Peter. (2008). "Monday Morning QB." (April, 20). sportsillustrated.cnn.com/2008/writers/peter_king/04/20/mmqb/3.html.

Klosterman, Chuck. (2008). "What a Difference a Freakishly Long, Ungodly Talented, Defensive Wizard of a Man Makes." *New York Times Play Magazine*. (March 2).

Kovash, Kenneth and Steven D. Levitt. (2009). "Professionals Do Not Play Minimax: Evidence from Major League Baseball and the National Football League." NBER Working Paper No. 15347 (September).

Krautmann, Anthony, Peter Von Allmen, and David J. Berri. (2009). "The Underpayment of Restricted Players in North American Sports Leagues." *International Journal of Sport Finance*, 4, n3; (August): 155-169.

Kubatko, Justin, Dean Oliver, Kevin Pelton, and Dan Rosenbaum. (2007). "A Starting Point for Analyzing Basketball Statistics." *Journal of Quantitative Analysis in Sports*, v3, n3.

Kuper, Simon and Stefan Szymanski. (2009). *Soccernomics: Why England Loses, Why Germany and Brazil Win, and Why the U.S., Japan, Australia, Turkey—and Even Iraq—Are Destined to Become the Kings of the World's Most Popular Sport*. New York: Nation Books.

Lee, Edmund. (2008). "The Thomas Tax." *Conde Nast Portfolio. com*. (April 4).

Lee, Young Hoon and David J. Berri. (2008). "A Re-Examination of Production Functions and Efficiency Estimates for the National Basketball Association." *Scottish Journal of Political Economy*, 55, n1; (February): 51-66.

Leeds, A. Michael and Sandra Kowalewski. (2001). "Winner Take All in the NFL: The Effect of the Salary Cap and Free Agency on the Compensation of Skill Position Players." *Journal of Sports Economics*, 2: 244-256.

Leeds, Michael A. and Peter Von Allmen. (2008). *The Economics of Sports*. Pearson, Addison-Wesley, 3rd ed.

Lehrer, Jonah. (2009). *How We Decide*. Houghton Mifflin.

Leonhardt, David. (2004). "Ideas & Trends: Super Bowl Economics; Incremental Analysis, with Two Yards to Go." *New York Times* (February 2). www.nytimes.com/2004/02/01/weekinreview/ ideas-trends-super-bowl-economics-incremental-analysis-with-two-yards-to-go.html.

Levitt, Dan. (2006). "Empirical Analysis of Bunting." (July 13). baseballanalysts.com/archives/2006/07/empirical_analy_1.php.

Levitt, Steven D. and John A. List. (2007). "What Do Laboratory Experiments Measuring Social Preferences Reveal About the Real World?" *Journal of Economic Perspectives*, 21(2):153-74.

Levitt, Steven D. and John A. List. (2006). "What Do Laboratory Experiments Tell Us About the Real World?" University of Chicago and NBER (June).

Levy, Alan H. (2003). *Tackling Jim Crow: Racial Segregation in Professional Football*. Jefferson, NC: McFarland & Company, Inc.

Lewin, David. (2008). "College Stats Don't Lie." (April 17). sports.espn.go.com/nfl/news/story?id=3350135.

Lewin, David and Dan Rosenbaum. (2007). "The Pot Calling the Kettle Black: Are NBA Statistical Models More Irrational Than "Irrational" Decision-Makers?" Working paper.

Lewis, Michael M. (2003). *Moneyball: The Art of Winning an Unfair Game*. W. W Norton & Company, Inc.

Lewis, Michael. (2006). "If I only had the nerve." *ESPN the Magazine*. (December 18). sports.espn.go.com/espnmag/ story?section=magazine&id=3641375.

Lindsey, G. (1963). "An Investigation of Strategies in Baseball." *Operations Research*, 11, 447-501.

Massey C., and R. Thaler. (2005). "Overconfidence vs. market efficiency in the National Football League." NBER Working Paper No. 11270.

McCarthy, Ryan. (2008). "Change You Can't Believe In: Why hiring a new coach won't solve your favorite NBA team's problems. (Unless the old coach was Isiah Thomas.)" Posted: November 18, 2008. (slate.com/id/2204834).

McCloskey, Deirdre. (1996). *The Vices of Economists, the Virtues of the Bourgeoisie*. Amsterdam University Press.

McCloskey, Deirdre. (1998). *The Rhetoric of Economics*. University of Wisconsin Press, 2nd ed.

McCloskey, Deirdre. (2002). *The Secret Sins of Economics*. Prickly Paradigm Press.

McCraken, Voros. (2001). "Pitching and Defense: How Much Control Do Hurlers Have?" www.baseballprospectus.com/article.php?articleid=878.

Miller, George. (1956). "The Magical Number Seven, Plus or Minus Two: Some Limits on Our Capacity for Processing Information." *The Psychological Review*, 63: 81-97.

Neyer, Rob. (1996). "Who Are the 'True' Shooters?" In *STATS Pro Basketball Handbook, 1995–96* (pp. 322–323). New York: STATS Publishing.

Oliver, Dean. (2004). *Basketball on Paper: Rules and Tools for Performance Analysis*. Potomac Books, Inc.

Pitino, Rick. (1998). *Success Is a Choice: Ten Steps to Overachieving in Business and Life*. Broadway Books.

Pitino, Rick. (2001). *Lead to Succeed: 10 Traits of Great Leadership in Business and Life*. Broadway Books.

Pluto, Terry and Earl Weaver. (1984). *Weaver on Strategy: Classic Work on Art of Managing a Baseball Team*. Potomac Books, Inc.

Price, Joseph, Brian Soebbing, David Berri, and Brad Humphreys. (2009). "Tournament Incentives, League Policy, and NBA Team Performance Revisited." Presented at the 2009 Western Economic Association meetings, Vancouver, British Colombia, June.

Price, Joseph and Justin Wolfers. (2007)."Racial Discrimination Among NBA Referees." Presented at the 2007 Western Economic Association meetings, Seattle, Washington, June.

Price, Paul. (2006). "Are You as Good of a Teacher as You Think? http://www2.nea.org/he/heta06/images/2006pg7.pdf.

Quinn, Kevin. (2008). "Player drafts in the major North American sports leagues." In *The Business of Sport*, eds. Brad Humphreys and Dennis Howard, 3 volumes, Westport, Conn.: Praeger: 191-217.

Quirk, James and Rodney Fort. (1992). *Pay Dirt: The Business of Professional Team Sports*. Princeton, N.J.: Princeton University Press.

Rhoden, William. (2003). "Sports of The Times; The Long-Drifting Knicks Have Finally Found an Anchor." *The New York Times*. December 27.

Riley, Pat. (1993). *The Winner Within: A Life Plan for Team Players*. Berkley Trade Books.

Romer, David H. (2006). "Do Firms Maximize: Evidence from Professional Football." *Journal of Political Economy*, 114: 340-65.

Ross, Charles. (1999). *Outside the Lines: African Americans and the Integration of the National Football League*. New York: New York University Press.

Rottenberg, Simon. (1956). "The Baseball Players' Labor Market." *Journal of Political Economy*, 64(3): 242-258.

Schatz, Aaron. (2006). "Keeping Score: N.F.L. Kickers Are Judged on the Wrong Criteria." (November 12). *New York Times*.

Schmidt, Martin B. and David J. Berrri. (2003). "On the Evolution of Competitive Balance: The Impact of an Increasing Global Search." *Economic Inquiry*, 41: 692-704.

Schulz, R. and C. Curnow. (1988). "Peak performance and age among superathletes: Track and field, swimming, baseball, tennis, and golf." *Journal of Gerontology*, 43:113–120.

Schwarz, Alan. (2004). *Numbers Game: Baseball's Lifelong Fascination with Statistics*. New York: Thomas Dunne Books, St Thomas Press.

Scott, Frank Jr., James Long, and Ken Somppi. (1985). "Salary vs. Marginal Revenue Product Under Monopsony and Competition: The Case of Professional Basketball." *Atlantic Economic Journal*, 13(3):50–59.

Seifert, Kevin. (2009). "Stafford Contract Holding Up." (August 25). espn.go.com/blog/nfcnorth/post/_/id/2458/stafford-contract-holding-up.

Siler, Ross and Steve Luhm. (2008). "Jazz Notes." *Salt Lake City Tribune*. (October 10). blogs.sltrib.com/jazz/2008/10/jazz-96-suns-89.htm.

Smith, Adam. (1776). *An Inquiry into the Nature and Causes of the Wealth of Nations* (1963 edition). Illinois: R.D. Irwin.

Sports Biz with Darren Rovell. www.cnbc.com/id/15837629.

Staw, B.M. and Ha Hoang. (1995) "Sunk costs in the NBA: why draft order affects playing time and survival in professional basketball." *Administrative Costs Quarterly*, 40: 474-94.

Szymanski. (2003). "The Economic Design of Sporting Contest." *Journal of Economic Literature*, 41, 1137-87.

Szymanski, Stefan. (2009). *Playbooks and Checkbooks: An Introduction to the Economics of Modern Sports*. Princeton University Press.

Taylor, Beck A. and Justin G. Trogdon. (2002). "Losing to Win: Tournament Incentives in the National Basketball Association." *Journal of Labor Economics*, 20: 23-41.

Thaler, Richard H. and Cass R. Sunstein. (2008). *Nudge: Improving Decisions About Health, Wealth, and Happiness*. Yale University Press.

Thorn, John and Pete Palmer. (1984). *The Hidden Game of Baseball*. Doubleday Publishers.

Veblen, Thorstein. (1898). "Why Is Economics Not an Evolutionary Science?" *The Quarterly Journal of Economics*, 12: 373-97.

Walker, James. (2008). "McNair's 'kinship' with Favre continues into retirement." (April 17). sports.espn.go.com/nfl/columns/story?columnist=walker_james&id=3351356.

Winston, Wayne. (2009). *Mathletics: How Gamblers, Managers, and Sports Enthusiasts Use Mathematics in Baseball, Basketball, and Football*. Princeton University Press.

Wolff, Alexander. (2009). "The NFL's Jackie Robinson." *Sports Illustrated*, October 12:60-71.

Young, Michael. (2008). "Nonlinear judgment analysis: Comparing policy use by those who draft and those who coach." *Psychology of Sport and Exercise*, 9, 760-774.

Zumsteg, Derek. (2002). "Walking Bonds usually not a smart choice." (October 18). a.espncdn.com/mlb/playoffs2002/s/2002/1016/1446990.html.

Web Sites

82games.com

www.advancednflstats.com

www.baseball-reference.com

www.basketball-reference.com

BasketballValue.com.

www.bls.gov/data/inflation_calculator.htm

www.cbamuseum.com/cbaisiah.html

Centers for Disease Control and Prevention, cdc.gov

espn.go.com/classic/biography/s/auerbach_red.html

espn.go.com/nfl/afc/draftsignings2002.html

Forbes.com

www.footballoutsiders.com

Freakonomics.com

www.hockey-reference.com

www.macmirabile.com/wonderlic.htm

myespn.go.com/nba/truehoop

mvn.com/bucksdiary

NCAA Football Statistics: web1.ncaa.org/d1mfb/
    mainpage.jsp?site=org

NFL.com

Patricia's Various Basketball Stuff, www.eskimo.com/
    ~pbender/index.html

www.predictablyirrational.com

proathletesonly.com/news/tag/nfl-minimum-salaries

www.profootballhof.com

www.Pro-Football-Reference.com

www.seinfeldscripts.com

Sport: Football, Nov. 26, 1934. www.time.com/time/magazine/article/0,9171,882323-1,00.html

sportsmediawatch.blogspot.com/2009/05/weekend-ratings-predictions.html

www.stumblingonwins.com

content.usatoday.com/sports/baseball/salaries/default.aspx

content.usatoday.com/sports/basketball/nba/salaries/default.aspx

content.usatoday.com/sports/football/nfl/salaries/default.aspx

content.usatoday.com/sports/hockey/nhl/salaries/default.aspx

The Wages of Wins Journal, www.dberri.wordpress.com

sports.yahoo.com/nfl/stats

INDEX

Note: Page numbers followed by *n* are located in the Endnotes.

A

Abbott, Henry, 125, 180*n*, 205*n*
Abdul-Jabbar, Kareem, 84, 131, 206*n*
Abdur-Rahim, Shareef, 94-95
ACC (Atlantic Coast Conference), 49
Adelman, Rick, 123
adjusted field goal percentage (NBA), 16
adjusted plus-minus statistic, 183-184*n*
Adjusted Production per 48 minutes played (AdjP48), 203*n*
AFL (American Football League), 50
African-American quarterbacks
    history of, 50-55
    pay discrepancy between black and white quarterbacks, 63-66
    performance of, 55-63
age and performance, 126-129, 205*n*
Aguirre, Mark, 88-89
Aikman, Troy, 66, 168-170
Albeck, Stan, 124
All-Rookie Team (NBA), voting factors for, 27
Allen, Ray, 84
Allmen, Peter Von, 189*n*
Almond, Morris, 24
American Football League (AFL), 50

American International Group, Inc., 174*n*
Anderson, Dave, 202*n*
Anderson, Ken, 88-89, 168-170
Ariely, Dan, 173*n*
Ariza, Trevor, 178*n*
Arizona Cardinals, 113
Armstrong, Hilton, 152-153
Ashenfelter, Orley, 174*n*
assigning wins and losses, 47-48
assists (NBA), 16
Atlantic Coast Conference (ACC), 49
Auerbach, Red, 23, 133, 179-180*n*
Ayres, Ian, 174*n*

B

Banks, Don, 188*n*
Banks, Tony, 52-53, 71-73
Barkley, Charles, 194*n*
Barzilai, Aaron, 184*n*
base stealing, efficiency of, 103-106, 198-199*n*
Baseball-Reference.com, 181*n*
baseball. *See* Major League Baseball
Basketball-Reference.com, 176*n*, 182*n*
basketball. *See* National Basketball Association
BasketballValue.com, 183*n*
Batch, Charlie, 52-53
batting average, 33, 135

Theodore, Jose, 43
Thomas, Isiah, 84, 88-89, 123-124, 138, 205*n*
   career as manager of New York Knicks, 14-20, 28-32
   career averages, 16-18
   ownership of Continental Basketball Association, 176*n*
Thomas, Tim, 43
Thompson, Mychal, 88-89
Thorn, John, 182*n*
Thrower, Willie, 51
Tisdale, Wayman, 88-89
Trogdon, Justin, 194*n*
True Hoop, 180*n*
Tversky, Amos, 115

V

Vallone, Robert, 115
Vanbiesbrouck, John, 43
variation in winning percentage, 176*n*
Veblen, Thorstein, 2
Vick, Michael, 52-53, 71

W-X-Y-Z

Wade, Dwayne, 44, 121
The Wages of Wins (Berri), 18, 177*n*
Walker, Antoine, 122
Walker, James, 188*n*
Walker, Moses Fleetwood, 186*n*
Walker, Weldy, 186*n*
walks (MLB), efficiency of, 106, 199*n*
Wallace, Gerald, 44
Wallace, Seneca, 52-53
Walters, Stephen, 101, 174*n*
Warner, Kurt, 72, 168-170
Washington Redskins, 13, 106
Washington, Kenny, 50
Weaver, Earl, 103
Webber, Chris, 88-89
Weil, Sandy, 202*n*
West, David, 152-153
Westhead, Paul, 205*n*
Westphal, Paul, 123
Wilkens, Lenny, 122
Williams, Doug, 51-53, 57, 63, 187*n*

Williams, Jay, 88-89
Williams, Marvin, 93, 195*n*
Willihnganz, Ty, 149
Willis, Bill, 50
Win Score, 154-156, 177*n*
wine vintage quality, statistical models of, 174*n*
The Winner Within: A Life Plan for Team Players (Riley), 203*n*
Wins per 48 Minutes (NBA), 18
Wins Produced, 18
   assigning wins, 47-48
   measuring for NBA players
      adjusting for position played, 150-151
      adjusting for production of teammates, 148-150
      alternative statistics, 156-157
      basics of regression analysis, 141-143
      calculating value of player's production, 148
      calculating WP48 and Wins Produced, 151-154
      modeling wins in NBA, 143-146, 148
      objections, 158-159
      Win Score and PAWS48, 154-156
   measuring for NFL players, 161-162, 166-167, 170-171
   relationship between payroll and wins, 13-14
Winston, Wayne, 184*n*, 190*n*, 207*n*
Wolff, Alexander, 186*n*
Wonderlic test, 78-79, 191*n*, 193*n*
Wonderlic, Eldon F., 191*n*
Worthy, James, 84, 88-89
WP48 (Wins per 48 Minutes), 18, 151-154
wrath of randomness, 7
Wright, Anthony, 52-53
Wright, Julian, 152-153

Young, Steve, 168-170, 187*n*
Young, Vince, 52-53